THE TOUGH GUY SURVIVAL KIT WORKBOOK

G. BRENT DARNELL

The Tough Guy Survival Kit Workbook By G. Brent Darnell

Copyright © 2020 G. Brent Darnell.
All rights reserved.

Printed in the USA on sustainably harvested paper. No part of this book may be copied or reproduced in any form without express written consent of the publisher except in the case of brief quotations embodied in critical articles and reviews.

For information, contact
BDI Publishers, Atlanta, Georgia, *bdipublishers@gmail.com*.

ISBN 978-1-946637-14-7

Cover Design and Layout: Tudor Maier

Back cover photo Courtesy of CMAA

BDI Publishers
Atlanta, Georgia

How to Use This Workbook:

The first step is to take the EI test (pages 5-11) to see what your emotional profile is. The second step is to take the Symptom Survey (pages 12-15) to see what your most stress body systems are. The third step is to work through the EI Roadmap (pages 16-57). Fill in your development plans with activities from The EI Activity Guide (pages 59-144). Refer to page 60 for a list of the emotional and physical areas to improve. The fourth step is to read through the Tough Guy Survival Kit (pages 145-230) to reinforce the learning and create behavioral change. The Appendix begins on page 232 with evaluations, worksheets, and other resources.

Ghyst Emotional Intelligence Test and Workbook

Name:_____ Date:_____

Work your way through the test, then read through the interpretive guidelines for the various typical profiles and pairings of competencies. Then, read through how these typical profiles affect the different areas of your life and work.

Emotional and Social Skills

		STRONGLY AGREE(SA)	AGREE(A)	NEUTRAL(N)	DISAGREE(D)	STRONGLY DISAGREE(SD)
	Point Value	5	4	3	2	1
1	I have a healthy level of self-respect.					
2	I'm comfortable with my general appearance.					
3	If someone criticizes me, I'm able to put their feedback into perspective and keep my emotional balance.					
4	I make it a habit to take time for personal and professional development.					
5	My plans for the future are motivating and energizing.					
6	It's easy for me to stay active doing things that I find most fulfilling.					
7	My emotional life is rich and varied.					
8	I'm in touch with the way I feel in most situations.					
9	I'm seldom, if ever, "hijacked" or caught off guard by my emotional responses to situations.					
10	I easily express my feelings.					
11	I enjoy showing my feelings to others.					
12	People tell me they always know how I feel about things.					
13	I am able to express my needs and opinions to others.					
14	I let others know when I believe they are ignoring my rights in a situation.					
15	I believe that expressing my honest opinion is important in maintaining good relationships.					
16	I prefer to make my own decisions.					
17	When working alone, I maintain a sure sense of purpose and directions.					
18	When working with others, I take the initiative on independent projects.					
19	I am comfortable sharing my deep feelings with good friends.					
20	My life is enriched by family and close friends.					
21	Others feel comfortable confiding in me.					
22	I'm good at discerning the way other people perceive their situations, even if different from mine.					
23	I easily tune into the feelings of others around me in order to assess the 'emotional climate' of any group.					
24	I appreciate it when people treat others with respect and kindness.					
25	Helping others outside my immediate family and group of friends is important to me.					
26	I impress others as dependable and reliable.					
27	It's not in my nature to take advantage of others.					
28	When confronted by a new challenge, I find it easy to decide on the best course of action.					
29	Even if it takes a long time to deal with a problem, I rarely get discouraged and give up.					
30	Even with an overload of information about all the options, I can still make the tough decisions.					
31	I'm aware of how my thoughts and beliefs impact my evaluation of circumstances.					
32	I learn about different aspects of any issue or problem before taking action.					

Emotional and Social Skills	STRONGLY AGREE(SA)	AGREE(A)	NEUTRAL(N)	DISAGREE(D)	STRONGLY DISAGREE(SD)
Point Value	5	4	3	2	1
33 I like to double check my facts to ensure the accuracy of assumptions.					
34 I'm not quick to anger or hot-headed.					
35 I am steady, patient and focused in achieving goals.					
36 I don't give in easily to temptations or distractions.					
37 It's my nature to remain balanced and calm even when things don't go as planned.					
38 Others tell me that I deal well with change.					
39 I am energized by the excitement, even the uncertainty, of beginning a new project.					
40 I usually calm down quickly after a crises has passed.					
41 I seldom get annoyed or stressed out by events.					
42 People look to me for calm assurance and guidance when things get tough.					
43 I move forward with confidence despite setbacks.					
44 I am confident about my ability to handle the unexpected.					
45 In my experience, disappointments, in the longer term, are just stepping stones to success in disguise.					
46 I'm an upbeat person who enjoys life.					
47 People consider me uplifting and fun.					
48 I'm seldom, if ever, depressed or 'down' about things.					

DIRECTIONS

For each competence below, go to the statements listed and add up your total results for those three statements. **For each 3-statement competency**:

If you scored **3-9 total**, this is probably an area that needs improvement.

If you scored **10-11 total**, your score is better, but still indicates you'd likely benefit from improvement.

If you scored **12-13 total**, you are probably in the average range.

If you scored **14-15 total**, you are probably above average in this area.

Often the most revealing aspect of this assessment is the degrees of difference between different scores, an amazingly helpful indicator of performance and behavior. Graph your results on the graph page.

SELF-PERCEPTION

Self-Regard (Statements 1-3) is respecting oneself while understanding and accepting one's strengths and weaknesses. Self-regard is often associated with feelings of inner strength and self-confidence.

Total points: _____

Self-Actualization (Statements 4-6) is the willingness to persistently try to improve oneself and engage in the pursuit of personally relevant and meaningful objectives that lead to a rich and enjoyable life.

Total points:_____

Emotional Self-Awareness (Statements 7-9) includes recognizing and understanding one's own emotions. This includes the ability to differentiate between subtleties in one's own emotions while understanding the cause of these emotions and the impact they have on the thoughts and actions of oneself and others.

Total points:_____

SELF EXPRESSION

Emotional Expression (Statements 10-12) is openly expressing one's feelings verbally and non-verbally.

Total points:_____

Assertiveness (Statements 13-15) involves communicating feelings, beliefs, and thoughts openly, and defending personal rights and values in a socially acceptable, non-offensive, and non-destructive manner.

Total points:_____

Independence (Statements 16-18) is the ability to be self-directed and free of emotional dependency on others. Decision-making, planning, and daily tasks are completed autonomously.

Total points:_____

INTERPERSONAL

Interpersonal Relationships (Statements 19-21) refers to the skill of developing and maintaining mutually satisfying relationships that are characterized by trust and compassion.

Total points:_____

Empathy (Statements 22-24) is recognizing, understanding, and appreciating how other people feel. Empathy involves being able to articulate your understanding of another's perspective and behaving in a way that respects the feelings of others.

Total points:_____

Social Responsibility (Statements 25-27) is willingly contributing to society, to one's social groups, and generally to the welfare of others. Social Responsibility involves acting responsibly, having social consciousness, and showing concern for the greater community.

Total points:_____

DECISION MAKING

Problem Solving (Statements 28-30) is the ability to find solutions to problems in situations where emotions are involved. Problem solving includes the ability to understand how emotions impact decision making.

Total points:_____

Reality Testing (Statements 31-33) is the capacity to remain objective by seeing things as they really are. This capacity involves recognizing when emotions or personal bias can cause one to be less objective.

Total points:_____

Impulse Control (Statements 34-36) is the ability to resist or delay an impulse, drive, or temptation to act. It involves avoiding rash behaviors and decision making.

Total points:_____

STRESS MANAGEMENT

Flexibility (Statements 37-39) is adapting emotions, thoughts, and behaviors to unfamiliar, unpredictable, and dynamic circumstances or ideas.

Total points:_____

Stress Tolerance (Statements 40-42) involves coping with stressful or difficult situations and believing that one can manage or influence situations in a positive manner.

Total points:_____

Optimism (Statements 43-45) is an indicator of one's positive attitude and outlook on life. It includes remaining hopeful and resilient, despite occasional setbacks.

Total points:_____

WELL BEING INDICATOR

Happiness (Statements 46-48) is the ability to feel satisfied with one's life, to enjoy oneself and others, and to have fun.

Total points:_____

Note: Although this evaluation may give an indication of areas which need improvement, it should not be used for in-depth, personal development. In order to do that, we recommend that you take the Emotional Quotient Inventory (EQ-i) 2.0, the validated and most widely-used emotional intelligence evaluation in the world. You can then obtain feedback on your results from a qualified, certified emotional intelligence professional. Visit our website and online store for more information.

GRAPHING YOUR RESULTS FOR ANALYSIS / DISCUSSION

```
              3   4   5   6   7   8   9   10  11  12  13  14  15
```

SELF-PERCEPTION
Self-Regard _____
Self-Actualization _____
Emotional Self-Awareness _____

SELF-EXPRESSION
Emotional Expression _____
Assertiveness _____
Independence _____

INTERPERSONAL
Interpersonal Relationships _____
Empathy _____
Social Responsibility _____

DECISION MAKING
Problem Solving _____
Reality Testing _____
Impulse Control _____

STRESS MANAGEMENT
Flexibility _____
Stress Tolerance _____
Optimism _____

WELL BEING INDICATOR
Happiness _____

INTERPRETIVE GUIDELINES

It is desirable to have a balanced profile. Avoid the trap of thinking that a high number is good and a low number is bad. Any strength taken to the extreme may become a weakness, especially if the balancing competency is low. For example: assertiveness is a great leadership skill, but if it is high and empathy is low, you may be perceived as someone who doesn't listen, doesn't ask for input or opinions, and doesn't understand others. Empathy is a great emotional skill. Too much empathy without the balance of assertiveness and you may have a tendency to put other people's needs ahead of your own. Look at the highs and lows of your EI profile. Put an "H" beside your four highest scores and an "L" beside your four lowest scores. Do you have any of the characteristics listed for the following highs and lows?

SELF PERCEPTION COMPOSITE

SELF-REGARD
High: Arrogant, full of yourself.
Low: Shy, lack confidence.

SELF-ACTUALIZATION
High: Have a clear plan for your future, feel good about the direction of your life.
Low: No plan, aimless, no clear vision for future, unhappy in present situation, you may see no way out.

EMOTIONAL SELF AWARENESS
High: Overly sensitive to comments, to others, and possibly to your environment.
Low: Unaware of others, your surroundings, and even your body, you "check out" often.

SELF EXPRESSION COMPOSITE

EMOTIONAL EXPRESSION
High: Easy to win the trust of those who appreciate exuberant expressiveness, though may alienate those who are more reserved.
Low: The opposite: more likely to fail to connect with those who are expressive but generally better received by emotionally reserved types.

ASSERTIVENESS
High: Bowl people over, don't take into account others' feelings or input - often perceived as aggressive.
Low: Don't speak what is on your mind, don't stand up for yourself, aren't clear in setting expectations or declaring own needs.

INDEPENDENCE
High: Would rather work alone and be alone, not comfortable in groups or teams or social settings.
Low: Dependent on others for self worth, would rather be told what to do, thrive in groups and teams.

INTERPERSONAL COMPOSITE

INTERPERSONAL RELATIONSHIPS
High: Gregarious, have a lot of friends, create instant rapport, stay in touch.
Low: Uncomfortable in social settings and meeting new people, do not stay in touch, may come across as a wallflower.

EMPATHY
High: Very sensitive to the needs of others and their feelings.
Low: Oblivious to others and their needs and feelings.

SOCIAL RESPONSIBILITY
High: Great team member, good neighbor, joiner, like to interact with groups, very social.
Low: You do not do well in groups or teams, not social; don't like to be a member of groups.

DECISION MAKING COMPOSITE

PROBLEM SOLVING
High: Able to arrive at workable solutions to problems quickly and understand how emotions can affect problem solving.
Low: You struggle with defining problems and arriving at solutions and are often overwhelmed emotionally by the problem-solving process.

REALITY TESTING
High: You see things as they really are despite emotions surrounding the situation.
Low: See all of the possibilities, do not investigate or reflect on the specific facts of a situation, live in a world where objective reality is unclear.

IMPULSE CONTROL
High: 'Paralysis of analysis,' over-thinks things, won't pull the trigger.
Low: You may have compulsive or addictive behavior such as eating, drinking, gambling, smoking, sex, spending, talking, etc., in which there is a consistent 'hijacking' of your long-term best interests resulting in possible profound physical as well as emotional effects.

STRESS MANAGEMENT COMPOSITE

FLEXIBILITY
High: Trouble saying no, take on too much, float from one thing to the next, trouble finishing things.
Low: Very rigid in your approach to things, want to maintain control.

STRESS TOLERANCE
High: Have the ability to handle a lot of stress, good coping skills. Note: We have found that some people with very high stress tolerance may first start to show physical signs of stress like fatigue, headaches or other pains, stomach issues, trouble sleeping, irritability, diminished sex drive, lowered immune response, and depression.
Low: Cluttered, harried, hurried, reactive, unable to stay on top of things, probably have symptoms of stress, feel overwhelmed.

OPTIMISM
High: You consistently see your future as bright and sunny, sometimes to your own detriment. - Glass half full.
Low: The curmudgeon who always looks on the dismal side of life. - Glass half empty.

WELL BEING INDICATOR

HAPPINESS:
High: Shiny, happy person who always seems to be in a good mood and full of joy.
Low: Always seem down and out, life is not fun, you find no joy,

Symptom Survey: Physical Profile

Instructions: Number ONLY the boxes that apply to you.

For no symptoms, leave blank
- **1** for **MILD** symptoms or ones that occur rarely.
- **2** for **MODERATE** symptoms or ones that occur several times a month.
- **3** for **SEVERE** symptoms or ones that occur almost constantly

If you are taking a medication that eliminates the symptoms mark the box the way you felt PRIOR TO taking the medicine.

Sympathetic Dominance
- ☐ Acid food upset
- ☐ Get chilled often
- ☐ "Lump" in throat
- ☐ Dry mouth-eyes-nose
- ☐ Pulse speeds after meal
- ☐ Keyed up - fail to calm
- ☐ Cut heals slowly
- ☐ Gag easily
- ☐ Unable to relax; startles easily
- ☐ Extremities cold, clammy
- ☐ Strong light irritates
- ☐ Urine amount reduced
- ☐ Heart pounds after retiring
- ☐ "Nervous" stomach
- ☐ Appetite reduced
- ☐ Cold sweats often
- ☐ Fever easily raised
- ☐ Neuralgia (nerve-like) pain
- ☐ Staring, blinks little
- ☐ Sour stomach often

TOTAL: ☐

Parasympathetic Dominance
- ☐ Joint stiffness on arising
- ☐ Muscle-leg-toe cramps at night
- ☐ "Butterfly" stomach, cramps
- ☐ Eyes or nose watery
- ☐ Eyes blink often
- ☐ Eyelids swollen, puffy
- ☐ Indigestion soon after meals
- ☐ Always seems hungry; feels "lightheaded" often
- ☐ Digestion rapid
- ☐ Vomiting occasionallly
- ☐ Hoarseness frequent

- ☐ Breathing irregular
- ☐ Pulse slow; feels "irregular"
- ☐ Gagging reflex slow
- ☐ Difficulty swallowing
- ☐ Constipation; diarrhea alternating
- ☐ "Slow starter"
- ☐ Rarely gets "chilled"
- ☐ Perspire easily
- ☐ Circulation poor, sensitive to cold

TOTAL: ☐

Sugar Handling
- ☐ Eat when nervous
- ☐ Excessive appetite
- ☐ Hungry between meals
- ☐ Irritable before meals
- ☐ Get "shaky" if hungry
- ☐ Fatigue, eating relieves
- ☐ "Lightheaded" if meals delayed
- ☐ Heart palpitates if meals missed or delayed
- ☐ Afternoon headaches
- ☐ Overeating sweets upsets
- ☐ Awaken after few hours sleep - hard to get back to sleep
- ☐ Crave candy or coffee in afternoons
- ☐ Moods of depression - "blues" or melancholy
- ☐ Abnormal craving for sweets or snacks

TOTAL: ☐

Cardio Vascular
- ☐ Hands and feet go to sleep easily, numbness
- ☐ Sigh frequently, "air hunger"
- ☐ Aware of "breathing heavily"
- ☐ High altitude discomfort
- ☐ Opens windows in closed rooms
- ☐ Susceptible to colds and fevers
- ☐ Afternoon "yawner"
- ☐ Get "drowsy" often
- ☐ Swollen ankles, worse at night
- ☐ Muscle cramps, worse during exercise; get "charley horses"
- ☐ Shortness of breath on exertion
- ☐ Dull pain in chest or radiating into left arm, worse on exertion
- ☐ Bruise easily, "black and blue" spots
- ☐ Tendency to anemia
- ☐ "Nose bleeds" frequent
- ☐ Noises in head, or "ringing in ears"
- ☐ Tension under the breastbone, or feeling of "tightness", worse on exertion

TOTAL: ☐

Biliary/Liver
☐ Dizziness
☐ Dry skin
☐ Burning feet
☐ Blurred Vision
☐ Itching skin and feet
☐ Excessive falling hair
☐ Frequent skin rashes
☐ Bitter, metallic taste in mouth in mornings
☐ Bowel movements painful or difficult
☐ Worrier, feels insecure
☐ Feeling queasy; headache over eyes
☐ Greasy foods upset
☐ Stools light colored
☐ Skin peels on foot soles
☐ Pain between shoulder blades
☐ Use laxatives
☐ Stools alternate from soft to watery
☐ History of gallbladder attacks or gallstones
☐ Sneezing attacks
☐ Dreaming; nightmare type bad dreams
☐ Bad Breath (halitosis)
☐ Milk products cause distress
☐ Sensitive to hot weather
☐ Burning or itching anus
☐ Crave sweets
TOTAL: [   ]

Digestive
☐ Loss of taste for meat
☐ Lower bowel gas several hours after eating
☐ Burning stomach sensations, eating relieves
☐ Coated tongue
☐ Pass large amounts of foul-smelling gas
☐ Indigestions 1/2 - 1 hour after eating; may be up to 3-4 hours
☐ Mucous colitis or "irritable bowel"
☐ Gas shortly after eating
☐ Stomach "bloating" after eating
TOTAL: [   ]

Adrenal
☐ Dizziness
☐ Headaches
☐ Hot Flashes
☐ Increased blood pressure
☐ Hair growth on face or body (female)
☐ Sugar in urine (not diabetes)

- ☐ Masculine tendencies (female)
- ☐ Weakness, dizziness
- ☐ Chronic fatigue
- ☐ Low blood pressure
- ☐ Nails weak, ridged
- ☐ Tendency to hives
- ☐ Arthritic tendencies
- ☐ Perspiration increase
- ☐ Bowel disorders
- ☐ Poor circulation
- ☐ Swollen ankles
- ☐ Crave salt
- ☐ Brown spots or bronzing of skin
- ☐ Allergies - tendency to asthma
- ☐ Weakness after colds, influenza
- ☐ Exhaustion - muscular and nervous
- ☐ Respiratory disorders

TOTAL: []

Foundational

- ☐ Muscle weakness
- ☐ Lack of Stamina
- ☐ Drowsiness after eating
- ☐ Muscular soreness
- ☐ Rapid heart beat
- ☐ Hyper-irritable
- ☐ Feeling of a band around your head
- ☐ Melancholia (feeling of sadness)
- ☐ Swelling of ankles
- ☐ Diminished urination
- ☐ Tendency to consume sweets or carbohydrates
- ☐ Muscle spasms
- ☐ Blurred vision
- ☐ Loss of muscular control
- ☐ Numbness
- ☐ Night sweats
- ☐ Rapid digestion
- ☐ Sensitivity to noise
- ☐ Redness of palms of hands and bottom of feet
- ☐ Visible veins on chest and abdomen
- ☐ Hemorrhoids
- ☐ Apprehension (feeling that something bad will happen)
- ☐ Nervousness causing loss of appetite
- ☐ Gastritis (stomach irritation)
- ☐ Forgetfulness
- ☐ Thinning hair

TOTAL: []

Add up your total points for each body system. Rank them with the highest number of points first down to the lowest number.

Body system with the highest number: []

Body system with the second highest number: []

Body System with the third highest number: []

Your EI Roadmap

Name: _____

Date: _____

Note: This book is protected by copyright laws and is intended for use by one person. No part of this book may be copied or used without the consent of the author. Portions of this book are copyrighted by Kate Cannon and used with permission.

"Mastering others is strength.
Mastering yourself makes you fearless."
Lao Tzu

"The seat of knowledge is in the head, of wisdom, in the heart."
William Hazlitt

"There are two pains in life:
the pain of discipline and the pain of regret. The choice is yours."
Bill Curry

"We are made of dreams and bones."
Dave Mallet

More Quotes:

"If we could give every individual the right amount of nourishment and exercise, not too little and not too much, we would have found the safest way to health."
—**Hippocrates**

"Even in such technical lines as engineering, about 15 % of one's financial success is due to one's technical knowledge and about 85 % is due to skill in human engineering-to personality and the ability to lead people."
—**Dale Carnegie**

"It is more important to know what sort of person has a disease than to know what sort of disease a person has."
—**Hippocrates**

"All things being equal, we will work harder and more effectively for people we like…and we like them in direct proportion to how they make us feel."
—**Irwin Federman**

"The doctor of the future will give no medicine, but will interest his patients in the care of the human frame, in diet, and in the cause and prevention of disease."
—**Thomas Alva Edison**

"Treat people right and they will eat nails for you."
—**Thomas Stemberg**

Part 1: Where am I now?

Tell us a little bit about yourself, a short bio that includes high points and low points of your life. Start as far back as you wish. Include all of the major events of your life and write down how you think it has shaped who you are today. Look for any patterns. Were there common themes at the high points and low points? How do those patterns inform the present?

Be sure to include early childhood, teen years, young adult years, adult years, education, major life events such as marriages, divorces, children, struggles with finances or health, how you overcame struggles, and any hobbies or interests outside of work.

Don't forget family (your definition of family), spouses, children (ages and genders), relatives, and pets!

The Four Quadrants: Fill in the boxes with words and pictures that represent these areas of your life. Also, tell us your:
Favorite Piece of Music:
Favorite Quote:

Personal	Work
Family	Future Vision
Challenges	

How Do You Feel Today?
(see feeling word vocabulary and feeling wheel on next pages)

Take a look at the feeling word vocabularies on the following pages and write down a few of the words that describe how you feel in this very moment. The aim here is to increase your self-awareness, your emotional vocabulary, and the ability to distinguish the subtle differences among the various emotions.

Date: _____

Feelings:

Happy	**Scared**	**Sad**	**Confident**
elated	fearful	hopeless	determined
exuberant	panicked	sorrowful	secure
ecstatic	afraid	defeated	capable
jubilant	overwhelmed	drained	strong
energized	terrified	dejected	hopeful
joyful	insecure	empty	proud
cheerful	shaken	distraught	competent
alive	anxious	demoralized	effective
loving	unsure	alienated	sharp
peaceful	nervous	disheartened	self-reliant
optimistic	apprehensive	resigned	successful
fortunate	vulnerable	disappointed	assured
content	intimidated	crushed	accomplished
gratified	desperate	depressed	encouraged

Excited	**Frustrated**	**Angry**	**Tired**
alert	distressed	upset	exhausted
curious	helpless	exasperated	apathetic
energetic	let down	offended	worn out
thrilled	dissatisfied	outraged	stressed
engaged	stuck	humiliated	numb
enthusiastic	hindered	hostile	checked out
involved	restless	enraged	empty
eager	irritable	betrayed	weary
ready	futile	agitated	weak
anticipatory	confused	used	vulnerable
stimulated	uneasy	furious	disengaged
optimistic	stifled	disgusted	lethargic
open	aggravated	provoked	fatigued
connected	annoyed	resentful	shut down
cooperative	uptight	mad	listless

"Plutchik's Feeling Wheel"

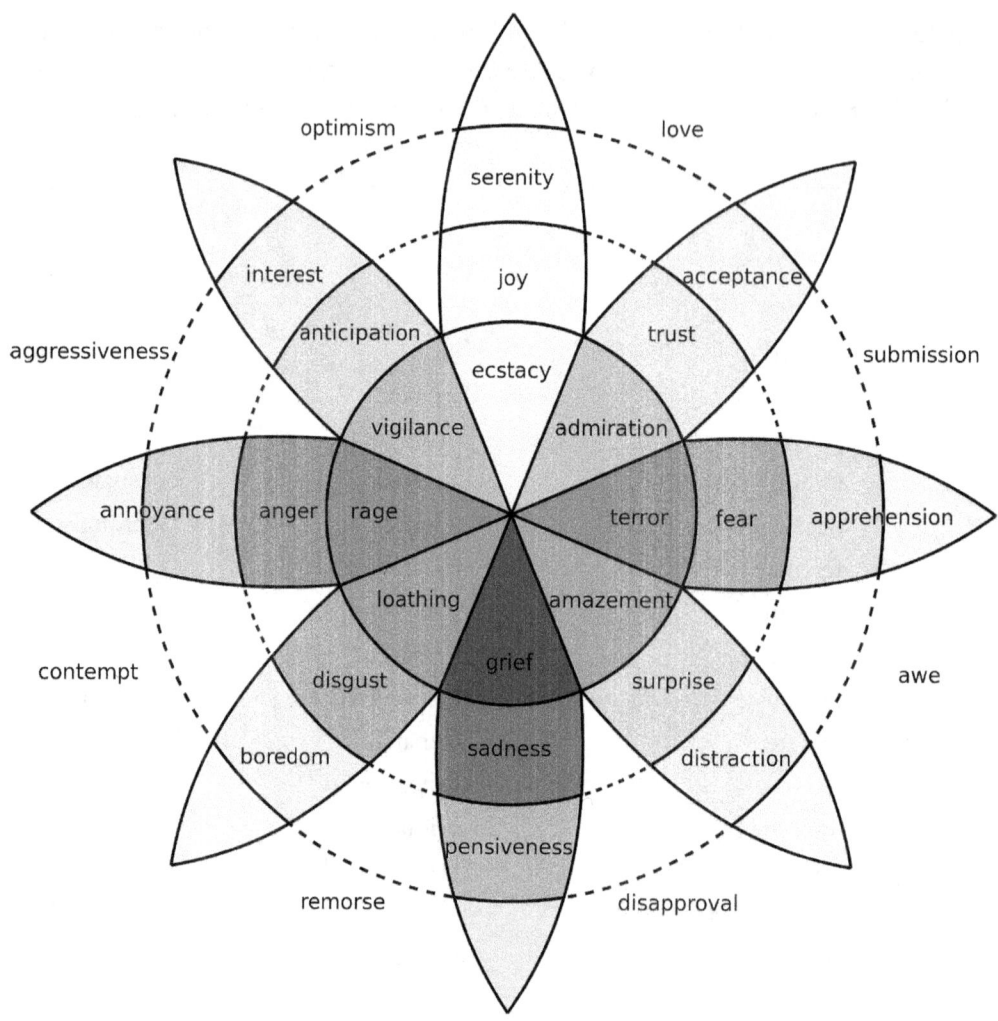

Pay special attention to the progression of emotion. The emotions on the inner circle don't just happen. They progress from the outside in. If your emotional self-awareness is good, you can feel the emotions on the outside of the wheel and manage them. If the emotion is not desired, you can prevent it from getting to the inner circle by managing your emotional state through reframing. If the emotion is desired, you can focus on your emotional state from the outside in until that emotion is achieved.

Physical

How is your body feeling? Are you feeling: Heavy? Tired? Fatigued? Uneasy? Full of energy? Do you have any symptoms or discomforts? Pains? Burning? Mobility issues? An easy feeling? Overall well-being?

Physical check:

_____

_____

What do you most want to accomplish with your physical health? How would your life be if you didn't have these symptoms that may be holding you back (fatigue, pain, headaches, stress-related illnesses, etc)?

_____

_____

_____

_____

_____

_____

Interpretive Guideline Review

Basic Definitions of the EI competencies:

SELF-PERCEPTION COMPOSITE

Self-Regard is respecting oneself while understanding and accepting one's strengths and weaknesses. Self-regard is often associated with feelings of inner strength and self-confidence.

Self-Actualization is the willingness to persistently try to improve oneself and engage in the pursuit of personally relevant and meaningful objectives that lead to a rich and enjoyable life.

Emotional Self-Awareness includes recognizing and understanding one's own emotions. This includes the ability to differentiate between subtleties in one's own emotions while understanding the cause of these emotions and the impact they have on the thoughts and actions of oneself and others.

SELF EXPRESSION COMPOSITE

Emotional Expression is openly expressing one's feelings verbally and non- verbally.

Assertiveness involves communicating feelings, beliefs, and thoughts openly, and defending personal rights and values in a socially acceptable, non- offensive, and non-destructive manner.

Independence is the ability to be self-directed and free of emotional dependency on others. Decision-making, planning, and daily tasks are completed autonomously.

INTERPERSONAL COMPOSITE

Interpersonal Relationship refers to the skill of developing and maintaining mutually satisfying relationships that are characterized by trust and compassion.

Empathy is recognizing, understanding, and appreciating how other people feel. Empathy involves being able to articulate your understanding of another's perspective and behaving in a way that respects other's feelings. Don't confuse empathy with sympathy. Empathy means that you understand and appreciate the other person's feelings. Sympathy means you feel sorry for the other person.

Social Responsibility is willingly contributing to society, to one's social groups, and generally to the welfare of others. Social Responsibility involves acting responsibly, having social consciousness, and showing concern for the greater community.

DECISION MAKING COMPOSITE

Problem Solving is the ability to find solutions to problems in situations where emotions are involved. Problem solving includes the ability to understand how emotions impact decision-making.

Reality Testing is the capacity to remain objective by seeing things as they really are. This capacity involves recognizing when emotions or personal bias can cause one to be less objective.

Impulse Control is the ability to resist or delay an impulse, drive, or temptation to act and involves avoiding rash behaviors and decision making.

STRESS MANAGEMENT COMPOSITE

Flexibility is adapting emotions, thoughts, and behaviors to unfamiliar, unpredictable, and dynamic circumstances or ideas.

Stress Tolerance involves coping with stressful or difficult situations and believing that one can manage or influence situations in a positive manner.

Optimism is an indicator of one's positive attitude and outlook on life. It involves remaining hopeful and resilient, despite occasional setbacks.

WELL BEING INDICATOR

Happiness is the ability to feel satisfied with one's life, to enjoy oneself and others, and to have fun.

INTERPRETIVE GUIDELINES

It is desirable to have a balanced profile. Avoid the trap of thinking that a high number is good and a low number is bad. Any strength taken to the extreme may become a weakness, especially if the balancing competency is low. For example: assertiveness is a great leadership skill, but if it is high and empathy is low, you may be perceived as someone who doesn't listen, doesn't ask for input or opinions, and doesn't understand others. Empathy is a great emotional skill. Too much empathy without the balance of assertiveness and you may have a tendency to put other people's needs ahead of your own. Look at the highs and lows of your EI profile. Make a mental note or put an "H" beside your four highest scores and an "L" beside your four lowest scores. Do you have any of the characteristics listed for the following highs and lows?

SELF PERCEPTION COMPOSITE

SELF-REGARD

High: Arrogant, full of yourself.
Low: Shy, lack confidence.

SELF-ACTUALIZATION

High: Have a clear plan for your future, feel good about the direction of your life.
Low: No plan, aimless, no clear vision for future, unhappy in present situation, you may see no way out.

EMOTIONAL SELF AWARENESS

High: Overly sensitive to comments, to others, and possibly to your environment.
Low: Unaware of others, your surroundings, and even your body, you "check out" often.

SELF EXPRESSION COMPOSITE

EMOTIONAL EXPRESSION

High: Easy to win the trust of those who appreciate exuberant expressiveness, though may alienate those who are more reserved.
Low: The opposite: more likely to fail to connect with those who are expressive but generally better received by emotionally reserved types.

ASSERTIVENESS

High: Bowl people over, don't take into account others' feelings or input - often perceived as aggressive.
Low: Don't speak what is on your mind, don't stand up for yourself, aren't clear in setting expectations or declaring own needs.

INDEPENDENCE

High: Would rather work alone and be alone, not comfortable in groups or teams or social settings.
Low: Dependent on others for self-worth, would rather be told what to do, thrive in groups and teams.

INTERPERSONAL COMPOSITE

INTERPERSONAL RELATIONSHIP

High: Gregarious, have a lot of friends, create instant rapport, stay in touch.
Low: Uncomfortable in social settings and meeting new people, do not stay in touch, may come across as a wallflower.

EMPATHY

High: Very sensitive to the needs of others and their feelings.
Low: Oblivious to others and their needs and feelings.

SOCIAL RESPONSIBILITY

High: Great team member, good neighbor, joiner, like to interact with groups, very social.
Low: You do not do well in groups or teams, not social; don't like to be a member of groups.

DECISION MAKING COMPOSITE

PROBLEM SOLVING

High: Able to arrive at workable solutions to problems quickly and understand how emotions can affect problem solving.
Low: You struggle with defining problems and arriving at solutions and are often overwhelmed emotionally by the problem-solving process.

REALITY TESTING

High: You see things as they really are despite emotions surrounding the situation.
Low: See all of the possibilities, do not investigate or reflect on the specific facts of a situation, live in a world where objective reality is unclear.

IMPULSE CONTROL

High: 'Paralysis of analysis,' over-thinks things, won't pull the trigger.
Low: You may have compulsive or addictive behavior such as eating, drinking, gambling, smoking, sex, spending, talking, etc., in which there is a consistent 'hijacking' of your long-term best interests - resulting in possible profound physical as well as emotional effects.

STRESS MANAGEMENT COMPOSITE

FLEXIBILITY

High: Trouble saying no, take on too much, float from one thing to the next, trouble finishing things. Physical correlation: Sugar Handling.
Low: Very rigid in your approach to things, want to maintain control.

STRESS TOLERANCE

High: Have the ability to handle a lot of stress, good coping skills. **Note:** We have found that some people with very high stress tolerance may first start to show <u>physical</u> signs of stress like fatigue, headaches or other pains, stomach issues, trouble sleeping, irritability, diminished sex drive, lowered immune response, and depression.
Low: Cluttered, harried, hurried, reactive, unable to stay on top of things, probably have symptoms of stress, feel overwhelmed.

OPTIMISM

High: You consistently see your future as bright and sunny, sometimes to your own detriment. Glass half full.
Low: The curmudgeon who always looks on the dismal side of life. - Glass half empty.

WELL BEING INDICATOR

HAPPINESS:

High: Shiny, happy person who always seems to be in a good mood and full of joy.
Low: Always seem down and out, life is not fun, you find no joy,

Categories of Organ Systems from Symptom Survey

Conversion of Energy (E); food to fuel.

Biliary and Liver: The liver is the industrial center of the body. It's a chemical factory making new body chemistry and breaking down toxic waste. The gallbladder (biliary) handles fat and fat is necessary to make hormones. The liver is responsible for the breakdown of all non-food substances such as food preservatives and colorings, medicines, caffeine and alcohol.

Sugar handling: Food to fuel. All sugars and carbohydrates are converted to glucose in the blood. If the body doesn't do this well or you overeat these foods, you'll have shifts in energy and mood; sometimes dramatic shifts. This also weakens the adrenals and the nervous system.

Digestive: Deals with breakdown of protein which is necessary for healing and repair, and to keep us from aging too rapidly. Protein transports the minerals which are spark plugs for every action in the body.

Note: If you see the previous three, we call it the **Trilogy**. It means you are extremely low in energy and are not converting energy from the foods you eat or that you are eating poor quality foods. You will be exhausted and everything in your life will suffer from that low energy. Start by working on nutrition; especially Sugar Handling.

<u>**Foundation**</u>: relates to nerve and muscle function including heart function and brain chemistry. Heavily reliant on B vitamins. Stress depletes Vitamin B and adding B vitamins helps handle stress better. This is especially important to weak Adrenals or Nervous System weakness.

Autonomic Nervous System: The electrical circuitry of the body

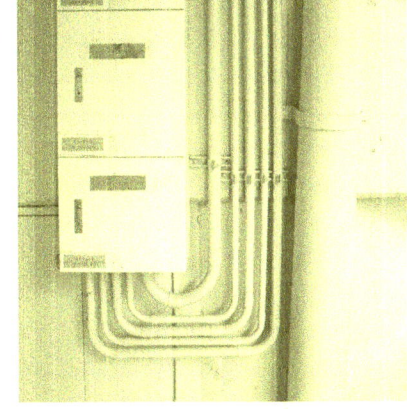

Sympathetic dominance (Fight or Flight): Responds to stress. It's the gas pedal, fight flight mode. If weak we see anxiety, revved up mind, loose bowels, and the many other signs of stress.

Parasympathetic dominance: Is the resting side of the nervous system; the brakes; things we don't have to think about like digestion, breathing, blood pressure. If weak we see low energy and motivation, poor coping and depression.

Adrenals: The emergency backup system of the body that jumps in when you need a boost; the jumper cable and battery. Greatly affected by stress. The adrenals aid in sugar handling and are weakened by too much sugar. If they're tired, they are priority. Caffeine to adrenals is like taking a whip to an exhausted horse.

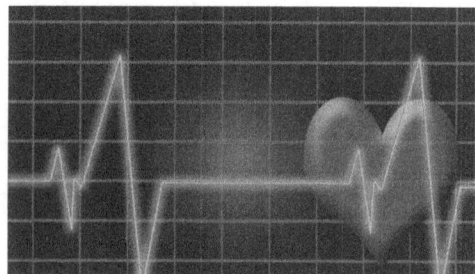

Cardiovascular:

Relates to the heart and circulatory system including oxygenation of the blood.

INTERPRETING YOUR HIGH-LOW SCORE DIFFERENCES

Again, the most revealing aspect of this assessment is often the degree of difference between scores. These differences are relative. The relative scores of one competence to another is often an excellent indicator of behavior and performance. Any strength taken to extreme can become a weakness, especially if the balancing emotional competence is low. For example, reality testing is a great decision-making skill, but if it is high and flexibility is low, a person may come across as overly controlling. It is always good to have balance in your profile. **For the EQi 2.0, if you see a difference of five points between the highs and lows, that can be significant. For the Ghyst EI Test, a difference of even one point can be significant.**

Look at your graphs from the EQi 2.0 or your Ghyst EI Test:

What are my high scores?

A. _____

B. _____

C. _____

D. _____

What are my low scores?

A. _____

B. _____

C. _____

D. _____

Look at your Symptom Survey Results:

What are my most stressed body systems?

A. _____

B. _____

C. _____

If you see these relative emotional highs and lows, ESPECIALLY the underlined competencies, you may have the

ALPHA PROFILE:

High: <u>assertiveness</u>, self-regard, and/or independence

Low: <u>empathy</u>, self-awareness, social responsibility, interpersonal relationships, impulse control, emotional expression, flexibility

Take a special look at assertiveness and empathy. These are the main indicators of this profile. If you have the other highs and lows as well, it means that it is highly likely that you have this profile.

PHYSICAL CORRELATIONS: <u>Biliary-Liver</u>, Sugar Handling

Note: If you see a difference of 10 points on the EQi 2.0 or 2 to 3 points on the Ghyst EI evaluation, you may be perceived as abrasive, abrupt, and without tact. You likely don't listen well, don't ask for opinions or input from others, and tend to take charge or take over. If coupled with high self-regard, you may be seen as arrogant. At its most extreme, these ultra alphas can be seen as aggressive, abusive, or bullying.

Alpha Strengths: Strong personality, driver, gets things done, results driven, high performer.

How does this Alpha Profile affect the following?:

Time Management: You may take on way too much because you don't think anyone can do it as well as you can. You may have trouble delegating.

Relationships: Doesn't listen, doesn't ask for opinions or input from others. Takes charge, takes over. If coupled with high self-regard, may be seen as arrogant.

Team Interactions: Has a tendency to take over and not work in a collaborative way.

Communication: Poor listening skills. Lack of understanding of others and their needs.

Presentation Skills: Usually good presenters, but lower empathy prevents a connection with the audience and understanding what they want.

Stress Management: Alphas are frequently stressed and hurried. They rarely take the time for themselves or build in daily reflection and recovery time.

Safety: Alphas may intentionally or unintentionally compromise good safety practices in the name of getting things done. Lower emotional self-awareness may mean low proprioception (how their body moves in time and space) and not aware of how they are feeling (tired, stressed, angry, etc)

Innovation: Alphas may be set in their ways (control/perfectionism). Alphas are usually masters, so the possibilities of doing things differently rarely occur to them.

Diversity and Inclusion: Because of lower empathy, Alphas may not be able to relate to and understand folks who are different than them.

Things to Work On: Empathy is a big key for alphas. By tuning in more to the needs of others, you create more intimate connections with others, which will help with your success both personally and professionally.

If you see these relative emotional highs and lows, ESPECIALLY the underlined competencies, you may have the

SELF-SACRIFICE PROFILE:

High: empathy, self-awareness, interpersonal relationships, social responsibility, flexibility

Low: assertiveness, independence, emotional expression, stress tolerance, self-regard, problem solving

PHYSICAL CORRELATIONS: Sugar Handling, Adrenals, Parasympathetic Dominance. Many self-sacrificers eat a lot of carbs and/or sugar. This adds to this dynamic. When you help people, you get a dopamine rush and feel good. Sugar and carbohydrates gives you the same feeling. We also see problem solving issues with many self-sacrificers due to this glucose imbalance.

Take a special look at assertiveness and empathy. These are the main indicators of this profile. If you have the other highs and lows as well, it means that it is highly likely that you have this profile.

Self-Sacrifice Strengths: Great team player, very helpful to others, good with people.

How does this Self-Sacrifice Profile affect the following?:

Time Management: Because you may not set proper limits and boundaries and are reluctant to say no, you will likely take on too much and be pulled into other people's agendas. This adds to stress levels and your work suffers.

Relationships: You may have scored lower in relationship skills because your relationships may not be mutually satisfying. You may give more than you get. Self-sacrificers think that when they start setting better limits and boundaries, that people won't like them anymore. The opposite is true. These limits create clear expectations and communication.

Team Interaction: You are a great team member, but you may not speak up and contribute your ideas.

Communication: Because you may be reluctant to say what you are thinking and feeling, there may be miscommunications. You may overpromise and under-deliver because you don't want to say no.

Presentation Skills: You may be reluctant to "put yourself out there" and connect with the audience.

Stress Management: Because you say yes a lot and don't set limits, you will likely take on too much and be overwhelmed much of the time. Stress levels stay high.

Safety: Self-sacrificers care about safety of the group, but may not have good self-care, so their own health and well-being may suffer. This may create a safety risk for them (stress, lack of sleep, etc).

Innovation: Self-sacrificers are rarely risk-takers, so they may not embrace innovation the same way others do.

Diversity and Inclusion: Self-sacrificers are quite good at being inclusive and understanding those who are different than themselves, sometimes to their own detriment.

Things to Work On: Assertiveness is the key to this profile. Be clear in your communications. Set better limits and boundaries. Begin each day with YOUR list of things to accomplish and don't be pulled off track by others. Have times when your door is closed. When these communications are clear, there is a deeper level of understanding from the people in your life and work. Reduce carbohydrates and sugar and always defer a decision. If someone asks if you can help, tell them that you will let them know in an hour or tomorrow. Then, you will have time to formulate a response. You can also say, "I can't say yes to that at this time."

If you see these relative emotional highs and lows, ESPECIALLY the underlined competencies, you may have the

CONTROLLER /PUPPET MASTER/PERFECTIONIST PROFILE:

High: reality testing, problem solving, impulse control

Low: flexibility

Take a special look at reality testing, problem solving and flexibility. These are the main indicators of this profile. If you have high impulse control as well, it means that it is highly likely that you have this profile.

Look at self-regard. If self-regard is **low**, you may be a perfectionist who beats yourself up because you don't live up to your own standards. If self-regard is **high**, you may think that no one else can do it better than you. Either way, people with this profile have a hard time letting go of control and delegating. You may tend to be a workaholic, but are rarely seen as a leader. **This is one of the biggest stumbling blocks to moving past a middle management position.**

PHYSICAL CORRELATIONS: Biliary-Liver and Sympathetic Dominance (Fight or Flight)

Control/Puppet Master/Perfectionist Strengths: Very detail oriented, good at planning and adherence to specifications, high quality work.

How does this Control/Puppet Master/Perfectionist Profile affect the following?:

Time Management: Trouble delegating. You tend to work a lot, but never get everything done. You won't let others do things their way. You won't let them make their mistakes. You are the "go to" problem solver. You stay in the details.

Relationships: You may try to control too many things in relationships, which leads to conflicts. Remember, you can be right or you can be happy.

Team Interaction: You tend to try and control the process and control the direction of the team. Negatively affects collaboration and the team process.

Communication: Preconceptions on how things should be may prevent understanding and connection with others.

Presentation Skills: May be rigid in your approach to presenting. Try being more spontaneous and improvisational. You don't have to have a perfect speech.

Stress Management: Overwhelmed because of lack of delegation. Works too much. Wants to be in on all decisions and know all information and details.

Safety: They are usually good at setting and implementing rules, but may not be as adept at the human side of safety and how to motivate others to work safely.

Innovation: Because they like to exert and maintain control, they are not as adept at innovation, which requires some element of risk, especially if the risk involves others or situations that are out of their area of control.

Diversity and Inclusion: Since they like the status quo and they don't like things to change drastically, diversity and inclusion may not be their best area. Diversity and inclusion require some thinking outside the box.

Things to Work On: Flexibility: with yourself, with others, with outcomes. By having a more flexible approach. Delegate more. Ask yourself: Is it wrong, or is it just different? Also, better stress tolerance can be helpful.

If you see these relative emotional highs and lows, ESPECIALLY the underlined competencies, you may have the

ANGER, FRUSTRATION, IMPATIENCE PROFILE:

High: <u>Assertiveness</u>,

Low: <u>Impulse Control</u>, Flexibility

Take a special look at assertiveness and impulse control. These are the main indicators of this profile. If you have low flexibility as well, it means that it is highly likely that you have this profile.

PHYSICAL CORRELATIONS: Biliary-Liver and Sugar Handling. Work on keeping your glucose levels even throughout your day by eating protein whenever you eat carbs and always eat breakfast.

How does this Anger, Frustration, Impatience Profile affect the following?:

Time Management: When experiencing anger, your thinking brain shuts down. This cognitive impairment reduces efficiency.

Relationships: Explosions directed toward others creates negative experiences and diminishes relationships. People won't come to you with anything negative for fear of an explosion.

Team Interaction: Team members may not connect with you. Your explosive nature diminishes interactions.

Communication: Anger, frustration, and impatience limits your communication skills. People will avoid you and not share information because of your overreactions.

Presentation Skills: May have trouble settling into a calm, easy presentation.

Stress Management: This is a huge factor that adds to stress levels. You are in a low-level fight or flight most of your day, which wears you out. By the end of the day, you are likely exhausted.

Safety: Being angry tends to shut down the thinking part of your brain, resulting in diminished problem solving and awareness. Also, physical awareness may be diminished. Their anger and ranting (especially when someone reports a possible safety issue) may limit future reporting.

Innovation: Frustration/impatience/anger usually involves focusing on all things that are "wrong". There is usually very little focus on the future or how to do things differently or better.

Diversity and Inclusion: When someone is seen as an angry person, they will likely be seen as unapproachable. This lack of connection with others will likely lead to a diminished focus on diversity and inclusion.

Things to Work On: Work on impulse control and empathy. Empathy will decrease assertiveness and impulse control will help with the reactions. Remember, take a deep breath and respond instead of reacting.

If you see these following relatively low scores, you may have the

BURNOUT PROFILE:

Low: self-regard, interpersonal relationships, self-actualization, stress tolerance, optimism, happiness

Five or six out of six = total burnout. Three to four out of six = highly stressed. Two out of six = pay attention. These six competencies contribute to an overall level of happiness and well-being.

Low **stress tolerance** indicates an inability to handle stressful situations, especially when there are strong emotions involved. You feel overwhelmed and hurried.

NOTE: *If you believe you are having mental health issues such as anxiety, depression and/or suicidal thoughts, please reach out to the suicide prevention hotline at 1-800-273-8255 or visit: preventconstructionsuicide.com*

for information, risk assessments, and support material.

PHYSICAL CORRELATIONS: 1. Parasympathetic Dominance (tired) 2. The Trilogy of (Digestive, Biliary-Liver, and Sugar Handling) 3. Adrenals

NOTE: *If you have high stress tolerance, but also are experiencing the physical symptoms of stress (trouble sleeping, headaches or other pain, fatigue, stomach problems, diminished immunity: frequents colds or flu, diminished sex drive, diminished cognitive ability, melancholy or depression) you are racing toward burnout. Just because you have the capacity to cope with stress emotionally doesn't mean it's not taking its toll on your body.*

PHYSICAL CORRELATION: Sympathetic Dominance (Fight or Flight)

How does this Burnout Profile affect the following?:

Time Management: Don't have the energy to get all of your work done. Overwhelmed, in fight or flight, cognitive processes impaired.

Relationships: Very little time and energy for the relationships in your life and work. May come across as withdrawn and disinterested.

Team Interaction: In survival mode, don't create connections and interactions, also too tired to contribute, you do the minimum.

Communication: Cognitive impairment reduces communication ability. Also, because you are exhausted, you may come across as disinterested.

Presentation Skills: Great presentation is all about energy. When your energy is low, there is no connection with the audience.

Stress Management: Self-explanatory.

Safety: When you are in burnout, many times, your body is in a low level fight or flight (adrenaline and cortisol). When this happens, your thinking brain shuts down and you can problem solve or perceive potential safety hazards. If you add lack of sleep, drug and alcohol use, poor nutrition, and lack of exercise, you may have an incident waiting to happen.

Innovation: When all of your energy is going to fight or flight (survival), your thinking is short term and you are in a reactive mode and you don't have the energy to try and do something differently. This does not bode well for innovation.

Diversity and Inclusion: Because of lack of energy, you will likely not be able to cultivate relationships or connect with others in a meaningful way. This will likely diminish your diversity and inclusion efforts.

Things to Work On: Stress Management is a key here. Build in recovery throughout your day. In addition, if your emotional self-awareness is low, that is the place to begin. You must be able to identify when you are tired, overwhelmed, etc. You must know what is happening in your body. Also, focusing on taking care of yourself, finding purpose and meaning in your life, connecting with others, and cultivating an optimistic outlook will help with this profile.

If you see this high and low pair, you may have the

CHAOS, REACTIVE MANAGEMENT PROFILE:

High: Stress Tolerance

Low: Impulse Control

PHYSICAL CORRELATIONS: Biliary-Liver, Sugar Handling, The Trilogy

How does this Chaos/Reactive Management Profile affect the following?:

Time Management: You get a lot of work done, but you are just reacting to things. You do not plan proactively. You will usually have low problem-solving skills as well. Workplace usually cluttered and cramped.

Relationships: No time for meaningful relationships. Reacts to everything.

Team Interaction: Living in a world of chaos, team interactions are usually frantic and frazzled.

Communication: You don't take the time to cultivate relationships. You may be trying to check emails and work while you are interacting with others.

Presentation Skills: Disorganization contributes to poor presentations.

Stress Management: Always feeling behind, on the treadmill. Feeling stress constantly.

Safety: Hurrying up, not preplanning, not looking ahead and being reactive is a safety nightmare!

Innovation: Innovation requires forward thinking, which this profile does not do well.

Diversity and Inclusion: With a lack of forward thinking, diversity and inclusion will likely take a back seat.

Things to Work On: Increase impulse control while working on managing stress. Remember to respond instead of react.

If you see this high and low pair, you may have the

OVERLY OPTIMISTIC PROFILE: Glass half full

High: Optimism

Low: Reality Testing

Overly Optimistic strengths: They always think positively about people and situations and sometimes change the outcome.

How does this Overly Optimistic Profile affect the following?:

Time Management: You think you can get more done than you actually can, so you tend to try to schedule too much.

Relationships: People like to be around optimistic, upbeat people. Sometimes over-commitment can lead to misunderstandings and not honoring promises.

Team Interaction: Unrealistic expectations that cannot be met.

Communication: May over-reach with expectations and not communicate clearly with details.

Presentation Skills: Good for presenting. Optimistic, upbeat energy is a magnet.

Stress Management: Mostly good for stress management. Optimistic people tend to cope with stress better, but over- committing and taking on too much may add to stress.

Safety: Overly optimistic people, when taken to the extreme, will think that everything will be okay and there will be no safety issues. These people will need a reality checker.

Innovation: Overly optimistic people are generally quite good with innovation as they are positive that they can work out the issues and make something work. The downside is they may not know when to give in or give up.

Diversity and Inclusion: Optimistic people are positive about the future and will likely be able to engage with any diversity and inclusion efforts.

Things to Work On: Would benefit from reality checks with someone you trust. Try to temper your optimism with reality checks and working on your reality testing.

If you see this high and low pair, you may have the

PESSIMIST OR REALIST PROFILE: Glass half empty

High: Reality Testing

Low: Optimism

Overly Pessimistic Strengths: They bring a reality check to their social and work groups.

How does this Pessimist Profile affect the following?:

Time Management: Negative attitude may reduce performance and results. May get mired down in all of the things that are impediments to progress.

Relationships: People shy away from negative people.

Team Interaction: Bring the team down. Be the curmudgeon who always looks at the negative side.

Communication: May take communications down a negative path by focusing on the negative.

Presentation Skills: Audiences may not connect with a negative presentation of a message.

Stress Management: Pessimistic people have higher levels of stress.

Safety: Pessimists can be good for safety programs. They are going to try and envision every single solitary thing that could possibly go wrong.

Innovation: Not a pessimists' strength. They tend to have a yes, but mentality and will find every possible thing that could go wrong with any innovation initiative. It could stall the process.

Diversity and Inclusion: Pessimists may be seen as negative and unapproachable, which may limit diversity and inclusion, especially if it is a new initiative. They may be able to contribute to a plan for D&I and let you know all of the things that won't work before you roll it out.

Things to Work On: Increase optimism and create more balance. Would benefit from reality checks with someone you trust.

If you see this high and low pair, you may have the

TEAM PLAYER PROFILE:

High: Social Responsibility

Low: Independence

Team Player Strengths: Works well in groups or teams.

PHYSICAL CORRELATIONS: Sugar Handling

How does this Team Player profile affect the following?:

Time Management: You may take on too much for the team and not be able to complete your own work.

Relationships: Generally good at relationships, especially in a team setting.

Team Interaction: Excellent with team and collaboration. But may be reluctant to contribute your own ideas.

Communication: Your lower independence may hinder good communication if you hold back saying what is on your mind. But generally, these folks are good communicators.

Presentation Skills: Good presenters. Good connections with audiences.

Stress Management: You may take on too much, which adds to stress levels.

Safety: Team players are safety players. They care for the group and will look out for others.

Innovation: You want some team players on your innovation initiatives. They will move the ball forward in a collaborative way.

Diversity and Inclusion: Team players generally embrace D&I and will be an asset to any program.

Things to Work On: If there is a large gap between independence and social responsibility (10 points or more on the EQi 2.0 or 3 points or more on the Ghyst EI Test), you may want to work on independence to create some balance. Assertiveness would also be helpful to create the balance.

If you see this high and low pair, you may have the

THE LONE WOLF PROFILE:

High: Independence

Low: Social Responsibility

The Lone Wolf Strengths: Can work well alone and be self-motivated.

Lone Wolf Liabilities: Can be held back by lack of motivation to invest in interpersonal potential with others.

How does this Lone Wolf profile affect the following?:

Time Management: Watch isolation that may lead to overwhelm and not relying on others for help.

Relationships: Generally, relationships are not strong.

Team Interaction: Sometimes a good contributor, but usually behind the scenes.

Communication: Without meaningful connections and relationships, sometimes communication is on a superficial level.

Presentation Skills: Generally low energy for presentations and not a great connection with the audience.

Stress Management: Stress levels can be high, especially if you don't ask for help.

Safety: Lone wolves may not be a big contributor to safety programs as they do not connect with others.

Innovation: As long as Lone Wolves can work alone, they are fine, but if innovation requires collaboration, they will likely be less adept.

Diversity and Inclusion: They are seen as wanting to be left alone, so their D&I efforts may be limited.

Things to Work On: Work on social responsibility and relationships (especially if there is a difference of 10 points or more on the EQi 2.0 or 3 points or more on the Ghyst EI Test.)

If you see this high and low pair, you may have the

CHASES SHINY OBJECTS PROFILE:

High: Flexibility

Low: Impulse Control

Chases Shiny Objects Strengths: Able to embrace something new in a moment's notice.

PHYSICAL CORRELATIONS: Sugar Handling

How does this Chases Shiny Objects profile affect the following?:

Time Management: Generally cluttered workspace. You start more than you finish and go from one thing to the next.

Relationships: You may come across as scattered and unfocused. This may negatively affect relationships.

Team Interaction: Scattered and unfocused, team members may not trust you to complete and contribute.

Communication: Hard to pin down. Unclear communication at times. Unfocused.

Presentation Skills: Presentations seem to be scattered. Goes down rabbit trails and loses the audience.

Stress Management: Stress levels can be high. You rarely slow down and build in recovery.

Safety: Unable to focus, safety may not be CSO folks' best thing.

Innovation: Generally good at initial ideas for innovation, CSO folks may need some help in bringing the innovation to fruition.

Diversity and Inclusion: As long as there are no other initiatives, CSO folks may be okay with D&I, but it may not be sustainable over time.

Things to Work On: Increase impulse control and assertiveness, which will reduce flexibility. Would benefit from learning rhetoric for communication and presentations.

Self-Regard Respecting oneself, confidence **Self-Perception Composite**	**Self-Actualization** Pursuit of meaning, self improvement **Self-Perception Composite**
Emotional Self-Awareness Understanding own emotions **Self-Perception Composite**	**Emotional Expression** Constructive expression of emotion **Self-Expression Composite**
Assertiveness Communicating feelings, beliefs, in a non-offensive way **Self-Expression Composite**	**Independence** Self-directed; free from emotional dependency **Self-Expression Composite**
Interpersonal Relationships Mutually satisfying relationships **Interpersonal Composite**	**Empathy** Understanding, appreciating how others feel **Interpersonal Composite**

Social Responsibility

Social consciousness, helpfulness

Interpersonal Composite

Problem Solving

Find solutions when emotions are involved

Decision Making Composite

Reality Testing

Objective; sees things as they really are

Decision Making Composite

Impulse Control

Resist or delay impulse to act

Decision Making Composite

Flexibility

Adapting emotions, thoughts and behaviors

Stress Management Composite

Stress Tolerance

Coping with stressful situations

Stress Management Composite

Optimism

Positive attitude and outlook on life

Stress Management Composite

Happiness

Satisfied with life; content

Well Being Indicator

EI Competence Ranking

Date: _____

Part 1: Rank the sixteen emotional competencies from the most important to the least important in your personal and professional life (NOT how you scored or what you want to work on). You may cut out the competencies (on the previous pages) if that helps you to rank them. Put today's date on this page and write them below:

1. _____
2. _____
3. _____
4. _____
5. _____
6. _____
7. _____
8. _____
9. _____
10. _____
11. _____
12. _____
13. _____
14. _____
15. _____
16. _____

Part 2:

Now that you have ranked your competencies from the most important to least important, How do your scores compare with your EI competence ranking (cards) on previous pages? Are your low scores also at the bottom of your ranking? Should you focus on those areas so they can be higher? If something is at the top of your ranking and you scored low, how might you be working on that competence?

Part 2: Where do I want to be?

GOALS

Personal:

1 year

_____

_____

5 years

_____

_____

10 years

_____

_____

Professional:

1 year

_____

_____

5 years

_____

_____

10 years

_____

_____

Health or Other Goals:

1 year

_____
_____

5 years

_____
_____

10 years

_____
_____

How well aligned is your EI to meet your future personal and professional goals? Example: Do you have a high enough level of independence and self-regard to move into a higher position?

_____
_____
_____
_____
_____

What are your physical concerns?

Example: weight, stress, fatigue, pain, sleep, physical symptoms

_____
_____
_____
_____

Do you have an EI strength that may eventually become a weakness? Example: Do you so much empathy that you neglect to take care of yourself, so much assertiveness that you are viewed as too aggressive, so much self-regard that you are viewed as arrogant?

How do your scores compare to your EI ranking cards? Are your low scores at the bottom of your ranking? Should you focus on those?

Do you have a lower emotional competence that could become problematic?

What would your family like you to improve?

What additional information do you need/want?

_____
_____
_____
_____

How does your physical state affect your emotions? How do your emotions affect your physical state? Does your physical state affect happiness? Does your health affect self-regard? Is impulse control an issue with eating and healthy habits? Does nutrition affect problem solving and energy levels? Is sleep a vital factor for overall performance? Does exercise make a difference in how you think and feel? Discuss these issues here in more detail:

_____
_____
_____
_____

Review your short and long-term goals that you wrote down in your personal information as well as the challenges that you listed in the 4 Quadrants. How well aligned is your EI to meet your future personal and professional needs? Will your profile help you to overcome your challenges and attain your goals? Example: Do you have a high enough level of independence and self-regard to move into a higher position? What about physically? Are you too tired to do the things you need to do? Will illness force you into a work situation that you don't want?

_____
_____
_____
_____

Part 3: How do I get there from here?

Now it's time to create your development plans! Go through the following steps to create your plans and don't forget to go all the way to the end of the workbook in order to build in the accountability to implement your plans!

Development Plan:

1. Use the analysis you've just completed to help you decide what to work on going forward.

2. You will get the best results if you combine the activities from the emotional sections and the physical sections.

3. Consult the **EI Activity Guide** or search the internet to find development activities on how to improve. Fill those activities in the blanks of your Development Plan.

4. **It is highly recommended that you choose at least ONE PRACTICAL DAILY APPLICATION activity for both the emotional and the physical.** Refer to the **EI Activity Guide** on page 56. And remember: it is daily application and daily reflection that create the most and the fastest behavioral change.

Development Plan Sample

Name: **Brent Darnell**

My goal is to (increase, **decrease**, improve, develop): **my weight**

When I achieve this goal, I will realize the following benefits:
1. more energy
2. higher self-regard and confidence
3. better health, longer life

Development activities (from EI Activity Guide):	**Target completion date:**
1. Dr. Berg fat burning book	1. November
2. Food log, monitor eating	2. Daily, ongoing
3. Exercise daily-yoga, P90X	3. Daily, ongoing
4. Self-hypnosis weight loss	4. Daily, ongoing

Accountability:
List specific accountability folks here:
Me, my wife, my brother-we are doing this together, my scale-weigh each day

How will I know that I am achieving this goal?
    Measure 1: The scale
    Measure 2: Higher energy
    Measure 3: Better fitting clothes

Development Plan Sample

Name: **Brent Darnell**

My goal is to (increase, decrease, **improve**, develop): **sugar handling**

When I achieve this goal, I will realize the following benefits:
1. Lose weight, less fatigue
2. Less explosive, better impulse control. My sugar lows contribute to angry outbursts.
3. Think more clearly, better problem solving

Development activities (from EI Activity Guide):   **Target completion date:**
1. Keep a food diary   1. ongoing
2. Start reading labels to decrease sugar intake   2. ongoing
4. Read Beat Sugar Addiction Now-Teitelbaum   3. December
5. Watch Fast Food Nation   4. November

Accountability:
List specific accountability folks here:
Me. My wife. My brother. We are doing this together.

How will I know that I am achieving this goal?
    Measure 1: I will feel better.
    Measure 2: Weight will decrease.
    Measure 3: Won't explode as often.

Development Plan Sample

Name: **Brent Darnell**

My goal is to (**increase**, decrease, improve, develop): **Impulse Control**

When I achieve this goal, I will realize the following benefits:
1. Fewer outbursts, less anger and frustration.
2. Better able to manage my emotions, which will help my physical state
3. Less stress because I will not expend that energy and go into fight or flight.

Development activities (from EI Activity Guide):	Target completion date:
1. Eat for mood management. Decrease sugar	1. ongoing
2. Practice the 20-minute solution	2. ongoing
3. Read the Anger Control Workbook	3. December
4. Watch The Godfather and focus on Sonny	4. November

Accountability:
List specific accountability folks here: Me. My wife. My brother.

How will I know that I am achieving this goal?
    Measure 1: Fewer outbursts.
    Measure 2: Less stress, anger, and frustration.
    Measure 3: Make better eating choices.

Development Plan

Name:

My goal is to (increase, decrease, improve, develop):

When I achieve this goal, I will realize the following benefits:
1. _____
2. _____
3. _____

Development activities (from EI Activity Guide):   **Target completion date:**
1.   1.
2.   2.
3.   3.
4.   4.

Accountability:
List specific accountability folks here: _____

How will I know that I am achieving this goal?
        Measure 1: _____
        Measure 2: _____
        Measure 3: _____

Development Plan

Name: _____

My goal is to (increase, decrease, improve, develop):

When I achieve this goal, I will realize the following benefits:
1. _____
2. _____
3. _____

Development activities (from EI Activity Guide):	**Target completion date:**
1.	1.
2.	2.
3.	3.
4.	4.

Accountability:
List specific accountability folks here: _____

How will I know that I am achieving this goal?
    Measure 1: _____
    Measure 2: _____
    Measure 3: _____

Development Plan

Name:

My goal is to (increase, decrease, improve, develop):

When I achieve this goal, I will realize the following benefits:
1. _____
2. _____
3. _____

Development activities (from EI Activity Guide):	**Target completion date:**
1.	1.
2.	2.
3.	3.
4.	4.

Accountability:
List specific accountability folks here: _____

How will I know that I am achieving this goal?
    Measure 1: _____
    Measure 2: _____
    Measure 3: _____

Accountability Partners

Accountability is a huge key for creating changes. Build in as much accountability as possible. Let your partners know what you are working on and ask them to hold you accountable. Meet with them often with scheduled check-in meetings.

Program Accountability Partner:

Name: _____

Mentor (may be the same as "Above me" or may be someone else above you):

Name: _____

Contact info (email and phone): _____

Above me:

Name: _____

Contact info (email and phone): _____

Beside me:

Name: _____

Contact info (email and phone): _____

Below me:

Name: _____

Contact info (email and phone): _____

Family/Friend (someone who knows you well):

Name: _____

Contact info (email and phone): _____

Client/Other Business Contact (outside your company):

Name: _____

Contact info (email and phone): _____

Development Success: How are you doing?

This is for your accountability partners to track weekly/monthly progress.

Name: _____

Date: _____

How successful were you in implementing your plans? For each week (1-52), write in the % of success (from 0-100%)

Activities	Week #	Week #	Week #	Week #

Journal: Add any victories or challenges especially those that you would like to discuss at your next meeting with your accountability partner or coach.

Week #

Week #

Week #

Week #

How to Create Lifelong Learning:

Here are a few tips to create lifelong learning and not let this powerful work go away in time.

1. Create a future vision for yourself. Sit with your eyes closed and imagine your perfect future life. Then write down what you imagined.

2. Write down a few affirmations to put into words what your future vision is. Put them in present tense as if you have already attained this vision.

3. Another great way to change those old tapes in your subconscious (I'm not good enough, I'm a failure, I'm fat, I don't deserve to be successful or happy, I'm a bad father or mother, etc) is self-hypnosis (www.instant-hypnosis.com or www.innertalk.com). There are many websites that have hypnosis audios that will reprogram your subconscious with positive thoughts. Find the ones that are applicable to what you are trying to accomplish or overcome. This accomplishes a lot of things. Even if you aren't consciously thinking about it, your subconscious is and creating your future.

4. Have a plan. This could be your EI development plan or your personal mission statement or some type of weekly worksheet with your roles and goals that you have for your life. IT MUST BE WRITTEN! Don't keep it in your head. Make it easy and simple and portable. Carry it with you always. Put it in your day timer or electronically in your Smartphone.

5. Work your plan. You must make a commitment to be proactive and work your plan. Always have a plan A, B, and C. Plan A is the best (exercise five times a week), Plan B is for when you get busy (exercise two times per week), Plan C is for when things get insane (walk for 20 minutes during lunch).

6. You must continually measure your progress. How will you tell if you are attaining your goals? You can re-take the EQi or the Ghyst EI Test, but there are many other ways to measure success and change.

7. Build in accountability. Find an accountability partner or several partners. Let them know what you are working on and have them hold you accountable. You can help each other to stay focused. Roll this into your review process at work. Let your boss know what you are working on.

8. Write a letter to yourself dated one year from the date you begin your plan. Or you can create a mind movie that is a future diary in video format. This plants these future visions in your subconscious so that you are working on them even when you aren't consciously thinking about them.

9. Example: Dear Brent, Congratulations for losing that last 20 pounds and for improving your empathy and impulse control. You have better relationships with your colleagues and your family and friends. Also, congratulations for your recent promotion and for winning the President's Award. You are firing on all cylinders. Keep up the great work! All the best, Brent

10. If you are in a group, listen to your music on your playlist. If you are working on your own, listen to the music that inspires you. The same goes for books and movies. Go to the sources that motivate you.

11. You will have setbacks. Don't beat yourself up. Be kind to yourself and get back on track. Go to the places and people and sources that give you encouragement.

12. Pay attention to your measurements, then follow up continuously and make adjustments. Ask people how you are doing. Continually look for ways to improve-read books, take classes, discuss this work with others. Revisit your EI Roadmap and look for more development strategies.

13. Check in at least once a year and take the EQi or Ghyst EI Test every year to two years. Revisit your development plans, see what has changed in your life and revise, as necessary.

14. <u>You MUST HAVE reflection time</u> every day if possible-call it meditation time, prayer time, quiet time, visualization time or whatever you want to call it. Be alone with your thoughts and start seeing yourself as you want to be. This is the <u>single most important thing</u> you can do.

EI Activity Guide:
Resources for Development

G. BRENT DARNELL

THE TOUGH GUY SURVIVAL KIT WORKBOOK

EI Activity Guide: TABLE OF CONTENTS

EI Activity Guide	61
Self-Regard	63
Self-Actualization	68
Emotional Self-Awareness	71
Emotional Expression	91
Assertiveness	92
Independence	95
Interpersonal Relationship	97
Empathy	99
Social Responsibility	106
Problem Solving	108
Reality Testing	111
Impulse Control	112
Flexibility	115
Stress Tolerance	117
Optimism	121
Happiness	123
Biliary and Liver	123
Sugar Handling: Food to Fuel	128
Digestive	131
Foundation	133
Sympathetic Dominance (The Gas)	135
Parasympathetic Dominance (The Brakes)	137
Cardiovascular Stress	139
Adrenals	141

EI Activity Guide

The guide is filled with development activities for your emotional development. We have included many different approaches from many different sources including secular, Christian, Eastern philosophies and religions, academic, philosophical, psychological, medical, childhood learning, and new age. There are many different types of development activities as well including books, plays, operas, fables, movies, television, videos, exercises, and websites and apps. These activities will be applicable to your personal life as well as your professional life.

There are two approaches to these activities:

1. Take away the things that are "bad" for you; whether they are behaviors, emotions, or thoughts. These deplete you.
2. Add the things that are "good" for you; whether they are behaviors, emotions, or thoughts. These build you up.

Don't try to set aside time for these activities! Try to weave these activities throughout your day. Do a little something each day rather than a big something once a week.

Choose the activities that resonate with you. If the one you choose does not work for you, try another one. If you are not a reader, stay away from the books. If you are an experiential learner, choose the experiential exercises. If you are a movie lover, check out the movies and find opportunities to discuss the emotional content with others. Determine the EI profiles of the various characters, which will give clues as to their behaviors in the movies. Do this emotional exploration with various types of music as well. What emotions do certain pieces of music evoke? If you practice a certain religion or philosophy, gravitate toward or away from the strategies listed. If you have suggestions for development ideas, please let us know. We are constantly adding to these lists.

We recommend that you choose at least ONE or TWO activities from the daily application section. It is the daily application of this work and the daily reflection on how you are doing that will create behavioral changes and lasting results.

It is vital to practice some form of reflection, meditation, prayer, pondering, and/or visualization each day. First of all, check in with yourself and how you are feeling. Identify your feelings and be specific. Then check in with all of your senses: sight, sound, touch, smell, and taste if you are enjoying your morning beverage. Become hyper-aware of these senses and feelings. Don't think, plan, or solve future problems. Just be. After this exercise, go through the previous day and think about your emotional management and reactions and try to make tweaks in your mind and heart to create a different outcome the next time this situation arises again.

What do athletes do when they are about to execute a shot or physical action? They visualize the positive outcome. Try to visualize yourself in your daily situations and how you will react to those situations. Work on the competencies you have chosen by seeing yourself as you want to be. If you are working on impulse control, see yourself in control. If you are working on your assertiveness, visualize yourself being assertive. Be as specific as possible and try to involve all of your senses. The brain doesn't know the difference between visualization and the real thing, and it will create new neural pathways necessary for behavioral change.

Measure your results. It is not enough just to read a book or try an exercise. **You must apply it in your daily life in the form of behavioral change. When you do that, watch for and measure the outcome. Look for changes in yourself and people's response to you.** Write down the exercises that you do along with the outcome. Use the Development Success form in the EI Roadmap to track progress and celebrate successes.

Enlist trusted people (accountability partners) to observe you and let you know how you are doing. If you work for a company, incorporate your learning process into your annual review process for accountability. You can help each other to stay on track by holding each other accountable for the things that you are attempting. Contact each other at least weekly and let each other know what you are working on, then debrief each other periodically. Ask: Did you do that exercise? Did you read that book? Did you apply the information? Have you noticed any different outcomes? Have you noticed any behavioral shifts? Has anyone else noticed any behavioral shifts? Again, the Development Success sheet in your EI Roadmap is an excellent way to track and discuss this process.

Tap into Technology! If you can't find a resource that you like here, do a search: How do I increase/improve my . . . ? Also, search for apps that track and teach exercise, breathing, food choices, meditation, sleep, etc. Also, look into wearable technology like Fitbit and Apple Watch. These devices track just about everything and offer ways to improve all areas of your wellness and peak performance.

There are six main categories of development activities, and one category to be used if you are trying to decrease that particular competence:

1. **Practical Daily Application:** These are activities that you can apply every single day to help you to shift your behavior. Choose the ones that you are sure to do each day.

2. **Exercises and General Improvement Ideas:** These are ideas, activities, and hands on exercises that you can do. Some are thought exercises. They are more involved. They will take more time to implement than the activities that are applied daily. Practice them and find ways to make them your own.

3. **Books/Plays/Operas/Fables/CDs/Magazines (written and performance materials):** This category has stories and information that are relevant to emotional competencies and physical body systems. Books may be academic or psychological or fiction. Plays can demonstrate complex emotional situations from which the audience can learn. Operas are classic stories with strong emotional content. Fables contain archetypes from which emotional literacy was first imparted to us as children. Music can be a powerful way to explore emotions. Ask yourself what emotions are evoked while listening. There are also instructional CD's on meditation and other skills. There are certain magazines that touch on emotional competencies and increase awareness. Don't just read or watch these, but write a review from an emotional perspective. Use the competencies you are working on and integrate them into the experience. For instance, if you are working on empathy, try to determine the EI profiles of the characters. Subscribe to a magazine that embodies the emotional competencies you are working on.

4. **Movies/TV/Videos:** It's a Wonderful Life is a movie that relates each of the 16 emotional competencies. This is a great movie to begin with. Watch the movie and discuss all of the emotional competencies with someone. Also determine the EI profiles of the main characters and why the act and react the way that they do. Write a movie review from an emotional perspective. Two other movies that touch upon all 16 emotional competencies is The Godfather-Parts I and II. If you have the soundtracks to movies, listen to the music only and determine which emotions the music evokes. There are many opportunities to work on emotional competencies while watching your favorite television shows. Whether it is a

sitcom, reality TV, drama or talk show, you can discuss the emotional content, determine how the people feel and determine the EI profile of the characters.

5. **Websites/Apps:** It is up to you to find the websites that contain the information that you need. Search and find your own. A few good general development and peak performance websites and apps.

6. **Inspirational Quotes:** Find a quote that interests you, print it out and put it in a prominent place such as your morning mirror, your desktop, your refrigerator, or your workstation. Use it to center you and to remind you of your plans and goals.

7. **To decrease the competency:** Some of these competencies are detrimental if they are too high. This section tells you how to decrease a competency.

Help Your Insurance Costs!: We have cross referenced the big five for insurance companies (Body Mass Index or BMI, Glucose, Blood Pressure, Tobacco Use, and Cholesterol) with our Development Activities. If you are trying to quit tobacco or get any of these metrics into the normal range, pay special attention to those Development Activities.

Choose and obtain your activities and resources:

You may be wondering which activities and resources are right for you. Go to www.amazon.com where you will be able to see many of the resources prior to buying. For many of these resources, listen to them, see a table of contents, a front and back cover, or a video clip. This will ensure that you choose a resource that is right for you.

There are many ways to obtain the resources listed. Visit your local library. Go online:

www.amazon.com
www.barnesandnoble.com
www.audible.com (This website has audio books you can download.)
www.audiobooks.com (This website has audio books you can download.)
www.awesound.com

For movies, visit your local library or go online to download. Go to www.amazon.com, www.netflix.com, or www.hulu.com.

When all else fails, **start surfing the web for your own resources**. There are thousands out there. Just search on what you want to accomplish and find more resources that are right for you.

Self-Regard:

is respecting oneself while understanding and accepting one's strengths and weaknesses. Self-regard is often associated with feelings of inner strength and self-confidence.

Practical Daily Application: (some ideas courtesy of Texas Women's University)

1. Ask the people closest to you to make a list of all of the things that they like, love, admire about you. Compile the list and keep in handy. When you hear negative self-talk, take out the list as a reminder.

2. Identify all the things about yourself that you can take pride in. Write them down if you need to. Don't be embarrassed to feel or express that pride. Review the list daily if needed.

3. Respect your own needs. Recognize and take care of your own needs and wants first. Identify what really fulfills you- not just immediate gratifications. Write down this fulfillment list and keep it handy. Respecting your deeper needs will increase your sense of worth and well-being.

4. Act as if you are feeling confident, even when you are not.

5. At the beginning of the day, talk positively to yourself. Tell yourself you are worthy and go over all of the things you will accomplish during the day.

6. At the end of the day, reflect on what went well. Reward yourself if that is appropriate.

7. Practice being as accepting and forgiving to yourself as you are to others.

8. Talk to yourself positively. Stop listening to your "cruel inner critic". When you notice that you doubt or judging yourself, replace such thoughts with self-accepting thoughts, balanced self-assessment and self-supportive direction.

9. When you talk negatively about yourself, reframe it. For example, if you are telling yourself that you are incompetent and unworthy, focus on all of the areas in which you are competent. Focus on the positive things-even if a negative event triggered the negative self-talk. Use it as a learning experience for the future.

10. Reward yourself when you reach your goals.

11. Use a time management system to document your accomplishments.

12. Free yourself from "should." Live your life on the basis of what is possible for you and what feels right to you instead of what you or others think you "should" do. "Shoulds" distract us from identifying and fulfilling our own needs, abilities, interests and personal goals. Find out what you want and what you are good at, value those, and take actions designed to fulfill your potential.

13. Set achievable goals. Establish goals on the basis of what you can realistically achieve, and then work step-by-step to develop your potential. To strive always for perfection, to pursue absolute goals (e.g., "Anything less than an 'A' in school is always unacceptable") invites stress and failure.

Exercises and General Development Ideas: (some ideas courtesy of Texas Women's University)

1. Validate your self-perceptions by gathering feedback from others about yourself. Use formal assessment instruments as well as informal methods.

2. Learn to recognize the physiological states you experience when you are feeling self-confident, e.g. slow, rhythmic breathing. Go to those feeling states when your self-confidence is low.

3. To tackle something for which your confidence is low, break the project or activity into small tasks at which you can succeed.

4. Seek out and spend more time with people who affirm your skills, self-worth, and your contribution.

5. Spend as little time as possible with people who make you feel badly about yourself.

6. Don't take yourself too seriously. Laugh at your mistakes and learn from them.

7. Adopt a "learning" orientation toward life, i.e. be in the habit of learning something new all the time.

8. Test your reality. Separate your emotional reactions, your fears and negative feelings, from the reality of your current situation. For example, you may feel stupid, anxious and hopeless about a project, but if you think about it, you know that you still have the ability and opportunity to accomplish something on it.

9. Experience success. Seek out and put yourself in situations in which the probability of success is high. Look for projects, which stretch but don't overwhelm your abilities. Imagine yourself succeeding. Whatever you accomplish, let yourself acknowledge and experience success and good feelings about it.

10. Take chances. New experiences are learning experiences that can build self-confidence. Expect to make mistakes as part of the process; don't be disappointed if you don't do it perfectly. Feel good about trying something new, making progress and increasing your competence.

11. Solve problems. Don't avoid problems, and don't worry about them. Face them, and identify ways to solve them or cope with them. If you run away from problems you can solve, you threaten your self-confidence.

12. Make decisions. Practice making and implementing positive decisions flexibly but firmly, and trust yourself to deal with the consequences. When you assert yourself, you enhance your sense of yourself, learn more and increase your self-confidence.

13. Develop your skills. Know what you can and can't do. Assess the skills you need, learn and practice those.

14. Emphasize your strengths. Focus on what you can do rather than what you cannot. Accept current limitations and live comfortably within them, even as you consider what strengths you might want or need to develop next.

15. Rely on your own opinion of yourself. Entertain feedback from others, but don't rely on their opinions excessively. Depend on your own values in making decisions and deciding how you feel about yourself and what is right for you to do.

Books/Plays/Operas/Fables/CDs/Magazines:

1. Read <u>Psychology of Self Esteem</u> by Nathaniel Branden.

2. To identify your career strengths, weaknesses, and preferences, read <u>What Color is My Parachute?</u> By Richard Bolles.

3. Read <u>Shyness</u> by Barnardo J. Carducci, PhD.

4. Read <u>Self-Power</u> by Maria Arapakis.

5. Read <u>Talking with Confidence</u> and other books by Don Gabor.

6. Read <u>Your Best Life Now</u> by Joel Osteen.

7. Read <u>The New Secrets of Charisma</u> by Doe Lang, PhD.

8. Read <u>How to Develop Self Confidence and Influence People by Public Speaking</u> by Dale Carnegie.

9. Read <u>ReFraming, Neuro-Linguistic Programming and the Transformation of Meaning</u> by Richard Bandler and John Grinder.

10. Read <u>The Adventures of Pinocchio</u> by Carlo Collodi.

11. Read <u>The Ugly Ducking</u> by Hans Christian Andersen.

12. See the opera Porgy and Bess and watch how Porgy increases his self-regard to be able to win Bess over.

13. Read the story of Samson and Delilah in the Bible to see how too much self-regard was Samson's downfall.

14. Read <u>The Ragamuffin Gospel</u> by Brennan Manning.

15. Read <u>The Wisdom of Accepted Tenderness</u> by Brennan Manning.

16. Read <u>Ruthless Trust</u> by Brennan Manning.

17. Read <u>What's so Amazing About Grace?</u> By Philip Yancey.

18. Read <u>The Fountainhead</u> by Ayn Rand.

19. Read <u>The Confidence Makeover</u> by Dr. Keith Johnson.

20. Read <u>Confidence</u> by Moss Kanter.

<u>Movies/TV/Videos:</u>

1. The Good Girl-Jennifer Anniston's character develops good self-regard despite obstacles.

2. Risky Business. Notice how Joel is transformed from someone lacking self-confidence into someone with good self-regard.

3. The Elephant Man-Despite his outward appearance, John Merrick displays remarkable self-regard.

4. Citizen Kane-Orson Welles character has high self-regard to the point of arrogance, and it contributes to his undoing.

5. Lawrence of Arabia-T.E. Lawrence's high self-regard allows him to do remarkable things.

6. The Fountainhead-Howard Roark has the confidence to walk his own path.

7. Schindler's List-People in search of their own worth in a horrific time.

8. Raging Bull-Jake Lamotta's struggle to accept himself.

9. Patton-General George Patton's arrogance is his downfall and redemption.

10. Groundhog Day-Phil Connors learns a lesson about too much self-regard.

11. The Hustler-Fast Eddie Felson's high self-regard is his downfall. Also watch Minnesota Fats' confidence.

12. The Man Who Shot Liberty Valance-James Stewart's character fights for his own self-worth and confidence.

13. Marty-Earnest Borgnine finds his self-worth.

14. A Patch of Blue-Selena finds the confidence to break away from her domineering mother.

15. Watch The Best Years of Our Lives and how Homer develops his self-regard despite the loss of both of his arms in World War II. Fred's self-regard is tested as well when he comes back home.

16. Watch The Greatest Game Ever Played and see how far confidence can take you.

Websites/Apps:

1. Visit www.growthcentral.com
2. Visit www.self-confidence.co.uk
3. Visit www.more-selfesteem.com
4. Visit www.selfgrowth.com
5. Download the app: How to Develop: Self-Confidence for Success
6. Download the app: Confidence Coach
7. Download the app: Increasing Your Self-Confidence

Inspirational Quotes:

1. "The first step in handling anything is gaining the ability to face it." L. Ron Hubbard

2. "Fight! Be somebody! If you have lost confidence in yourself, make believe you are somebody else, somebody that's got brains, and act like him." Sol Hess

3. "Man must be buttressed from within, else the temple will crumble to dust." Marcus Aurelius Antoninus

4. "Other people's opinion of you does not have to become your reality." Les Brown

5. "There are admirable potentialities in every human being. Believe in your strength and your youth. Learn to repeat endlessly to yourself, 'It all depends on me.'" Andre Gide

6. "I was always looking outside myself for strength and confidence, but it comes from within. It is there all the time." Anna Freud

7. "Attempt easy tasks as if they were difficult, and difficult as if they were easy; in the one case that confidence may not fall asleep, in the other that it may not be dismayed." Baltasar Gracion.

8. "Self-confidence is the first requisite to great undertakings." Samuel Johnson

9. "I want you to take your ego out of the equation and judge the situation dispassionately. Arrogance and self-awareness seldom go hand in hand." Ian Fleming (M talking to James Bond in Casino Royale)

To decrease Self-Regard:

Too much self-regard can become arrogance. To decrease self-regard, work on the development strategies in the Interpersonal Skills, especially Social Responsibility and Empathy.

Self-Actualization:

is the willingness to persistently try to improve oneself and engage in the pursuit of personally relevant and meaningful objectives that lead to a rich and enjoyable life.

Practical Daily Application:

1. Create a personal mission statement for your life that encompasses the following areas: work, relationships, money, spirituality, and health.

2. Make a list of short-term and long-term goals and make plans to accomplish them. Schedule time daily to propel yourself toward your goals.

3. Make a list of your twenty favorite things to do and examine how frequently you actually do them. Schedule time for the ones you don't do often.

4. Ask yourself, "Why not?" when insecurity prevents you from pursuing your dreams.

5. Keep a daily diary and write down your hopes, dreams, aspirations and thoughts. The first step is to create that future. The second step is to assess current reality, confront the brutal facts. The third step is to focus on turning those dreams into realities by writing down concrete steps that propel you toward that future.

6. Schedule time each week explicitly for self-actualization pursuits.

7. Develop a daily habit of reflection, meditation, relaxation or prayer.

8. Email to your accountability partner 5 things you are grateful for each day.

Exercises and General Development Ideas:

1. Identify and develop your unique talents.

2. Share your interests with others by teaching or coaching them.

3. Identify those people who are your role models.

4. Identify your personal values and live by them.

5. Identify what interferes with pursuit of your goals. Examine your attitudes, your responsibilities, and your priorities.

6. Take career aptitude tests to identify your talents and opportunities.

7. Write down 5 to 10 things you want. Then write down 5-10 things you need. Then write down 5-10 things you love. Then ask yourself if you had a year to live, what would you do? Then list three things that are stopping you from doing the things you want to do. Review and see if there is any correlation/crossovers. This will give you some perspective on things.

8. Visualize outrageously successful scenarios for your future. Jim Collins calls these BHAGS (Big, Hairy, Audacious Goals). Then create a plan to get there.

Books/Plays/Operas/Fables/CDs/Magazines:

1. Read The Power of Purpose by Dick Leider.
2. Read The Power of Full Engagement by Jim Loehr and Tony Schwartz.
3. Read The 7 Habits of Highly Effective People by Stephen Covey.
4. Read The 8th Habit by Stephen Covey.
5. Read The Purpose Driven Life by Rick Warren
6. Read The Empowerment Book by David Gershon.
7. Read Good to Great by Jim Collins and apply it to your life. Find your hedgehog, the one thing that fulfills these three ideas: Are you passionate about it? Can you be the best at it? Does it drive your economic engine?
8. Read or see the play Pygmalion by George Bernard Shaw. The play shows the transformation of Eliza Doolittle, someone from a lower class background who finds purpose in life.
9. Read the book The War of Art by Steven Pressfield.
10. Read Think and Grow Rich by Napoleon Hill.
11. Read any books by Og Mandino.
12. Read Your Best Life Now (7 Steps to Living at Your Full Potential) by Joel Osteen.
13. Read Seabiscuit by Laura Hillenbrand and see how a trainer finds a horse with potential and develops it through training.
14. Read The Secret Power of Persuasion by Roger Dawson.
15. Read How to Turn Your Everyday Experiences into Zingers! By Joanna Henderson and Betty Lou Marple.
16. Read Zen Flesh, Zen Bones by Paul Reps.
17. Read Coming to Our Senses: Healing Ourselves and the World through Mindfulness by Jon Kabat-Zinn.
18. Read Full Catastrophe Living by Jon Kabat-Zinn.
19. Read Wherever You Go, There You Are by Jon Kabat-Zinn.
20. Read any books of self-exploration by Alan Watts.
21. Read any books of self-exploration by Ram Dass.
22. Read Zen Mind, Beginner's Mind by Shunryu Suzuki.
23. Read The Longevity Factor by Lydia Bronte, Ph.D..
24. Read Seven Keys to Spiritual Renewal by Stephen Arterburn and David Stoop.
25. Read 40 Days to Personal Revolution by Baron Baptiste.
26. Read The Adventures of Pinocchio by Carlo Collodi.
27. Read The Tao of Pooh or The Te of Piglet by Benjamin Hoff.
28. Read Your Best Life Now by Joel Osteen.
29. Read What's so Amazing About Grace? By Philip Yancey.
30. Read The Fountainhead by Ayn Rand.
31. Read The Seven Spiritual Laws of Success by Deepak Chopra.
32. Read Seven Keys to Spiritual Renewal by Stephen Arterburn and David Stoop.

33. Read The Traveler's Gift by Andy Andrews.
34. Read The 360 Degree Leader by John Maxwell.
35. Read Talent is Never Enough by John Maxwell.
36. Read What Got You Here Won't Get You There by Marshall Goldsmith.
37. Read The Element by Ken Robinson.

Movies/TV/Videos:

1. Whale Rider-a twelve year old girl trusts that her gifts will be recognized and continues on her journey despite setbacks.
2. The Best Years of Our Lives-Homer finds his way after coming home from World War II with prosthetic arms.
3. It's a Wonderful Life-George Bailey is self-actualized by realizing what the world would be like without him.
4. Edward Scissorhands-Johnny Depp's character finds fulfillment despite his handicap.
5. My Fair Lady-Eliza Doolittle finds fulfillment.
6. The World's Greatest Indian. See one man fulfill his destiny.
7. What the Bleep do We Know?-Do we create our own reality?
8. The Fountainhead-Howard Roark fulfills his destiny to be a great architect.
9. The Shawshank Redemption-Andy Dufrane does what it takes to escape.
10. Million Dollar Baby-Despite the odds, a boxer fulfills her dream only to have it shattered.
11. Toy Story-Toys find their purpose.
12. The Flying Scotsman about an innovative cyclist.
13. The Natural and see Roy Hobbs fulfill his destiny.
14. The Straight Story-A man does what it takes to see his dying brother.
15. Miracle-The story of the 1980 Olympic hockey team.
16. Conversations with God-A man finds his mission in life.
17. The Miracle Worker and see Helen Keller find her direction.
18. Dreamer about a young girl and a horse.
19. Seabiscuit about the greatest racehorse in history.

Websites/Apps:

1. Visit www.performance-unlimited.com
2. Visit www.stevepavlina.com
3. Visit www.greatday.com
4. Visit www.personaldevelopment.ie
5. Download the app: Daily Motivation – A Month of Self Improvement Inspiration
6. Download the app: Ideal Me

Inspirational Quotes:

1. "Never forget: This very moment, we can change our lives. There never was a moment, and never will be, when we are without the power to alter our destiny. This second, we can turn the tables on resistance. This second, we can sit down and do our work." Steven Pressfield from <u>The War of Art</u>.

2. "My life has no purpose, no direction, no aim, no meaning, and yet I'm happy. I can't figure it out. What am I doing right?" Charles M. Schultz

3. "Real, constructive mental power lies in the creative thought that shapes your destiny, and your hour-by-hour mental conduct produces power for change in your life. Develop a train of thought on which to ride. The nobility of your life as well as your happiness depends upon the direction in which that train of thought is going." Laurence J. Peter

4. "Go confidently in the direction of your dreams! Live the life you've imagined. As you simplify your life, the laws of the universe will be simpler." Henry David Thoreau

Emotional Self-Awareness:

The ability to recognize and understand one's feelings and emotions, differentiate between them, and know what caused them and why.

Start with these pre-reading and self-study exercises. Other developmental resources are listed after this section.

Emotional Self-Awareness Pre-Reading and Self-Study Guide

Emotional self-awareness is the foundation of emotional intelligence and is critical to career success, health, learning, relationship satisfaction and individual performance. These emotional self-awareness exercises will improve your skill in understanding and working with emotions and facilitate your effectiveness at work and in your personal life.

By completing this self-study on emotional self-awareness you will improve your ability to:
- Identify the emotional and intellectual factors that contribute to your decisions
- Label your feelings
- Discriminate the intensity and range of feelings you experience
- Recognize the existence of multiple feelings in a given situation
- Identify what triggers feelings
- Appreciate the "contagious" nature of feelings
- Recognize that emotions can change over time
- Shift your emotional energy

Have you ever been confronted with an unexpected situation and scrambled to figure out what to do next? Think about the volatility of construction projects and how they are filled with such situations. Projects are in a constant state of flux. Think about your day-to-day situations. Or perhaps you walked into an OAC meeting fully prepared, only to be told that the topic of the meeting had changed but you didn't know it. Or scheduled a meeting with an important client and arrived late because you were held up by traffic. Most of us can identify with these kinds of situations where we are immediately called on to respond in an emotionally intelligent manner. Developing emotional self-awareness is a life-long process. Some people develop it naturally as they mature. But you have the opportunity to develop it on purpose!

Is it really possible to develop emotional self-awareness and improve emotional intelligence?

- Yes, the good news is that emotional intelligence can be learned. Your emotional skills develop through experience over your entire lifetime. While this self-study will give you tools to increase your emotional intelligence, the real classroom is your everyday life!

- Emotional learning is quite different than cognitive (intellectual) learning. It takes place in a different part of your brain. Cognitive learning primarily accesses the memory centers while emotional learning is literally hard wired into your nervous system. Developing new emotional skill actually retrains your neural pathways (the system in your body and brain which carries messages around). The more you practice your new emotional self-awareness skills, the stronger those emotional habits become. An old emotional habit (e.g. holding a grudge) atrophies from lack of use when replaced by another emotional habit (e.g. forgiveness). Emotional learning is more like learning to play a musical instrument or learning a language. It takes more time, repetition, application, reflection, follow up and coaching.

What are the benefits of emotional self-awareness?

Like many people, you probably make decisions without giving a great deal of conscious thought to many of them. For example, did you reflect on your rationale for purchasing your last car? You probably spent time evaluating cost, mileage, comfort, financing, color, and other factors. But, did you actually spend time analyzing why those factors were important? Was it that blue reminded you of your favorite bicycle? Or, that you chose the same car company as your parents? So much feeling goes into every decision you make – and most of the time you aren't even aware of it. Those feelings provide critical information. That information helps you make decisions. So, by getting better at using emotional information along with other rationale, you will be able to make better choices in your life. People who have developed their emotional self-awareness are more likely to:

- make career and job choices, which match their talents and give them satisfaction
- create and sustain healthy relationships
- be highly regarded as team players
- exhibit formal and informal leadership qualities
- take appropriate risks and understand the consequences of their actions
- maintain their composure and demonstrate resilience
- elicit trust from others
- enjoy a general sense of well-being
- identify their level of stress tolerance and manage their lives to avoid debilitating stress
- accurately assess their strengths and weaknesses and know what they need to develop
- trust their intuition and use it to be creative
- make thoughtful choices and take responsibility for their actions
- know their values and live in alignment with them
- recognize and respect differences in others
- manage their time and resources consistent with their priorities
- demonstrate integrity
- balance their work and home lives
- maintain flexibility in the face of challenges and change

What if I am not so good at it? The reverse is often true.

Sometimes people with low emotional self-awareness:
- are unhappy with their jobs and they don't know why
- are dissatisfied in their personal lives and they don't know why
- alienate the people they work with and they don't know why
- don't achieve their potential and they don't know why
- get passed over for promotions and they don't know why
- fail over and over in relationships and they don't know why
- make rational decisions that don't work out and they don't know why
- have a vague sense of restlessness or lack of fulfillment and they don't know why

There are several skills involved in being emotionally aware, such as recognizing and identifying feelings, understanding the reasons underlying your emotions, and understanding how emotions can be influenced. These skills allow you to be more in tune with your emotional life and use the skills to be effective in every aspect of your daily life. But, how you use these skills is, to a certain extent, a reflection of your beliefs about the value of emotion.

Next you will explore some of your attitudes toward emotion and how those attitudes might impact your effectiveness. Following are some common attitudes toward emotion. Check all that reflect your own thoughts and beliefs about emotion:

Attitudes toward emotion:

- [ ] "I try to keep my emotions in check. I have them, but I find that they aren't particularly helpful in the workplace."

- [ ] "I'm not big on thinking about my emotions. I prefer to work in the rational realm."

- [ ] "I am committed to being in touch with my emotions, and especially, the emotions of others. I think it's necessary for a productive and ethical business environment."

- [ ] "People let their emotions get the best of them too often. Too much emotion usually signifies faulty logic."

- [ ] "I don't like to think too much about my emotional state at any given time. I'd rather just live and let live."

So what does emotional self-awareness look like anyway?

1. Recognizing feelings
2. Identifying and labeling feelings
3. Identifying the intensity and range of feelings
4. Recognizing that you can hold multiple feelings at the same time
5. Identifying what triggers feelings
6. Appreciating that emotions are contagious
7. Recognizing that emotions can change over time
8. Demonstrating how to shift emotions

SKILL #1: RECOGNIZING FEELINGS

The very first step to becoming emotionally aware is to recognize your feelings and differentiate them from thoughts and body states. When you are aware of feelings, and the thoughts and sensations that go along with them, you are better able to make appropriate choices.

Over the course of your lifetime you will have developed some very consistent correlations between certain feelings and particular sensations in the body. For example, your palms may sweat when you are anxious, your heart might pound when you are excited, perhaps your face gets bright red when you are angry, sometimes you feel nauseated before a presentation, and probably you have difficulty breathing when you anticipate a confrontation. How you react in a given situation often dictates the outcome.

Consider safety. There are all kinds of approaches to safety (rules, consequences, personal protective equipment, best practices), yet no one has "cracked the code" in creating behaviors that lead to zero accidents. And consider the billions of dollars that organizations have spent on reengineering and restructuring, quality programs. Each of those initiatives was carefully planned out and yet few have ever succeeded in achieving their goals. Why? Each employee is tapping into their own emotional databank of information to help them decide what to do. That personal information often overrides any other influence and directly influences their behavior. So it just makes sense to learn to value emotional information at least as much as cognitive information in order to make the best decisions possible.

The process of recognizing your feelings requires practice in learning about their relationship to different thoughts and the body's responses. As you take the time needed to reflect on your emotional reactions you will find it easier to differentiate a thought from a feeling. And you can "tune in" directly to your body to help you understand your emotions. For example, you may not be consciously aware that someone is irritating you while she is giving a report. However, you may observe that your neck is getting sore. You could ask yourself, "What is this stiff neck about?" and find an interesting response that will guide you in your interaction with that individual. For example, you may recognize that your irritation is because she did not acknowledge your role in preparing the report. Once you are clear about the feeling and its cause you are more likely to be able to do something constructive with it, e.g. expressing your disappointment, rather than carrying it around with you and ruining your day.

Emotions are a critical source of information. Dr. Candace Pert, a respected neuroscientist at MIT and Georgetown Medical Center has found that human beings have receptors for emotion throughout the body. In other words, emotions don't "live" just in the brain or in the heart. They exist throughout the body. In her groundbreaking book, Molecules of Emotion, Dr. Pert explains that we are bombarded by more information each day than we can possibly absorb or process effectively. We naturally go to our emotions to help us determine what is and is not important, whom we respect and whom we do not, what will make us happy and what will make us miserable. Emotions are truly the beacon that guides the hundreds of choices and decisions we make each day. Most of it happens below our level of awareness but we can get better at tuning into this source of wisdom.

Reflection:

Do you tend to rely more on your thought or your feelings when making decisions? Are there different times/places where there is a difference, e.g. home versus work? Where my ego is involved, etc.?

Do you more easily communicate thoughts or feelings to others?

SKILL #2: IDENTIFYING AND LABELING FEELINGS

In many normal activities, you are exposed to situations or information that bring up emotions. Some emotions will be pleasant, some uncomfortable, some familiar and some hard to identify or even confusing. As you experience or feel an unfamiliar emotion, a question that may follow is, "what is this feeling?" Being able to identify a specific feeling is a basic emotional self-awareness skill. Some people call this skill "emotional literacy." Take a look at your EI Roadmap and the exercises on how you are feeling. Use the feeling words and feeling wheel to help.

You probably easily recognize common feelings such as happiness, impatience, and anger. However, it may be harder for you to identify and understand more subtle or complex feelings, sometimes leading to confusion or leading to difficulty relating to others.

So, why is identifying emotions important? What difference will it make?

- People do their best when their thoughts, feelings and behavior are in synch with each other. This requires being able to identify feelings. The more aware you are of feelings, the better able you will be to observe their impact on yourself and others and to choose actions that are appropriate to the feelings and to getting the results you are seeking.

- And … the easier it is for you to label and communicate your feelings, the easier it is to identify what you need and ask for it. For example: When faced with a difficult issue at work, instead of yelling "*@#% you! I quit!" a person can use feeling words to clearly communicate and improve a difficult situation. "Boss, I feel confused and anxious when your directions are vague. I would feel more confident if you would clearly explain it to me."

- Your feelings are the source of information you use to assess whether you are in the right job or career. Subconsciously you probably consult your feelings to answer such questions as, "Does this job use my talents well?" and "Are my opinions valued?" or "Do I want to do this kind of work for the rest of my life?" Those considerations determine how motivated you are to stay or leave, work hard or hardly work.

SKILL #3: IDENTIFYING THE RANGE AND INTENSITY OF FEELINGS

Because we are all individuals, each of us experiences the same situation in a different way. And because we each approach a situation from our own perspective, how we react and the extent to which our emotions are affected are also different. And when your identity (your role at work, your position in the family) is linked to that situation, the feelings elicited may be even more intense!

Being emotionally aware involves being able to recognize the way in which you react to situations, as well as your ability to recognize the subtle nuances that characterize your feelings. This awareness can help you communicate your reactions more clearly to others and understand their reactions.

So What?

All feelings exist on a continuum from very weak to very strong. In a typical day, you probably experience many different types of feelings, at varying degrees of intensity. Felt and expressed appropriately, those feelings are a rich resource. However, feelings at the outer edges of the continuum can be problematic.

When some emotions, e.g. anger, fear, insecurity, are experienced too intensely, they can lead to results such as workplace violence, underachievement, etc. On the job, behaviors such as a verbal outburst can be the result of a feeling, which is out of proportion to the trigger. Some people have the opposite problem. They experience and show so little feeling that others can't get a "read" on them. Either type of emotional experience (too much or too little) may be counter-productive on a team or in a customer service environment. And lots of time is wasted at the proverbial water cooler as employees try to figure out how to avoid a manager who is in a rage, or they try to guess the mood their laid back manager is in.

Reflection:

Are there situations in the workplace that you think you might feel more intensely or less intensely than other people? What are the consequences?

Identify one situation that triggers intense feelings for you and reflect on it. Consider some of the following questions and record your responses:

- What is the situation?
- Under what circumstances do I feel these intense feelings?
- Under what circumstances do I tend to NOT show feelings?
- How do I handle the intense feelings?
- What is the typical result?

SKILL #4: IDENTIFYING MULTIPLE FEELINGS

To add another rung in your climb up the ladder of emotional self-awareness, you need to recognize that emotions co-exist with each another. Just as what you feel is not isolated to one situation, the feelings you have are not independent of one another. Do you recall your feelings at the completion of a really great project? Surely you were happy to close out this amazing project and move on to the next one. But did you also feel somewhat saddened or even afraid of leaving that work environment where you felt confident and safe and successful? Did you feel unsure and a bit afraid of what you would encounter on the next project?

So What?

The following wise axiom has been credited to several authors: "the ability to hold two conflicting thoughts at the same time is the sign of the mature person." The same might be said regarding feelings. Life is complex and the mature person knows better than to try to oversimplify it.

Contemporary literature on leadership is full of descriptions of the "authentic" leader. This style of leadership requires honest and direct communication and it inspires motivation and loyalty. The authentic leader claims the right to hold and express multiple feelings, even if they appear contradictory. That authenticity generates trust and respect from others. For example, imagine your own response to the manager who announces that, while she is confident that a Joint Venture with another company will ultimately create exciting new opportunities, she feels that there will be some issues with your company's close-knit culture versus this other company, which is more cold and calculating.

Reflection:

Think of a time in your own life when you felt multiple (and/or mixed) emotions, such as a first day in a new position at work or the retiring of a mentor and friend? Describe and reflect on the different, and sometimes conflicting, emotions you experienced.

SKILL #5: IDENTIFYING WHAT TRIGGERS YOUR FEELINGS

A fairly advanced skill in emotional self-awareness is the ability to identify the cause of your feelings. This is not an easy task. Much of the time you may not have a clear sense of what triggers your emotions. But, being able to identify the reasons for your emotional states can assist you in managing them.

Many times the reasons people fail in jobs or careers is because of the way they handle (or don't handle) their emotions. Being unaware of your feelings and what causes them can lead to some pretty serious consequences. For example, discomfort in dealing with someone from another culture can lead to behavior that is discriminatory. Feelings of pressure to turn in good safety numbers or profit numbers can lead directly to questionable practices, under-reporting and inaccurate numbers. When you recognize these feelings when they are happening you can choose appropriate responses that serve you, rather than get you into trouble. After you have begun to see patterns, e.g. "I always start to lose my temper when other project stakeholders question me," then you can choose to take a proactive approach.

SKILL #6: RECOGNIZING THAT EMOTIONS ARE CONTAGIOUS

Can you remember a time when your mood changed after interacting with someone? You probably can. Sometimes this influence is dramatic, and sometimes it is subtle. In either case, emotional self-awareness allows you to recognize how other peoples' emotions impact your own, and in turn, how your emotions influence the people around you. When you are unaware of the contagious nature of emotional energy, you are vulnerable to catching an "emotional virus." With conscious effort you can "immunize" yourself so that you do not pick up others' negativity and let it interfere with your own motivation and drive.

Most people think events cause feelings when in fact it is thoughts surrounding feelings that cause other feelings.

So what?

The importance of creating the right emotional energy to support goals is implicitly understood by most successful organizations. Many team-building initiatives explicitly attempt to evoke this energy, calling it "esprit de corps" and hoping that it inspires team members to higher levels of performance. And, many organizations conduct annual employee morale surveys and create committees to change those aspects of corporate culture, which demotivate their employees.

Recent research has identified the overarching power of the leader in creating productive cultures. More than any other factor, it is the leader who creates the emotional climate in the organization. That emotional culture either inspires workers to perform at their best or it inhibits their optimal efforts.

Reflection:

Consider that you are "broadcasting" your feeling states to others all day long.   What emotional energy are you transmitting and what do you think the impact is? Using your workplace as your own personal laboratory, spend a day paying attention to the two-way transmission of emotional energy and record your insights.

Once you are more sensitive to the contagious nature of feeling, you will want to develop a practice of protecting yourself from others' negative energy. Some people like to create an imaginary "force field" around themselves to deflect negative energy.

SKILL #7: RECOGNIZING THAT YOUR FEELINGS CAN SHIFT OVER TIME

Emotions are related to time in two different ways:

1. You can undergo many different emotional states and hold many different feelings over a short period of time, as brief as the blink of an eye

2. An individual feeling that you hold regarding a particular event or circumstance can change over time, sometimes slowly, sometimes very fast.

Understanding how your emotions change is very important for recognizing and identifying what you feel and why you feel.

When your skill in emotional self-awareness increases, you will be able to predict the course of your emotional reactions. For example, if you are a project manager starting a new project, you might intuitively know that first you will feel a combination of exhilaration and anxiety. You may even find the anxiety strong enough to interfere with your performance. From past experience, you also know that the anxiety will diminish as you get into the project and will be replaced by a sense of mastery. You may assume that you need to go through the anxiety to get to the confidence, but you don't. By changing the way you talk to yourself, you can actually shift from the original feeling state (anxiety) to the final feeling state (confidence). That self-talk might sound like, "Jack, you've been through this drama every project for the past ten years. You're a great project manager, and you've got a great team, so knock it off! Just enjoy the excitement and let go of the nervousness." With that kind of a self "talking-to" your brain chemistry will literally change, providing you with the energetic resources to plan the project successfully.

Reflection:

Reflect on today, starting with when you woke up in the morning until right now. What do you think about the way in which your emotions evolved over time? How different were your feelings when you first woke up until now?

SKILL #8: SHIFTING YOUR EMOTIONS

Finally, the most practical aspect of being emotionally self-aware is knowing that you have the capacity to change your emotions. That is, once you have identified your emotions and their underlying causes, you become able to influence them so that you feel better and function more effectively in your environment.

So What?

As you read in the last section, you have the natural ability to shift your feelings at will. This is easier for some people than others. You will want to build up your own emotional "tool kit" of ways to shift emotions. These tools serve as "catalysts" to create a shift of emotional energy. In your personal life, you are probably using several catalysts from the following list:

- calling a friend you know will give you the inspiration you need to stay on your diet
- renting a favorite movie to make you laugh when you are sad
- scheduling a massage or a manicure when you need some pampering
- having dinner at a favorite restaurant to recognize your daughter's soccer win

At work, you can and already do employ the same strategy. A gesture as simple as bringing doughnuts is an attempt to shift the mood of the group. Surprising the project workers with a lunch or tee shirts can make both of you feel good. Recognizing the efforts of the team to meet a deadline can be accomplished by an afternoon spent together at a baseball game.

Following is a list of possible situations you may encounter at work on a daily basis. Read each of them and write down what you might say to yourself in that situation.

1. You missed a critical deadline.
2. A meeting you were running went very poorly and was unproductive.
3. A direct report of yours does not respond to your requests for information.
4. Your boss assigns a very important project to your friend.
5. You get a promotion.

Shifting your emotion state through reflection

You know that at the end of the day you are taking your entire family out to dinner and a moview. Throughout your day, you experience the following:

1. When you reach the project, several trade partners do not show up, putting you way behind on a pour.
2. There is an accident on site. Although it is not serious, it is recordable.
3. The client is angry about a change order and storms into your office to express his displeasure.
4. Your boss calls you and tells you that if you don't correct the schedule, you could be pulled off the project.
5. It's the end of the workday and you are heading home.

What do you do to shift the emotional energy and enjoy the time with your family? How do you process these difficult emotional situations?

Emotional Self-Awareness

Self-Directed Exercises

Emotional self-awareness Outcomes

At the end of the Emotional self-awareness exercises you will be able to:

- understand the impact that emotions have on your thoughts, actions, and ultimately, your leadership effectiveness

- identify your unique emotional response patterns and their implications for your health, happiness and performance

- have an appreciation for the power your emotional energy has on other's attitudes, motivation, behaviour, and productivity

- use practical skills for leveraging emotion and creating a productive team environment

Where Do I Feel…?

Draw an arrow from the listed emotion to where you feel it in your body.

Look at your feeling word exercise from the EI Roadmap and locate those feelings in your body as well.

APPRECIATION
ANGER
FRUSTRATION
LOVE
PRIDE
HAPPINESS
SHAME
FEAR
IRRATIBILTY
SADNESS
ANTICIPATION
CURIOSITY
HOSTILITY
PANIC
FATIGUE
ANXIETY

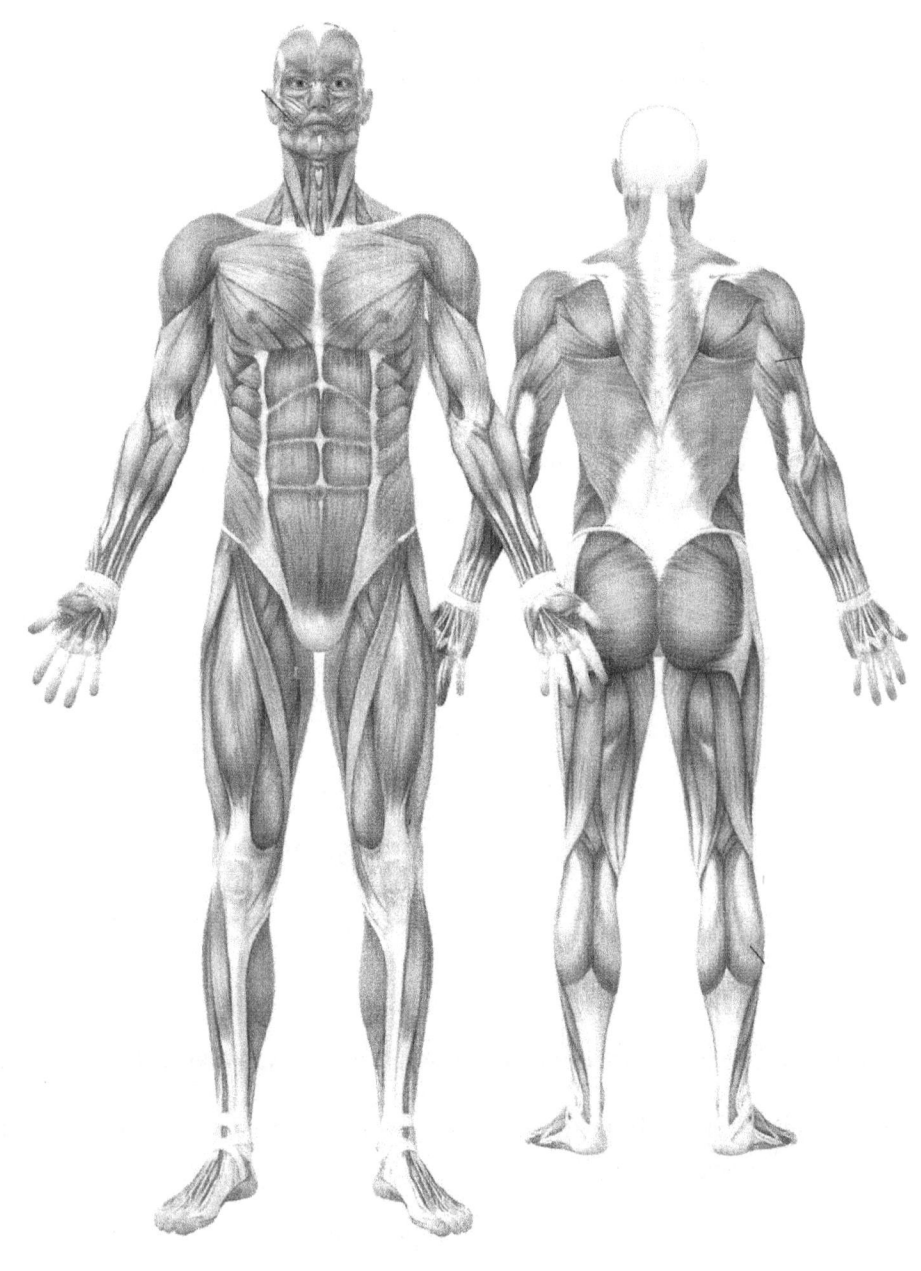

Think of several situations where you are aware of your emotions. Write down your various feelings, a summary of the situation, the intensity and the impact.

My Emotion Triggers

Feeling	Situation	Intensity	Impact

My Personal Values

Rank the following values: 1 for little or no value and 5 for high value

Success	Power	Making A difference
Truth	Health	Independence
Wisdom	Pleasure	Fame
Creativity	Aesthetics	Family
Spirituality	Reputation	Equality
Freedom	Achievement	Adventure
Status	Order	Fairness
Wealth	Loyalty	Efficiency
Security	Morality	Nature
Responsibility	Harmony	Competence
Excellence	Cooperation	Community
Relationships	Challenge	Altruism
Privacy	Peace	
Play	Acceptance	

How do these values affect your emotional states during various situations day-to-day?

Anatomy of an Emotional Hijack

1. Something happens which provides information: event, thought, image, feeling. This stimulus can be external or internal and the stimulus itself is neutral.

2. The information goes to the senses to the Thalamus (The Controller) and is sent immediately to the Amygdala (Emotional Brain). At the same time, it travels to the Neocortex, the largest part of the Cerebral Cortex (Thinking Brain).

3. The Amygdala contains all of our life experiences with any emotional content. The Amygdala asks, "Is this like anything that happened before?" The problem is a) there is a shorter distance from the Thalamus to the Amygdala. b) the Amygdala only gets 5% of the information. c) the Amygdala database is low tech. d) the brain doesn't have capacity to notice everything. e) The Amygdala is looking for negative content.

4. If the Amygdala answers yes (this negative thing has happened before), it causes an emotional highjack. The emotional brain "hijacks" the thinking brain. The body believes it is under attack and systems are deployed to fight, flee or freeze. Adrenaline and Cortisol (stress hormone) are released: for quick energy and focus with increased sensitivity to danger.

5. The attack reinforces and "grooves" our mental maps (the world is unsafe, people cannot be trusted, I am a good/bad person.) The body delivers these messages as physical feelings and internal dialogue. Over time, we develop patterned responses: aggression, fear, feeling paralyzed.

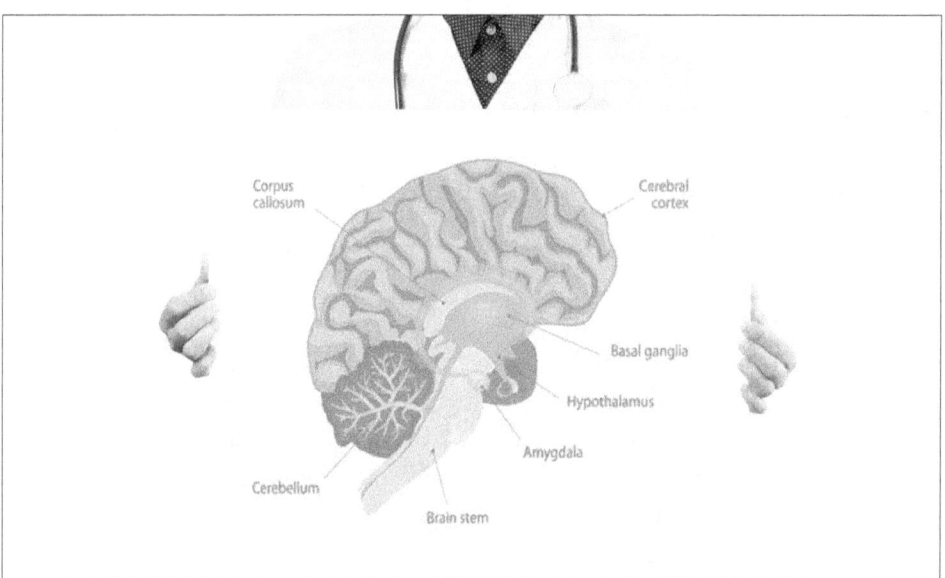

"In an emergency, the emotional brain hijacks the thinking brain."
Daniel Goleman

Early Warning Signs of an Emotional Hijack

Instructions:

- Put a check by all that are typical of you.
- Try to remember the last time you had each response. Record them.

☐ My heart starts to pound.

☐ My eyes tear up.

☐ Upsetting thoughts run over and over in my mind.

☐ My stomach feels queasy.

☐ My face flushes.

☐ I find it hard to focus on anything else.

☐ My muscles start to tighten in my neck, shoulders and back.

☐ I can feel a headache coming on.

☐ There is an edge in my voice.

☐ Disturbing images and pictures flash through my mind.

☐ I think about getting even.

☐ My forehead, hands, or underarms sweat.

☐ I pull away from other people.

☐ My breathing gets more rapid.

☐ I get an urge to eat something or I lose my appetite.

☐ I lose my train of thought.

☐ I get very critical of myself

Automatic Thoughts: Determine the situations where you have these automatic thoughts. Then determine the feelings surrounding those automatic thoughts and write them in the space provided.

TYPE OF AUTOMATIC THOUGHT	EXAMPLE	FEELING
1. Fortune Telling	"I'm going to blow it."	
2. Mind Reading	"He will think I'm incompetent."	
3. Catastrophic Thinking	"It's going to be a disaster."	
4. Over-generalization	"This is going to play out like every other time I started a new job."	
5. Shoulds	"I shouldn't be so anxious. I should be more adult about this."	

Reflection: What are your core beliefs around:

> You vs. others, e.g. people are good or bad
> The world, e.g. the world is safe or dangerous
> Accountability, i.e. whose fault is it?
> Hope, e.g. the glass is half full or half empty
> When you encounter these automatic thoughts, reframe them. See the next page.

Reframing Guidelines

The next time you find yourself thinking these automatic thoughts, reframe them using the following methodologies:

Finding Evidence

- Ask yourself "what are the facts?"
- Identify other, more accurate, interpretations.
- Consider how someone else would see the situation.
- Scan for all possible causes.

Shift Perspective

- Argue with yourself.
- Take the opposite point of view.
- Be your own "devil's advocate".

Take a Positive Outlook

- Ask yourself what good might come out of this.
- De-catastrophize.
- Find the silver lining.

The purpose of reframing is to help you shift from being your own worst critic to being your own best champion.

Think of a situation where you usually have negative self-talk and fill out this form as a rehearsal for next time. Name the situation. Name your desired outcome. List all of the negatives, objections, and yes, buts. Then list how you will turn this around to positive self-talk.

Self-Talk Turnarounds

Situation:	
Desired Outcome:	
Negatives, Objections, Yes Buts	**Turnarounds**
•	•
•	•
•	•
•	•
•	•
Turnaround Tips: Find evidence, talk back to yourself, take a positive stance.	

Example:

Situation: I chose to work late and missed my kid's play. I feel badly and I am a crappy human being and a poor excuse for a father. I hate myself for it.

Desired outcome: Don't go down the bad road of putting myself down as a father.

Negatives/Turnarounds:

1. You missed her play/I've made 75% of her events.
2. You CHOSE to work late/I am a great provider and sometimes work has to come first.
3. Your daughter likely resents you/My daughter loves me knows I love her.
4. Your wife resents you/My wife loves me and steps in whenever she needs to.
5. Your wife feels unsupported/We support each other and take up slack for the others.

The Rules of Engagement

Engagement is about emotion: yours and theirs.

Instructions:

- Go back to the feeling word wheel in your EI Road Map.
- Circle all the feelings that you are comfortable expressing at work.
- Cross out those you can't/won't express.
- Now circle those that are crossed out which you would be comfortable expressing outside of work.

Debrief with a partner:

- Where did you learn it wasn't OK to express those feelings?
- What are the consequences of not being able to express them?
    - To you
    - To the project
    - To the organization in general
    - On your team, department, etc.

Emotional Self-Awareness Development Activities

NOTE: If you believe you are having mental health issues such as anxiety, depression and/or suicidal thoughts, please reach out to the suicide prevention hotline at 1-800-273-8255 or visit: preventconstructionsuicide.com

for information, risk assessments, and support material.

Practical Daily Application:

1. Keep a daily journal to record what triggers strong feelings in you.
2. Develop a practice of asking yourself, "How do I feel about this?" with choices you need to make. Trust the answer you get and use the information to make your decision. Use the feeling word vocabulary.
3. Go for walks in nature and tune all your senses into the experience.
4. Do some form of meditation and/or reflection each day where you observe your emotions and all of your senses.
5. Create a contract with someone else to increase your expression of feelings.
6. Learn a centering technique (e.g. meditation, prayer) to use before identifying and expressing what you are feeling.
7. When you practice meditation or reflection, notice the feelings that fly in and out.
8. Ask family and friends closest to you to coach you: e.g. when you are upset about something, have them ask you to describe how you feel about the situation.
9. Listen to different kinds of music and identify the types of feelings each piece evokes.
10. Look at different images in Google Images and describe how they make you feel. Write down these descriptions.

11. Point at different objects in your environment and name them something different. You should do this out loud and do at least 20 objects. For instance, point at a lamp and say door. Point at a table and say book. Point at a shelf and say tub. This forces your brain into a hyper self-awareness as it tries to reconcile these two conflicting pieces of information. Afterward, sit and notice the difference in your level of awareness.
12. Engage in some form of creative self-expression (e.g. painting, writing) to identify feelings.
13. Clarify your personal values.
14. Don't be ashamed of your feelings.
15. Don't feel the need to DO. Just BE. Sit and fully experience the world around you.
16. Practice yoga, especially balance postures. When you are not in the moment, you will lose your balance.

Exercises and General Development Ideas:

1. Go on a quest. Pick a color and an emotion or emotional state (happy, sad, angry, tired, energized, assertive, empathetic, etc) You could throw a dart at the feeling wheel if you wish. Try to focus on an emotion that you are trying to cultivate more of. Walk around for a set period of time from 30 minutes to all day in any environment (city, rural, nature, etc) with the color and the emotion in mind. Find all of the ways you connect with your environment through all of your senses keeping in mind the emotion and color. You can have encounters with others as long as you keep your quest color and emotion in mind throughout. How does this focus affect your awareness of emotional states and how it is affected by all of the things that surround you? How does your awareness of a color and/or emotional state affect how you interact with others?
2. Increase your feeling word vocabulary-see word list in the back of this booklet.
3. Learn the difference between thoughts and feelings.
4. Learn the places in your body where you experience various feelings. The next time there is an emotionally charged situation, get some distance, take a few breaths and inventory your body.
5. Identify your attitudes or beliefs about emotions in general.
6. Identify people who are good at identifying and expressing their feelings and observe them.
7. Identify the subtle differences between feelings, e.g. irritation and frustration.
8. Notice what types of feelings are easier and harder for you to identify and express.
9. Recognize the relationship between thoughts, feelings and the resulting behavior.
10. Think of feelings as messages. When you experience a particular emotion in a situation, ask yourself what the message is.
11. Observe in which environments you are most comfortable expressing your feelings.
12. Discuss the emotional content of books, movies, plays, and other situations with others. One of the best movies for discussions about emotions is It's a Wonderful Life.
13. Analyze your own feelings rather than the actions or motives of other people.
14. For fun, turn off the sound when watching TV or videos and guess what the characters might be feeling. Ask yourself how you would feel if you were in the same situation.
15. Analyze your own feelings rather than the actions or motives of other people.
16. Read the emotional self-awareness work book at the end of this section.
17. Practice EFT (Emotional Freedom Technique) to rid yourself of negative emotions.

Books/Plays/Operas/Fables/CDs/Magazines:

1. Read Emotional Self-Awareness Pre-Reading and Self Study exercises following these pages.
2. Read What to Say When you Talk to Yourself by Shad Helmstettler.
3. Take the Questionnaire in Achieving Emotional Literacy by Claude Steiner.
4. Learn about how emotion works. Read The Emotional Brain: The Mysterious Underpinnings of Emotional Life by Joseph LeDoux.
5. Read The Power of Emotion by Michael Sky.
6. Read Emotional Alchemy by Tara Bennett-Goleman.
7. Read Emotional Literacy by Rob Bocchino.
8. Read The One Thing You Need to Know by Marcus Buckingham.
9. Read The Wisdom in Feeling by Peter Salovey and L. Feldman-Barrett.
10. Read Primal Leadership by Daniel Goleman.
11. Read Mind Wide Open by Steven Johnson.
12. Read Encouraging the Heart by Barry Posner and James Kouzes.
13. Read Hidden Dynamics by Faith Ralston.
14. Read How the Science of Feelings Can Transform Your Life by Normal Rosenthal.
15. Read The Molecules of Emotion by Candace Pert.
16. Read Learned Optimism by Martin Seligman.
17. Read Coming to Our Senses: Healing Ourselves and the World through Mindfulness by Jon Kabat-Zinn.
18. Read Full Catastrophe Living by Jon Kabat-Zinn.
19. Read Wherever You Go, There You Are by Jon Kabat-Zinn.
20. Read any books of self-exploration by Alan Watts.
21. Read any books of self-exploration by Ram Dass.
22. Read Zen Mind, Beginner's Mind by Shunryu Suzuki.
23. Read the novel Deliverance by James Dickey and see the self-discovery of the characters.
24. Read The Ragamuffin Gospel by Brennan Manning.
25. Read The Wisdom of Accepted Tenderness by Brennan Manning.
26. Read Ruthless Trust by Brennan Manning.
27. Read Man's Search for Meaning by Victor Frankl.
28. Read The Book of Secrets by Deepak Chopra.
29. Read Erfolg im Job mit EQ by Hendrie Weisinger.
30. Read Emotional Intelligence at Work by Dr. Michael Larrass.
31. Read The Artist's Way by Julia Cameron.
32. Read The Secrets Men Keep by Stephen Arterburn.
33. Read No Yelling: The Nine Secrets of Marine Corps Leadership You Must Know to Win in Business by Wally Adamchik.
34. Read any of the books by Gary Zukav including The Heart of the Soul: Emotional Awareness.
35. Read The Five Love Languages by Gary Chapman.

Movies/TV/Videos:

1. Watch any movie, then listen to the soundtrack alone and determine how the music makes you feel. Describe the feeling to someone.
2. The Manchurian Candidate-Marco, played by Frank Sinatra, keeps exploring his feelings until he uncovers an assassination plot.

3. Regarding Henry-Harrison Ford's character, a brilliant lawyer caught in an accidental shooting that reduces his cognitive function, learns self-awareness through his recovery.
4. Awakenings-The patients at a mental hospital become "aware" if only for a short period of time.
5. Invasion of the Body Snatchers-Aliens grow pods that replace humans. The new beings are void of emotional self-awareness.
6. Wings of Desire-Angels return to earth and long to be able to feel like a human again.
7. It's a Wonderful Life runs the gamut of emotions. Watch it and discuss all of the emotions that the movie depicts. All fifteen emotional competencies are well represented in this movie.
8. Miracle on 34th Street-Watch how Doris, played by Maureen O'Hara becomes more emotionally self-aware throughout the movie.
9. What the Bleep do We Know?
10. Groundhog Day-Watch Phil Connors as he becomes more emotionally self-aware.
11. Watch The Best Years of our Lives and struggle along with these returning soldiers.
12. Watch Slingblade and see the self-awareness of the various characters and how it affects their interaction with each other.

Websites/Apps:

1. Visit www.newlifeparadigm.com and sign up for their newsletter.
2. Visit www.higherawareness.com and sign up for their newsletter.
3. Visit www.mindfulness.com and learn about having your awareness fully in the moment.
4. Visit www.umassmed.edu/behavmed/faculty/kabat-zinn.cfm
5. Visit www.myfatherusedtosay.com
6. Awareness App
7. Mobile Therapy App
8. Download the app: Self Check-In
9. Download the app: MoodMinder
10. Download the app: iEmotion
11. Download the app: AWARENESS
12. Download the app: I Am Feeling…

Inspirational Quotes:

1. "What is necessary to change a person is to change his awareness of himself." Abraham Maslow
2. "The man who is aware of himself is henceforward independent; and he is never bored, and life is only too short, and he is steeped through and through with a profound yet temperate happiness." Virginia Woolf
3. "The ultimate value of life depends upon awareness, and the power of contemplation rather than upon mere survival." Aristotle
4. "The first step toward change is awareness. The second step is acceptance." Nathaniel Branden
5. "Let us not look backward in anger or forward in fear, but around in awareness." James Thurber
6. "I want you to take your ego out of the equation and judge the situation dispassionately. Arrogance and self-awareness seldom go hand in hand." Ian Fleming (M talking to James Bond in Casino Royale)

To decrease Emotional Self-Awareness: Google hypersensitivity and take a look at some ways to decrease your emotional self-awareness.

Emotional Expression:

is openly expressing one's feelings verbally and non-verbally.

Practical Daily Application:

1. Practice telling those close to you how you are feeling moment to moment. Tell them to ask you how you are feeling throughout your day.
2. Once you are comfortable with people close to you, start expressing your feelings more to others in the workplace and other places. Practice as much as possible, especially during conflicts during your day to day encounters with others.
3. Use powerful, not powerless language to express yourself. Avoid being tentative in your speech style. For example say, "I'd like you to do it this way," rather than, "Maybe you would like to try it like this." Avoid words and phrases such as maybe, perhaps, if you want, if you could, if it's convenient, almost, sort of, etc.
4. Check in daily with how you are feeling and express those feelings to others. If it is impossible to share those feelings immediately, create a journal and share it with someone periodically.
5. Think how the lack of emotional expression affects communication in business and personal settings.

Exercises and General Development Ideas:

1. Clarify what is important to you. Being clear about your objectives makes it easier to express yourself.
2. Create written scripts for you to follow in order to practice expressing yourself assertively.
3. Write down all of your feelings for a week, then ask yourself why you are not expressing those feelings in those moments.
4. Watch a two year old and how they express their emotions. It's clear.

Books/Plays/Operas/Fables/CDs/Magazines:

1. Self hypnosis CD: http://www.hypnosisdownloads.com/emotional-intelligence/express-emotions
2. Read Expressing Your Feelings, the Key to an Intimate Relationship by Roger T. Crenshaw.
3. Read Why Can't You Read My Mind by Jeffrey Bernstein and Susan McGee.
4. Read Communication Miracles for Couples by Jonathan Robinson. Then, take the principles and apply them in the workplace.
5. Read Self Expression by Mitchell S. Green.

Movies/TV/Videos:

1. Watch The Hunchback of Notre Dame and look at the hunchback's journey to self expression.
2. Watch Crazy, Stupid, Love, and Cal's journey to self-expression.
3. Watch Norma Rae.
4. Watch Mr. Smith Goes to Washington.
5. Watch Awakenings.
6. Watch Regarding Henry.
7. Watch Charly.
8. Watch One Flew Over the Cuckoo's Nest.

Websites/Apps:

1. http://www.drnadig.com/feelings.htm
2. http://www.ehow.com/how_4425349_express-emotions.html

3. http://www.counselingcenter.illinois.edu/?page_id=190
4. http://www.wikihow.com/Express-Your-Feelings
5. http://www.wikihow.com/Express-Your-Feelings-to-the-One-You-Love
6. http://www.hypnosisdownloads.com/emotional-intelligence/express-emotions

Inspirational Quotes:

1. "Every mind which has given itself to self-expression in art is aware of a directing agency outside its conscious control which it has agreed to label 'inspiration'." Norman Lindsay

2. "If you copy then it is not self-expression." Michael Schenker

3. "My interest lies in my self-expression - what's inside of me - not what I'm in." John Turturro

4. "No good poem, however confessional it may be, is just a self-expression. Who on earth would claim that the pearl expresses the oyster?" C. Day Lewis

5. "Self-expression must pass into communication for its fulfillment." Pearl S. Buck

6. "The desire for self-expression afflicts people when they feel there is something of themselves which is not getting through to the outside world. " Fay Weldon

7. "The key thing is, even if you only have a couple of hours a month, those two hours shoulder-to-shoulder, next to one student, concentrated attention, shining this beam of light on their work, on their thoughts and their self-expression, is going to be absolutely transformative, because so many of the students have not had that ever before. " Dave Eggers

8. "The universe must exist for the self-expression of God and the delight of God." Ernest Holmes

9. "Never apologize for showing feeling. When you do so, you apologize for the truth." Benjamin Disraeli

To Decrease Self Expression:

1. Work to increase impulse control and decrease assertiveness. Focus on keeping your mouth closed and not reacting to things.

Assertiveness:

Involves communicating feelings, beliefs, and thoughts openly, and defending personal rights and values in a socially acceptable, non-offensive, and non-destructive manner.

Practical Daily Application:

1. Identify the situations in your life where you have trouble asserting yourself. Create written scripts for you to follow in order to practice expressing yourself assertively. Think about assertiveness as being hyper-clear about communication, stating your needs and expectations of yourself and others.
2. When dining out, no matter what table the hostess chooses, ask for another. If your meal is not prepared exactly as you ordered, send it back. Send back a bottle of wine if it isn't up to your expectations. Practice finding ways to assert yourself daily.
3. Use powerful, not powerless language to express yourself. Avoid being tentative in your speech style. For example say, "I'd like you to do it this way," rather than, "Maybe you would like to try it like this."

Avoid words and phrases such as maybe, perhaps, if you want, if you could, if it's convenient, almost, sort of, etc.
4. Clarify what is important to you. Being clear about your objectives makes it easier to assert yourself.
5. Visualize yourself being assertive. Practice. Many people working on assertiveness are afraid that the other people won't like them any longer. Actually, what they find out is that the other people like them even better. They respect them because the communication is very Identify the situations in your life where you have trouble asserting yourself. Create written scripts for you to follow in order to practice expressing yourself assertively.

Exercises and General Development Ideas:

1. Get comfortable with saying "no" appropriately. Or you may have to say, "I just can't say yes."
2. If you are an assertive person, observe the impact your assertiveness has on others. Consider reducing your assertiveness if it has negative consequences.
3. Choose your battles. Decide in advance what your position is, how you will express it, and how far you will go with it.
4. Develop alternate ways of expressing your feelings, beliefs, and thoughts. If you are typically a person who expresses orally, use written communication as another means.
5. Put emotional energy into your requests. Show your excitement, disappointment, etc.
6. Plan ahead to be assertive. Consider whether the time and the place and the circumstances are appropriate.
7. Practice using whole messages: Communicate what you think, what you feel and what you want or need.
8. If being assertive feels self-centered or selfish to you, consider working with a counselor to increase your comfort with it.
9. Stay calm and state clearly what you want.
10. Remember that whenever you dominate a social or work situation, you decrease the opportunity for someone else to shine.
11. If you want to be a courageous leader, develop your assertiveness.
12. Ask someone you respect to videotape you during a meeting or other relevant situation, examine the videotape to determine whether your behavior is assertive or aggressive.
13. Make decisions. Practice making and implementing positive decisions flexibly but firmly, and trust yourself to deal with the consequences. When you assert yourself, you enhance your sense of yourself, learn more and increase your self-confidence.
14. Watch TED talk by Amy Cuddy on Power Poses. Practice your Power Poses often throughout your day and before meetings, encounters with others or presentations.

Books/Plays/Operas/Fables/CDs/Magazines:

1. Read Rejection Proof by Jia Jiang.
2. Read Your Perfect Right by Robert Alberti and Michael Emmons.
3. Create a personal Bill or Rights. Use The Anxiety and Phobia Workbook by Edward Bourne as a resource.
4. Read anything from the Harvard Negotiation Project, e.g. Getting to Yes by Roger Fisher, William Ury, and Bruce Patton.
5. Read Shyness by Bernardo J. Carducci, Ph.D.
6. Complete relevant exercises in The Assertiveness Workbook: How to Express Your Ideas and Stand Up for Yourself at Work and in Relationships by Randy Peterson.
7. Read Self Power by Maria Arapakis.

8. Read the book <u>The War of Art</u> by Steven Pressfield.
9. Read <u>You Can Negotiate Anything</u> or any books by Herb Cohen.
10. Read <u>The Negotiator's Handbook</u> by George Fuller.
11. Read <u>The Tao of Negotiation</u> by Joel Edelman and Mary Beth Crain.
12. Read <u>The Secret Power of Persuasion</u> by Roger Dawson.
13. Read <u>Women and the Art of Negotiating</u> by Juliet Nierenberg and Irene S. Ross.
14. Read <u>Wie sie lernen-nein-zu sagen</u> by Vera Pfeiffer.
15. Read any negotiating books by Gavin Kennedy.
16. Read <u>Crucial Conversations</u> and <u>Crucial Confrontations</u> by Kerry Patterson, Joseph Grenny, Ron McMillan, and Al Switzler.

Movies/TV/Videos:

1. Erin Brockovich-Julia Roberts plays Erin Brockovich, whose assertiveness results in a $333 million settlement.
2. Patton-George Patton may be too assertive at times, but this movie shows the positive results of assertiveness as well.
3. Pinocchio-Pinocchio's lack of assertiveness gets him in trouble.
4. The Godfather-Learn all about the assertiveness of the Corleones.
5. The Bridge on the River Kwai-A British Colonel oversees the building of a bridge to build morale.
6. The African Queen-Kathryn Hepburn's character is the epitome of assertiveness in this adventure tale.
7. Any one of a number of Clint Eastwood movies work here.
8. Saving Private Ryan-This small band will not give up.
9. A Streetcar Named Desire-Stanley Kowalski's assertiveness leads to dire consequences.

Websites/Apps:

1. Visit www.growthcentral.com.
2. Download the app: Assertiveness Pocketbook
3. Download the app: Assertiveness: ComboBook
4. Check out the assertiveness section on www.livestrong.com

Inspirational Quotes:

1. "It is one thing to study war and another to live a warrior's life." Telamon or Arcadia, mercenary of the fifth century B.C
2. "Courage is rightly considered the foremost of the virtues because upon it, all others depend." Winston Churchill.
3. "The basic difference between being assertive and being aggressive is how our words and behavior affect the rights and well-being of others." Sharon Anthony Bower
4. "Assertiveness is not what you do, it's who you are! Cal Le Mon
5. "All the mistakes I ever made were when I wanted to say 'no' and said 'yes'." Moss Hart
6. "The best way out is through." Robert Frost
7. "Never be bullied into silence. Never allow yourself to be made a victim. Accept no one's definition of your life; define yourself." Harvey Fierstein

To Decrease Assertiveness:

Too much assertiveness can be seen as aggression. To decrease your assertiveness, work on the development strategies in Empathy.

Independence:

is the ability to be self-directed and free of emotional dependency on others. Decision-making, planning, and daily tasks are completed autonomously.

Practical Daily Application:

1. Practice being alone. Develop a level of comfort with it.
2. For those relationships where you feel too dependent, have a talk with that person and talk to them about doing more things on your own.
3. Find ways throughout the day to establish your independence.
4. Don't give in to family or friend's pressure to be involved with them continuously. Make time for yourself daily.

Exercises and General Development Ideas:

1. Draw a dependency diagram. Identify on whom you are dependent for what.
2. Create your own behavior modification plan. Reinforce your efforts to be more independent, e.g. with appropriate rewards.
3. Reflect on when it is easier and harder to be independent.
4. Talk with others you observe to be independent and ask their advice and opinions as a guide for increasing your independence.
5. Identify the thoughts and feelings that prevent you from being independent.
6. Identify what you think are the risks of independence. Reframe your fears by identifying the positive outcomes of independent thoughts and actions.
7. Be reasonable and appropriate in expecting emotional support from others. Be your own best source of support.
8. Be more self-directed in your thinking and decision-making.
9. Be careful to not go overboard on independence. See below for how to reduce independence.
10. Identify decision options and confidently make your choice.
11. Discern when to exhibit your independence and when to step back to let others take the lead.
12. Take it seriously if you get feedback that you are too independent. It is likely that your independence is interfering with your own or others' well-being.
13. Think of something you are afraid to do or take on and find a way to do it without support from others if possible.
14. Sever yourself temporarily from others you are dependent upon, e.g., family, friends. Instead of time with family or friends for a holiday or special gathering, let them know that you need some time for yourself.
15. Take a day or a weekend or a week independence vacation that is just for you.

Books/Plays/Operas/Fables/CDs/Magazines:

1. Read The Emperor's New Clothes by Hans Christian Andersen.
2. Read Codependent No More and other books by Melody Beattie
3. Read Doormats And Control Freaks: How to Recognize, Heal or End Codependent Relationships by Rebekah Lewis
4. Do a search on www.amazon.com under the books section on codependency.
5. Read Pecos Bill, a folk tale.
6. Read Paul Bunyan, a folk tale.

7. Read Walden by Henry David Thoreau.
8. Read the story of David and Goliath in the Bible (I Samuel, chapters 16-18) to see how David fought the giant despite what others said.
9. Read The Ragamuffin Gospel by Brennan Manning.
10. Read The Wisdom of Accepted Tenderness by Brennan Manning.
11. Read Ruthless Trust by Brennan Manning.
12. Read The Fountainhead by Ayn Rand.
13. Read Crucial Confrontations by Kerry Patterson, Joseph Grenny, Ron McMillan and Al Switzler.

Movies/TV/Videos:

1. The Matrix-Neo rebels against the matrix and fights for truth.
2. Norma Rae-Despite pressure from almost everyone, Norma Rae fights for better working conditions and organizes a union.
3. High Noon-Gary Cooper's character does what he knows needs to be done despite the entire town not supporting him and trying to talk him out of it.
4. Erin Brockovich-Julia Roberts plays Erin Brockovich, an independent woman.
5. Cool Hand Luke-Paul Newman's character shows his independence in his quest to break out of a chain gang prison.
6. Apocalypse Now-Martin Sheen's character is single minded and independent in this war epic. Marlon Brando's character also has a high level of independence to the point of being a renegade.
7. Mr. Smith Goes to Washington-Despite pressure from the Senate, Mr. Smith stands up for what he believes.
8. Ghandi-Ghandi continues his campaign of civil disobedience for India's independence despite pressures from all sides.
9. The Fountainhead-Howard Roark's independence carries him through.
10. One Flew Over the Cuckoo's Nest-Jack Nicholson's character's independence cannot be diminished.
11. On the Waterfront-Terry Malloy's independence allows him to do the right thing.
12. Braveheart-Scottish clans battle for their independence.
13. Spartacus-A slave battles for independence and freedom.
14. A Man for All Seasons-Sir Thomas Moore follows his conscience despite the prevailing winds.
15. Casablanca-Rick Blaine is an icon of independence in this film.
16. Mr. Deeds Goes to Town-Mr. Deeds shows us all what it is like to be a little different than anyone else.

Websites/Apps:

1. Visit www.mentalhelp.net/psyhelp
2. Visit www.selfhelpmagazine.com

Inspirational Quotes:

1. "The greatest of all human benefits, that, at least, without which no other benefit can be truly enjoyed, is independence." Parke Godwin
2. A great step toward independence is a good-humored stomach. Seneca
3. "Voyager upon life's sea: To yourself be true, And whate'er you lot may be, Paddle your own canoe." Dr. Edward P. Philpots
4. "Maybe the greatest challenge now is to find a way to keep independence while also committing ourselves to the ties that bind people, families, and ultimately societies together." Jane O'Reilly

To decrease Independence: Too much independence can be problematic, especially if you are called upon to work in groups or teams. To decrease your independence, work on the development strategies for Social Responsibility.

Interpersonal Relationship:

refers to the skill of developing and maintaining mutually satisfying relationships that are characterized by trust and compassion.

Practical Daily Application:

1. Golden Rule: Treat everyone with the same respect that you would wish others to treat you.
2. Platinum Rule: Treat everyone as you think they would want to be treated.
3. Use the skill of self-disclosure to establish trust and rapport. Tell something about yourself that you would not normally share and let the person know you are doing that.
4. Avoid the over use of self-reference words "I", "me", "my", "mine".
5. Be generous with compliments.
6. Keep your promises.
7. Choose one day per week or one day per month to reconnect with friends and family.
8. Listen to others with purpose. Find out about them and what makes them tick.
9. Ask leading questions of people to find out more about them. Use the magic phrase, "Tell me more about that!"
10. Be explicit in identifying the expectations you have of others. Ask them to clarify their expectations of you.
11. Use reflective listening and clarify what others are telling you.
12. Don't make assumptions about behaviors or actions. Clarify and ask questions.
13. Take the time to listen and interact with others.

Exercises and General Development Ideas:

1. Learn and practice negotiation skills.
2. Love yourself first-improve self-regard.
3. Practice expressing appreciation on a regular basis - not just for extraordinary situations.
4. Remember people's names. Create an outrageous association with their name. Or you can ask for their business card and write down physical descriptions along with pertinent information such as family information, hobbies, interests, college, etc.
5. Develop and maintain appropriate interpersonal boundaries.
6. Remember that forgiveness can revive relationships. Think of a strained relationship and approach the other party with an apology. Ask for and give forgiveness.
7. Use Marshall Rosenberg's model of non-violent communication.

Books/Plays/Operas/Fables/CDs/Magazines:

1. Read People Skills by Virginia Satir.
2. Read Difficult Conversations by Douglas Stone, Bruce Patton, Sheila Heen and Roger Fisher.
3. Read The Art of Intimacy by Thomas Patrick Malone, MD
4. Read Friendships that Run Deep by Keith R. Anderson

5. Read <u>Coping with Toxic Managers, Subordinates, and Other Difficult People</u> by Roy H. Lubit, MD, PhD.
6. Read <u>How to Win Friends and Influence People</u> by Dale Carnegie.
7. Read <u>How to Talk to Anyone</u> by Leil Lowndes.
8. Read <u>Dealing with People You Can't Stand</u> by Dr. Rick Brinkman and Dr. Rick Kirschner.
9. Read <u>The Relationship Cure</u> by John Gottman.
10. Read <u>A Couple's Guide to Communication</u> by John Gottman.
11. Read <u>Raising an Emotionally Intelligent Child</u> by John Gottman.
12. Read <u>What am I feeling?</u> by John Gottman.
13. Read <u>Meta-Emotions: How Families Communicate Emotionally</u> by John Gottman.
14. Read <u>Coping with Difficult People</u> by Robert M. Abramson, PhD.
15. Read <u>You Can Negotiate Anything</u> by Herb Cohen.
16. Read <u>The Tao of Negotiation</u> by Joel Edelman and Mary Beth Crain.
17. Read <u>Winning with the Velvet Touch</u> by Richard Stern.
18. Read <u>The Bundle of Sticks</u> by Aesop.
19. Read <u>How We Love</u> by Milan & Kay Yerkovich.
20. Read <u>Winning with the Velvet Touch</u> by Richard Stern.
21. Read any networking books by Ivan Misner.
22. Read <u>A Survival Guide to Managing Employees from Hell: Handling Idiots, Whiners, Slackers and Other Workplace Demons</u> by Gini Graham Scott.
23. Read <u>The Connected Leader</u> by Emmanuel Gobillot.
24. Read <u>Working With You is Killing Me</u> by Katherine Crowley and Kathi Elster.
25. Read <u>Nonviolent Communication: A Language of Life</u> by Marshall Rosenberg.
26. Read <u>Words That Work</u> by Dr. Frank Luntz.
27. To remember names, get <u>The Memory Book</u> by Jerry Lucas.
28. Read <u>Relationship Skills for Tough Guys</u> by Brent Darnell.
29. Read <u>The Five Love Languages</u> by Gary D. Chapman.

Movies/TV/Videos:

1. Something's Got to Give-Jack Nicholson's and Diane Keaton's characters, both committed to their singleness, find a rewarding relationship.
2. When Harry Met Sally-Note the ups and downs of this long relationship.
3. Forrest Gump-Forrest is a master at establishing and maintaining relationships over time.
4. It's a Wonderful Life-George Bailey creates great relationships over his life.
5. Butch Cassidy and the Sundance Kid-Butch and Sundance form a lasting friendship over many years.
6. Papillion-Dustin Hoffman and Steve McQueen's characters form a lasting friendship despite many obstacles.
7. Harold and Maude-Two unlikely people forming a great relationship.
8. Crash-watch the interplay of relationships.
9. In the Heat of the Night-watch how the relationships develop in this mystery.
10. Freedom Writers.
11. The Pursuit of Happyness-Relationships are redeeming in this story.
12. King Kong-Watch the relationship between an ape and a girl.
13. Twelve Angry Men-The relationships between jurors unfold.
14. The Deer Hunter-Relationships drive the actions of these Viet Nam veterans.
15. Harvey-See the relationship between an amiable man and his six foot rabbit.
16. Stan by Me-The relationships of these young boys are wonderfully developed.

17. Dr. Zhivago-Relationships drive this drama.
18. Miracle-The story of the 1980 Olympic hockey team.
19. On Golden Pond-Watch the various relationships as they unfold.
20. Watch West Wing.
21. Watch The Office.
22. Watch Mon Meilleur ami (My Best Friend)

Websites/Apps:

1. Visit www.coping.org for information on relationships.
2. Visit www.mentalhelp.net/psyhelp
3. Visit www.selfgrowth.com
4. Visit www.myfatherusedtosay.com
5. Visit www.cnvc.org
6. Download the app: People Skills To Go

Inspirational Quotes:

1. "Relationships are like Rome. Difficult to start out, incredible during the prosperity of the 'Golden Age', and unbearable during the fall. Then, a new kingdom will come along and the whole process will repeat itself until you come across a kingdom like Egypt that thrives, and continues to flourish. This kingdom will become your best friend, your soul mate, and your love." Helen Keller
2. "Personal relationships are the fertile soil from which all advancement, all success, all achievement in real life grows." Ben Stein
3. "Without relationships, no matter how much wealth, fame, power, prestige and seeming success by the standards and opinions of the world one has, happiness will constantly elude him." Sidney Madwed
4. "Cherish your human connections: your relationships with friends and family." Barbara Bush
5. "Real magic in relationships means an absence of judgment of others." Wayne Dyer
6. "Assumptions are the termites of relationships." Henry Winkler (The Fonz)
7. "Eighty percent of life's satisfaction comes from meaningful relationships." Brian Tracy
8. "A cardinal principle of Total Quality escapes too many managers: you cannot continuously improve interdependent systems and processes until you progressively perfect interdependent, interpersonal relationships." Stephen R. Covey
9. "Friendship is the source of the greatest pleasures, and without friends even the most agreeable pursuits become tedious." Saint Thomas Aquinas

Empathy:

is recognizing, understanding, and appreciating how other people feel. Empathy involves being able to articulate your understanding of another's perspective and behaving in a way that respects other's feelings.

Practical Daily Application:

1. Practice reading other people's faces. What does their face convey?
2. Ask more questions. Take the time to clarify what people mean and how they are feeling.
3. Give others the opportunity to completely express themselves while you listen without interrupting, judging, or trying to solve their problems.

4. Practice reflecting others' thoughts and feelings. Paraphrase their thoughts or ideas and reflect back their feeling message.
5. Ask others how they feel on a scale of 1-10.
6. Ask: "How do you feel and what would help you feel better?"
7. Avoid saying "You need to," "You have to," "You better," You should," "You shouldn't," and "Why didn't you"? In fact, avoid "why" questions altogether. They sound accusatory, like an interrogation.
8. Empathy exercise. When you arrive home, turn off all the noise (TV, radio, etc.) and sit down with your partner or call a person close to you. Ask them to tell you about their day and listen intently, without judgment, without offering solutions, without comments. Be thinking about how what the other person would be feeling throughout their day. The only comment you should offer is, "That must have made you feel....."
9. Make clear what you expect of others.
10. Do an exchange with someone-switch roles for a day with your wife, colleague, friend, etc and experience what they experience.
11. When someone comes to you with a problem, do you: a) try to solve the problem or b) try to determine how this problem makes them feel. If the answer is a), then next time, try to determine how the other person is feeling and verify that emotion with them by saying, "That must make you feel . . . ".
12. Search for "Before Your Next Fight" by Daniel Shapiro
13. Double your questions to statements ratio. In other words, the statements that you make should be half the number of the questions that you ask.
14. Remember to listen, understand, and acknowledge when having a discussion with someone.

Exercises and General Development Ideas:

1. Learn to appreciate differences in people.
2. Improve your ability to read body language. Tune in more to nonverbal communication.
3. Use your own emotional self-awareness to recognize others' feelings.
4. Make an effort to be more sensitive and understanding of others.
5. Ask yourself how you would feel in a given situation and respond accordingly.
6. Improve your listening skills.
7. Respect others' interpersonal boundaries.
8. Treat the other person as you would like to be treated (Golden Rule) or better yet, how THEY would like to be treated (Platinum Rule).
9. Learn to validate and empathize without taking on responsibility for the problem.
10. Learn a new language and find out about the new culture as well.
11. Travel more and embrace differences in people. Try to understand them better.
12. When someone delivers bad news, this is the time to practice your empathy skills, especially when the news negatively affects you.
13. Utilize the empathy map (Google this).
14. Get into groups of 3-7 people. Ask a question: What is your favorite food? Major challenge facing company? What is your current mood? (an emotional empathy question) Everyone writes down a short answer for themselves. Choose one person in group. Person to the left makes a prediction what the response will be. Try to be as empathetic as possible. Put yourself in their shoes, what you know about them, what will be a human response. The person tells what they wrote. If you get it right, you get one point. Variation: Person to right and left of the answer person make predictions and whoever is right gets a point.
15. Minority report: If anyone is different from the group (African American, woman, etc). All of us guess what this person(s) are feeling right now or during a company social interaction. Start with any

other open ended question. They write down their answer. Other people take turns trying to predict what their answer will be and write it down. Variation: Can be answers to other company specific questions. What is the most difficult part of a project? Group decides which of the answers are the best. Then, see if they are right.

16. Pair up. Back to back. You look at a picture given to you (geometric shapes that you hand out) and describe it to the other person so they can draw it. Alternative: One person is blindfolded. You see what he is doing and you describe it so that he gets it right.
17. Empathy: Blindfold one person and other person gives directions on how to negotiate the room, get a pencil and bring it back. You can also do it with earplugs. Describe a process without sound to the other person through gestures.
18. Group of people. All are on a lifeboat. Lifeboat is overloaded. You have to throw two people out in a shark infested sea. Each one of you speak on behalf of someone else (to their left) and convince the group to spare that person.
19. Pair up with someone. Your job is to talk about things that are common between the two of you. Come up with the most unique, unusual similarity that is not obvious or visible. Each pair stands up and the group tries to guess what the unique similarity is. After they have all made statements, then the pair can tell them what it is. Discuss the common things and ask if they think they can find something in common even with people that may not be like them.
20. Small groups. Fill in the sentences: People with a lot of empathy always . . .on one side of the paper. People who lack empathy never . . . on the other side of the paper. Fill a page with these endings to the sentences. Collect all of the papers, distribute them randomly to another group. That group will look at the lists and come up with a definitive checklist on always and never.
21. Two large, even groups. Each person from group one stands like they would ordinarily stand. Each person from Group two goes and stands behind another person in Group one and stands exactly like they are standing. Now Group two stands normally and Group one mirrors how they stand, but now Group one people are standing face to face instead of behind them. Discuss what the experience is like from the person standing and the person mirroring. Was standing behind easier than standing face to face? Why?
22. People pair up. Think of a major or minor problem he/she is facing on the job. The problem person has a sheet of paper. On the paper, briefly state the problem you shared with your partner. The listener writes down the problem person's problem on another sheet of paper, but they have to make it sound like their own problem. One is faking it, one is the real problem. Audience doesn't know which. Switch up the paper pairs and read each out loud. The audience guesses which is the real problem and which is the listener's fake. How close can you pretend to be another person?
23. Pair up. Taller of the two or better looking person share a problem he is facing on the job. Other person, listen carefully and try to respond appropriately. You will hear: Oh I'm sorry to hear that. Or you should try this. Go for 3 minutes. Stop. How many of the listeners tried to solve the problem? How many reflected, listened empathetically, but didn't try to solve the problem? Can you take on the other's feelings as a way of expressing? Variation: One person has a problem and tells the listener. The listener can respond in any way, but he can't use any self-reference (I, me or my). Debrief with Was that hard? What made it hard? What did no self-reference force you to do? Sometimes people don't want you to solve their problem, they just want to be listened to and understood. Show video "It's not about the nail."
24. Dictionary. What the heck is empathy? In groups, come up with and write on a piece of paper, write 3 or 4 sayings about the nature of empathy. Some examples: It's an emotion, putting yourself in other's shoes. Collect everything. You will also have three real statements taken from book on empathy. Read all of the sayings/definitions and vote on which one is the official definition. Individuals get one point if they can determine the "real" definitions and five points if you convince the group that your definition is the right one.

25. Emotional contagion. Mingle and imitate the facial expressions of another person in the room. Keep moving around. No talking. 2 minutes. Ask people to maintain the expression that they have. What is the default emotion? Was it happy, sad, neutral.
26. Picture someone you are having a difficult time with, perhaps conflict.

    Go through the statements with that person in mind:
    - "Just like me, this person is trying to find happiness and meaning in his/her life."
    - "Just like me, this person is trying to avoid pain in his/her life."
    - "Just like me, this person has known heartache, loss, loneliness and despair."
    - "Just like me, this person wants to be loved and connected with others."
    - "Just like me, this person has people in his/her life who care about them."
    - "Just like me, this person is trying to get his/her needs met."
    - "Just like me, this person is trying his/her best to complete this project, make a profit, etc."
    - "Just like me, this person is trying his/her best to make this project successful."
    - "Just like me, this person wants to excel and be good at what he/she does."
    - "Just like me, this person is learning about how to navigate through this sometimes difficult life/project/work environment."

    Has your view of that person changed? Has your view of the situation changed? How?

27. Empathy exercise: For everyone you come into contact with (especially women, minorities, and other groups, especially those whom you have bias against), say the following in your mind. I wish you and every human being to be safe, happy, healthy and live a peaceful and joyful life.

28. Tragic Tour: (You can do this in a group or alone) The following is a list of people trapped in a cave rapidly filling with water. The rescue team will be here in 20 minutes. In that 20 minutes, you have to decide the order in which these people come out of the cave knowing that many of the ones at the bottom of the list will likely drown. How do you decide? Write down the list from first out to last out.

Tour Group Members

- **Pia:** A 22-year old African American university student and former heroin addict. She is transgender, being born a male, and is agnostic. She is an only child of a world-renowned artist who is described as having a brilliant future as a multi-media artist.

- **Sven:** Retired, 66-years old. Sven, originally from Sweden, is a naturalized, US citizen. He came on the trip as a break from his full-time responsibility of caring for his wife, who has Alzheimer's. He is a non-practicing Lutheran and is disabled. He walks with great difficulty with a cane.

- **Sandra:** 32-years old, an African American, full time mother of two children, ages four and six. She and her husband, Mark, have taken this trip to celebrate their tenth wedding anniversary and re-evaluate their relationship. She may be pregnant.

- **Mark:** Mark is a 40-year old, Caucasian stockbroker, husband to Sandra, and the father of her two children and possibly a third. He is Mormon. He is having an affair with his administrative assistant.

- **Aarav:** Aarav is from India. He is a 42-year old brilliant research scientist with a pharmaceutical firm. He believes he may be close to finding a cure for AIDS. He is a devout Hindu. He is gay and his partner is on his way to the tour site.

- **Kathleen:** Kathleen, 55-years old, is an Orthodox Jew. She is taking a break from an intense investigation. She heads up an international team of aviation specialists who have been studying a series of plane crashes. While on this trip, she has been reflecting on her work and believes she has come up with the common denominator that may be causing the air disasters.

- **Maria:** Maria, Hispanic, 34-years old, emigrated from Mexico ten years ago and owns a very successful landscaping business. She has a husband and five children. A devout Catholic, she is always helping the poor in her community.

- **Entifadh:** Entifadh, 28-years old, is an exchange student from Iraq with both US and Iraqi citizenship. He is a devout Muslim. He is a brilliant engineer, studying for his PhD in structural design. He hopes to take his knowledge back to the Middle East to help rebuild the region.

- **Blanche:** Blanche is a teenage girl who is dying of a rare form of cancer. She only has a few months to live has taken this trip before she is too weak to travel. She belongs to a group who follows a Hindu Avatar named Meher Baba.

- **Billy:** Billy, a Caucasian male, 45 years old, and is a construction Superintendent. He is a devout Christian and a veteran with six tours of duty. He has a purple heart and a medal of honor.

Debriefing: Thirty Questions (courtesy Thiagi, *thiagi.com*)

Phase 1. How Do You Feel?
On the whole, was this a pleasant or an unpleasant activity?
Which step in this activity was especially uncomfortable?
Which step in this activity was especially pleasant?

Phase 2. What Happened?
Did most people agree on the criteria for the order of removing people from the cave? If not, why not?
What types of criteria were used to choose the order? Did you agree with those criteria? If not, why not?
What happened when the time started to wind down?
What changed during the process of selection?

Phase 3. What Did You Learn?
Do people's values come into play when they view other people?

Were people's values and selection criteria different than your own? If so, how did you deal with that?

Which of these differences do you think would have the most significant impact on who you chose to come out first?: race, religion, gender, sexual orientation, physical ability, educational level, personality type, social class, or thinking style?

Phase 4. How Does This Relate to the Real World?

When you were imagining the impact of the decision on the order, did you think about some specific people who belonged to those groups? Were these thoughts positive or negative?

In the United States, we try to be unbiased and fair irrespective of such factors as his or her race, gender, physical abilities, or sexual orientation. Do you agree or disagree with this statement?

Some people find this activity extremely discomforting. What would you say to someone who has problems getting into this activity?

Would you feel uncomfortable discussing with your colleagues the issues implied in this activity? Why?

Does your organization accept differences among the employees and attempt to provide everyone with equal opportunities?

Do you know of any colleague who feels that he or she has been denied equal opportunities because of race, gender, physical ability, age, or sexual orientation? Do you agree or disagree with this colleague?

Which of the various differences in the tour group would have been the most difficult one for you to think about?

Phase 5. What If?

What would have happened if we had made the group all white males? Or all females? Or all one race? Would your process have been different?

What would have happened if the group that did this exercise was actually the group trapped in the cave? How would you decide?

What would have happened if we had asked you to role-play some of the people in the group to defend why you should come out first?

Phase 6. What Next?

If you were to talk about this activity with your significant other, what would be the first thing you would say?

What advice would you give to a friend of yours who is different from you?

How would you collect realistic data about the impact of the types of differences you thought about?

Some people claim that none of these differences would have made any difference in their selection order. What would you say to them?

What can you do to help your organization have a positive impact on the personal and professional development of everyone in spite of individual differences?

Books/Plays/Operas/Fables/CDs/Magazines:

1. Read <u>A General Theory of Love</u> by Thomas Lewis, Fari Amini, Richard Lannon.
2. Read <u>Emotions Revealed</u> by Paul Ekman.
3. Read <u>Telling Lies</u> by Paul Ekman.
4. Read <u>Unmasking the Face</u> by Paul Ekman and Wallace V. Friesen.
5. Read the novel, <u>The Curious Incident of the Dog in the Night-time</u>, by Mark Haddon. This is the story of an autistic boy who investigates the mysterious death of a neighborhood dog. It teaches us how the ability to perceive emotions in others plays such a vital role in our lives.

6. Read <u>Teaching Your Children Sensitivity</u> by Linda and Richard Eyre.
7. Read <u>A Christmas Carol</u> by Charles Dickens or see the play. See how Scrooge develops empathy through visits by three ghosts.
8. Read <u>Metamorphosis</u> by Franz Kafka. A man turns into a giant roach.
9. Read <u>Reading People: How to Understand People and Predict Their Behavior</u> by Jo-Ellan Dimitrius and Mark C. Mazzarella.
10. Read <u>The Art of Speed Reading People</u> by Paul D. Tieger and Barbara Barron-Tieger.
11. Read <u>The Art of Profiling</u> by Dan Korem.
12. Read <u>Teach Yourself Body Language</u> by Gordon Wainright.
13. Read <u>The Definitive Book of Body Language</u> by Barbara Pease and Allan Pease.
14. Read <u>Raising An Emotionally Intelligent Child</u> by John Gottman.
15. Read <u>Winning with the Velvet Touch</u> by Richard Stern.
16. Read <u>How Does it Feel? Exploring the World of Your Senses</u> by Mick Csaky.
17. Read <u>The Heart is a Lonely Hunter</u> by Carson McCullers.
18. Read <u>The 7 Habits of Highly Effective People</u> by Stephen Covey and focus on the 5th habit.
19. Watch The Sopranos. Mobsters with empathy?

Movies/TV/Videos:

1. Terms of Endearment-Jack Nicholson's character develops his empathy despite himself.
2. Gigot-Jackie Gleason plays a mute whose is empathetic to a fault. He is taken advantage of by a woman because of Gigot's empathy for her situation.
3. Zelig-Zelig takes empathy to a new level when he changes his physical characteristics to match the people around him.
4. It's a Wonderful Life-George Bailey gives up his dreams because of his empathy for others.
5. A Clockwork Orange-This movie shows what it is like to have no empathy for others. (Note, this is a very violent film.)
6. A Christmas Carol-My favorite version stars Alistair Sim. See how Scrooge develops empathy through visits by three ghosts.
7. Mr. Blandings Builds His Dream House. Hone your empathy skills while this poor man tries to build his dream home.
8. Watch Band of Brothers from the aspect of team and social responsibility.
9. Freedom Writers-How do these young people feel about their situations?
10. The Pursuit of Happyness-Figure out the feelings of the characters.
11. The Elephant Man-Put yourself in John Merrick's shoes.
12. To Kill a Mockingbird-Atticus teaches Jim and Scout the valuable lesson of empathy.
13. Schindler's List-Put yourself in the Jew's place. Also, as hard as it is, put yourself in the German's place. What could have led them to these horrific events?
14. Google Cleveland Clinic empathy. Watch the movie.

Websites/Apps:

1. Empathy Test app
2. Google "empathy map"

Inspirational Quotes:

1. "One of the most poignant of all human experiences is empathy-the ability to feel what others feel when suffering from pain or loss." Louis Jolyon West

2. "Some people think only intellect counts: knowing how to solve problems, knowing how to get by, knowing how to identify an advantage and seize it. But the functions of intellect are insufficient without courage, love, friendship, compassion and empathy." Dean Koontz
3. "Communication by empathy is a talent that few possess." Unknown
4. "Manners are a sensitive awareness of the feelings of others. If you have that awareness, you have good manners, no matter what fork you use." Emily Post
5. "Be kind, for everyone you meet is fighting a hard battle." Plato
6. "Three things in human life are important: The first is to be kind. The second is to be kind. And the third is to be kind." Henry James
7. "Anything done for another is done for oneself." Pope John Paul II
8. "Could a greater miracle take place than for us to look through each other's eyes for an instant?" Henry David Thoreau

To decrease Empathy:

If you have too much empathy, you are likely the type of person who has trouble saying no, who gets taken advantage of, who gets walked on at times. In order to not have empathy become a problem, work on increasing your assertiveness and self-regard.

Social Responsibility:

is willingly contributing to society, to one's social groups, and generally to the welfare of others. Social Responsibility involves acting responsibly, having social consciousness, and showing concern for the greater community.

Practical Daily Application:

1. Volunteer in your neighborhood, community, and at work.
2. Mentor someone else.
3. Plan time into every day to help others: at home, at work, and in the community.
4. Increase your level of participation as a team member.
5. Volunteer to take on responsibility rather than waiting to be asked.
6. Practice random acts of social responsibility: pick up trash that's not yours, pick up dog poop that's not yours, bus other's tables at restaurants, take other's shopping carts back to the store, let people in line ahead of you, pay the toll for cars behind you, offer to help people in need of assistance, stop to help a stranded car, hand out inexpensive umbrellas on a rainy day.
7. When sitting in a meeting with a team, keep your mouth shut and listen to others.
8. Focus on asking for the opinions and input from others.
9. Practice consensus where appropriate; even if you are the final decision maker, involve everyone in the process if you can.

Exercises and General Development Ideas:

1. Hire employees from different backgrounds than your own.
2. Do something beyond the limits of your usual job at work. Take on a project that will benefit others.
3. Encourage and support others to volunteer, mentor, and take responsibility at home, at work, and their communities.

4. Help build an atmosphere of cooperation and responsibility at work and in the community.
5. Participate in community initiatives that your employer supports, e.g. Junior Achievement, Habitat for Humanity, homeless shelters, etc.
6. Take advantage of diversity training programs at work.
7. Serve on the board of an organization you support.
8. Plan your charitable contributions thoughtfully and learn about the organizations you support.
9. Create family or team traditions, of service e.g. preparing meals for the homeless on holidays.
10. Learn a new language and find out about the new culture as well.
11. Travel more and embrace differences in people. Try to understand them better.
12. Emphasize the accomplishments of the team.
13. Join some social networks such as Facebook, My Space, Linked In, or other websites that connect you with people in your past.

Books/Plays/Operas/Fables/CDs/Magazines:

1. Read <u>Mercy Beyond Measure</u> by Lori Salierno.
2. Read <u>The Team Building Tool Kit</u> by Deborah Harrington-Mackin.
3. Read <u>When a Butterfly Sneezes</u> by Linda Booth Sweeney.
4. Read <u>The Tip of the Iceberg</u> by David Hutchens.
5. Read <u>Executive Marbles and Other Team Building Activities</u> by Sam Sikes.
6. Read <u>Gulliver's Travels</u> by Jonathan Swift.
7. Read <u>A Christmas Carol</u> by Charles Dickens or see the play. See how Scrooge develops social responsibility through visits by three ghosts.
8. Read the parable of The Good Samaritan in the Bible (Luke 10:25-37)
9. Read <u>The Ragamuffin Gospel</u> by Brennan Manning.
10. Read <u>The Wisdom of Accepted Tenderness</u> by Brennan Manning.
11. Read <u>Ruthless Trust</u> by Brennan Manning.
12. Read <u>When Cultures Collide</u> by Richard D. Lewis.
13. Read <u>Cultures and Organizations</u> by Geert Hofstede.
14. Read <u>The Heart and Art of Netweaving</u> by Robert S. Littell.
15. Read <u>International Business Culture</u> by Terry Garrison.
16. Read <u>Lord of the Flies</u> by William Golding and see how a group of children divide into two social groups.
17. Read <u>Leading at a Higher Level</u> by Ken Blanchard.
18. Read <u>Group Genius</u> by Keith Sawyer.

Movies/TV/Videos:

1. Remember the Titans-Herman Boone takes his players, who are African American and White, to a Civil War Battlefield and helps them to connect with the human pain and suffering that was common to everyone on both sides.
2. Schindler's List-Schindler sees something greater than himself.
3. The Grapes of Wrath-Tom Joad sees himself as not a single soul, but a piece of a "great big soul".
4. Shane-Farmers stand up for what is right for the community in this western.
5. Mr. Smith Goes to Washington-Senator Smith stand up for what is right for the country, not giving into special interest and greed.
6. The Magnificent Seven-Seven warriors help a small Mexican village defend their town against outlaws.
7. Ghandi-A great example social responsibility and the implications for independence.

8. A Christmas Carol-My favorite version stars Alistair Sim. See how Scrooge develops social responsibility through visits by three ghosts.
9. Bagdad Café. Watch how this unlikely group pulls together to save a diner in the middle of the desert.
10. Freedom Writers-Youths in trouble find meaning.
11. The Pursuit of Happyness-One man finds meaning and gives back.
12. The Man Without a Past (Finnish)-A man with amnesia battles the notion that without his identification number, he is nobody.
13. Watch Band of Brothers from the aspect of team and social responsibility.
14. Twelve Angry Men-Do social implications come into play during this trial?
15. To Kill a Mockingbird-Social mores are challenged in this story.
16. A Clockwork Orange-This movie shows a society with a lack of social responsibility. (Note, this is a very violent film.)
17. The Day the Earth Stood Still-This science fiction movie deals with our society's selfish motives.

Websites/Apps:

1. Visit www.cnvc.org
2. Download the app: The Extraordinaries
3. Download the app: Volunteer Match
4. Download the app: Trensy

Inspirational Quotes:

1. "Individual commitment to a group effort-that is what makes a team work, a company work, a society work, a civilization work." Vince Lombardi
2. "To be happy, you must learn to forget yourself." Edward George Bulwer-Lytton
3. "Never doubt that a small group of thoughtful committed people can change the world: indeed it's the only thing that ever has!" Margaret Mead
4. "The good neighbor looks beyond the external accidents and discerns those inner qualities that make all men human and, therefore, brothers." Martin Luther King, Jr.
5. "Everything is connected... no one thing can change by itself." Paul Hawken
6. "You must become what you want the world to be." Ghandi
7. "It is not enough to limit your love to your own nation, to your own group. You must respond with love even to those outside of it.... This concept enables people to live together not as nations, but as the human race." Clarence Jordan
8. "Two stone cutters were asked what they were doing. The first said, 'I'm cutting this stone into blocks.' The second replied, 'I'm building a cathedral'."

Problem Solving:

is the ability to find solutions to problems in situations where emotions are involved. Problem solving includes the ability to understand how emotions impact decision-making.

Practical Daily Application:

1. Identify all the stakeholders in a problem situation and what their interests/needs are.
2. Practice brainstorming solutions to problems before making a decision.

3. Attempt to achieve a win/win solution that meets the needs of all parties.
4. Use problem solving and analysis tools, e.g. mind maps, force field analysis.
5. Break big projects into small parts and tackle them step-by-step.
6. Identify the feeling component when undertaking any problem solving, conflict resolution, or change effort.
7. Play games such as chess and solve puzzles that test your problem solving skills. In Chess, you have to think several moves ahead and you cannot be impulsive with your approach. There are many puzzles out there that stretch your problem solving muscles.
8. Learn to delegate and bring in other parties with specialized knowledge to help solve the problem. You can't be an expert at everything.

Exercises and General Development Ideas:

1. Practice differentiating important from not-so-important problems to devote the appropriate amount of energy to solving them.
2. Develop your intuition and tap into it when solving problems and making decisions.
3. Study systems thinking methodologies and the systems archetypes such as reinforcing loops and balancing loops.
4. Learn to play chess.
5. Learn to do Sudoku or other types of puzzles daily.
6. Check out Mindmap software for planning your work and your life.
7. Check out Mind Manager software for getting things done.
8. Study Appreciative Inquiry.
9. Study the Stanford "D" School method: Empathize, Define, Ideate, Prototype, Test.

Books/Plays/Operas/Fables/CDs/Magazines:

1. Read any books by Edward De Bono, in particular, Lateral Thinking.
2. Read A Whack On the Side Of The Head by Roger Von Oech.
3. Read A Kick in the Seat of the Pants by Roger Von Oech.
4. Read The Fifth Discipline by Peter Senge.
5. Read The Fifth Discipline Field Book by Peter Senge.
6. Read How Would Confucius Ask for a Raise? by Carol Osborn.
7. Read The Endurance, Shackelton's Legendary Antarctic Expedition by Caroline Alexander.
8. Read Blink, the Power of Thinking Without Thinking by Malcolm Gladwell.
9. Read The Three Little Pigs.
10. Read The Crow and the Pitcher by Aesop.
11. Read Expect the Unexpected or You Won't Find It by Roger Von Oech.
12. Read Storm Rider: Becoming a Strategic Thinker by Rich Horwath.
13. Read Ahead of the Curve: A Guide to Applied Strategic Thinking by Steven Stowell and Melanie Mead.
14. Read The Artist's Way by Julia Cameron.

Movies/TV/Videos:

1. GI Jane-Demi Moore's character finds a way to solve all of the problems thrown her way as she trains to be a Navy Seal.
2. The Great Escape-The prisoners are constantly solving problem after problem in order to engineer their escape from a German prison camp.

3. The Castaway-Tom Hanks' character solves many problems in order to survive.
4. Das Boot-German U boat commander solves many problems in this taught story.

Websites/Apps:

1. Visit www.debonogroup.com
2. Visit www.thinkingmanagers.com
3. Visit www.mindtools.com
4. Visit www.braingle.com
5. Visit www.lumosity.com
6. Google Mind Mapping and check out this way to organize thoughts.
7. Download the app: The Art of Problem Solving
8. Download the app: Mobile Decision Maker
9. Download the app: Steps and Techniques to Solve Problems at Work
10. Download the app: Force Field Analysis
11. Download the app: Liberating Structures (also a book and website)

Inspirational Quotes:

1. "The reward for being a good problem solver is to be heaped and heaped with more and more difficult problems to solve." Buckminster Fuller
2. "Problems always appear big when incompetent men are working on them." William Feather
3. "Before it can be solved, a problem must be clearly stated and defined." William Feather
4. "The most important thing to do in solving a problem is to begin." Frank Tyger
5. "Leadership is solving problems. The day soldiers stop bringing you their problems is the day you have stopped leading them. They have either lost confidence that you can help or concluded you do not care. Either case is a failure of leadership." Karl Raimund Popper
6. "To raise new questions, new possibilities, to regard old problems from a new angle, requires creative imagination and marks real advance in science." Albert Einstein
7. "If you do not ask the right questions, you do not get the right answers. A question asked in the right way often points to its own answer. Asking questions is the A-B-C of diagnosis. Only the inquiring mind solves problems." Edward Hodnett
8. "A positive attitude may not solve all your problems, but it will annoy enough people to make it worth the effort." Herm Albright
9. "Snow and adolescence are the only problems that disappear if you ignore them long enough." Earl Wilson
10. "Most people are more comfortable with old problems than with new solutions." Charles Brower
11. "Problems are only opportunities in work clothes." Henry Kaiser
12. "I am not afraid of storms for I am learning how to sail my ship." Louisa May Alcott
13. "The best way to have a good idea is to have a lot of ideas." Linus Pauling
14. "We can't solve problems by using the same kind of thinking we used when we created them." Albert Einstein

Reality Testing:

is the capacity to remain objective by seeing things as they really are. This capacity involves recognizing when emotions or personal bias can cause one to be less objective.

Practical Daily Application:

1. Play devil's advocate with yourself, and when appropriate, with others.
2. Delay making decisions until you have collected objective data.
3. Make sure you don't "kill the messenger" when someone delivers bad news.
4. Ask others to do reality checks with you.
5. Conduct 'post mortems' at the conclusion of projects to get others' opinions of what went well, what could be improved, and what could be done differently.
6. Wrap up your meetings with an assessment that identifies what was accomplished and what still needs to be done.

Exercises and General Development Ideas:

1. Search for objective evidence to support what you are feeling and thinking when sizing up the situation.
2. Develop best and worst case scenarios.
3. Use formal goal setting techniques (e.g. management by objectives) and measure progress frequently.
4. Use formal project management techniques that include analysis of ongoing progress at regular intervals.
5. If you are a manager, use tools such as employee surveys administered by third parties to collect objective information.

Books/Plays/Operas/Fables/CDs/Magazines:

1. Read the book A New Guide to Rational Living by Albert Ellis.
2. Read the book Confronting Reality by Larry Bossidy and Ram Charan.
3. Read the book The War of Art by Steven Pressfield.
4. Read or see the play Death of a Salesman by Arthur Miller. Notice the low reality testing of the father, Willy Loman, and the higher reality testing of the sons, Happy and Biff.
5. Read or see the play A Streetcar Named Desire by Tennessee Williams. Notice the low reality testing of Blanche and the high reality testing of Stanley.
6. Read The Emporer's New Clothes by Hans Christian Andersen.
7. Read The Secret Life of Walter Mitty by James Thurber. Walter is continually going off into fantasy worlds of his own creation.
8. Read Shattered Dreams by Larry Crabb.
9. Read The Grasshopper and the Ants by Aesop.
10. Read any books by Edward De Bono, in particular, Lateral Thinking.
11. Read A Whack On the Side Of The Head by Roger Von Oech.
12. Read A Kick in the Seat of the Pants by Roger Von Oech.

Movies/TV/Videos:

1. Matchstick Men-Nicholas Cage's character has a distorted view of reality until something happens to challenge that. He ends up having a much grounded sense of reality and what it truly important.
2. Casablanca-Rick is a realist and is very good at staying grounded in reality when all around him people

live in a world of fantasy.
3. MASH-During the Korean War, reality is distorted in this mobile army hospital. Note the world of fantasy in which some of the characters reside.
4. Forrest Gump-Forrest has a way of cutting through the fog and seeing the real situation. His matter of fact statements bring us back to reality.
5. The Best Years of Our Lives-After World War II, veterans come back to face the harsh reality of civilian life.
6. A Christmas Story-Watch how Ralph goes off into fantasies that have little to do with reality.
7. The Secret Life of Walter Mitty-Walter goes off into fantasies.
8. Any of the Charlie Brown shows-Snoopy is the Walter Mitty of the cartoon world.
9. Taxi Drive-Travis Bickle gets lost in a world of violence.

Websites/Apps:

1. Download the app: Conscious

Inspirational Quotes:

1. "Things rumored lessen in importance as they assume reality." Proverb
2. "Leadership is the capacity to translate vision into reality." Warren G. Bennis
3. "This is too much reality for a Friday." From the movie As Good as it Gets
4. "We must learn to tailor our concepts to fit reality, instead of trying to stuff reality into our concepts." Victor Daniels
5. "Your goals, minus your doubts, equal your reality" Ralph Marston
6. "Reality leaves a lot to the imagination." John Lennon
7. "There are some people who live in a dream world, and there are some who face reality; and then there are those who turn one into the other." Douglas Everett
8. "Reality is merely an illusion, albeit a very persistent one." Albert Einstein

To decrease Reality Testing: If you Reality Testing is too high, you likely overanalyze things. To decrease this tendency, work on the strategies in Flexibility and Optimism. Don't overanalyze situations. Once you have thought about it adequately, make a decision and move on.

Impulse Control:

is the ability to resist or delay an impulse, drive, or temptation to act and involves avoiding rash behaviors and decision making. Low impulse control can manifest itself in different ways: eating, drinking, smoking, gambling, spending, anger, or impatience.

Practical Daily Application:

1. Eat for mood management. The brain needs adequate nourishment to maintain its proper function. Eat something every two hours.
2. Exercise regularly. It provides distraction and helps balance the brain chemistry associated with emotion. Tobacco
3. Think of impulse control preventatively and avoid the thoughts/feelings and situations that challenge your ability to manage your impulses. Tobacco

4. Develop scripts you can use to buy time to regain your composure. For example, "I'd like some time to think about it," and "I'm not in a good place to respond to that right now."
5. Practice "the 20 minute solution." Distract yourself for 20 minutes, which is how long the emotional brain needs to recover from a stressor. Tobacco
6. Put yourself in a "time-out."
7. Ask yourself, "Will this matter in five years, ten years, twenty years?"
8. Use the 24 hour rule. For big decisions, wait 24 hours before finally deciding.
9. When someone is telling you something and you know that they are not correct, control the impulse to be right. If it has no consequences for you, don't correct the person.
10. Remember to listen, understand, and acknowledge when having a discussion with someone.
11. Listen, listen, listen! You don't have to say what you are thinking all of the time. Let it go.

Exercises and General Development Ideas:

1. Avoid others who have impulse control problems. Tobacco
2. Ask someone you trust to give you honest feedback on the impact your low impulse control is having on others.
3. Get better at recognizing aggressiveness in yourself and others and observe the impact it has on people and situations.
4. Create your own "posture" of self-control (e.g. standing up straight with shoulders back) that you can go to when you are at risk of losing control.
5. Learn to be an objective observer of your feelings in the moment. While you are observing, you are preventing yourself from being flooded and overwhelmed by your emotions. While observing, you are likely to create more choices with which to respond.
6. Make lists or write out plans as a way to avoid acting impulsively.
7. Practice patience.
8. Make a habit of considering the consequences before acting. Tobacco
9. Make a pro and con list prior to acting. Tobacco
10. If impulse control manifests itself in anger, start learning anger management techniques.
11. Make rules of engagement surrounding circumstances where you naturally react impulsively.
12. Use stress management techniques. Tobacco
13. Practice detachment to emotionally distance yourself in the heat of the moment.
14. Keep a food log or any other kind of log to track your impulsive behavior. It can be a time log of how you spend your time as well.
15. Cut others some slack by giving them the benefit of the doubt.
16. Identify the feelings that lead to impulsivity. Recognize the physiological signs that indicate you are about to lose control.
17. Practice a martial art such as tai chi. Tai chi forces you to have patience and delay your impulses. You have to be completely in the moment.

Books/Plays/Operas/Fables/CDs/Magazines:

1. Learn about the underlying physiology of emotion.
2. Read The Emotional Brain: The Mysterious Underpinnings, of Emotional Life by Joseph LeDoux.
3. Read Wherever You Go There You Are by Jon Kabat-Zinn and practice the mindfulness exercises he offers.
4. Complete the exercises in The Anger Workout Book by Henrie Weisinger.
5. Read The Dance of Anger by Harriet Lerner.

6. Read Managing Your Mouth by Robert L. Genua.
7. Read The Anger Control Workbook by Matthew McKay, Peter Rogers.
8. Read I Am, a Common Sense Guide to Coping with Anger by Melvyn L. Fein.
9. Lean and practice conflict management techniques, such as those in The Magic of Conflict
10. by Thomas Crum.
11. See the opera Don Giovanni. Notice the deadly consequences of that lack of impulse control of Don Giovanni (Don Juan).
12. Listen to the CD Anger Releasing: Visualization Exercises for Releasing Negative Feelings and Maximizing Your True Potential by Louise L. Hay.
13. Read Settle It! By Karin Vagiste.
14. Read The Time Trap by Alec Mackenzie.
15. Read Every Man's Battle by Stephen Arterburn and Fred Stoeker.
16. Read Feeding Your Appetites by Stephen Arterburn.
17. Read Beyond Juggling by Sandholtz, Derr, Buckner, and Carlson.
18. Read If You Haven't Got Time To Do It Right, When Will You Find the Time To Do It Over? By Jeffrey J. Mayer.
19. Read Wherever You Go There You Are by Jon Kabat-Zinn and practice the mindfulness exercises he offers.
20. Read The Time Trap by Alec Mackenzie.
21. Read The Art of the Possible by Alexandra Stoddard.
22. Read the story of Samson and Delilah in the Bible to see how Samson's lack of impulse control led to his downfall.
23. Read The Grasshopper and the Ants by Aesop.
24. Read The Tortoise and the Hare by Aesop.
25. Listen to Cat's in the Cradle by Harry Chapin.
26. Listen to Vienna Waits for You by Billy Joel.
27. Read Mindful Eating by Jan Chosen Bays.
28. Read Getting Things Done by David Allen.
29. Read To Buy or Not to Buy by April Lane Benson.

Movies/TV/Videos:

1. Goodfellas. Notice the lack of impulse control of these good fellas.
2. Raging Bull. Jake Lamotta's impulse control needs much work. It manifests itself in many different ways.
3. The Godfather. Good impulse control-Don Corleone. Bad impulse control-Sonny Corleone.
4. To Kill a Mockingbird. Notice the incredible impulse control of Atticus Finch, even when a racist spits in his face. Lack of impulse control is epitomized by Tom Ewell.
5. Shane-Shane, a gunfighter, resists temptation to act, until he is left with no choice.
6. A Christmas Story-There are many scenes dealing with impulse control in this holiday movie.
7. Gladiator-models of impulse control and lack thereof.
8. Taxi Driver-Travis Bickle cannot control himself.
9. The Lost Weekend-An alcoholic cannot control his impulses.
10. The Hustler-Eddie Felson's impulse control gets him into trouble.
11. The Great Santini-Bull Meacham's lack of impulse control alienates his family.

Websites/Apps:

1. Visit www.coping.org for stress related issues.
2. Visit www.mindtools.com
3. Download the app: Patience – Practice the art of waiting

Inspirational Quotes:

1. "Know prudent, cautious, self-control is wisdom's root." John Bunyan
2. "A fool gives full vent to his anger, but a wise man keeps himself under control." Italian Proverb
3. "He who cannot agree with his enemies is controlled by them." Chinese Proverb
4. "The greatest power of ruling consists in the exercise of self-control." Proverb
5. "Who controls the past controls the future: who controls the present controls the past." George Orwell
6. "Anger is a great force. If you control it, it can be transmuted into a power which can move the whole world." Sivananda
7. "But the fruit of the Spirit is love, joy, peace, patience, kindness, goodness, faithfulness, gentleness, self-control." Galatians 5:23, 2
8. "The reputation of a thousand years may be determined by the conduct of one hour." Japanese Proverb
9. "The shortest way to do many things is to do only one thing at a time." Richard Cech.
10. "Nothing is so fatiguing as the eternal hanging on of the unfinished task." Anonymous.
11. "If you are patient in one moment of anger, you will escape a hundred days of sorrow." Chinese Proverb

To decrease Impulse Control:

If you have too much impulse control, you likely overanalyze things at times and are not spontaneous. In order to decrease impulse control, be consciously impulsive and don't think about things too much. Other ways to decrease impulse control would be to join an improvisation group. Learn improvisation and how to think on your feet. Make up stories for the children in your life. Join a dance class. Learn to juggle. Do an impulsive road trip with no destination and no reservations.

Flexibility:

is adapting emotions, thoughts, and behaviors to unfamiliar, unpredictable, and dynamic circumstances or ideas.

Practical Daily Application:

1. Practice relaxation techniques to calm your anxiety when you are uncomfortable.
2. Pursue an artistic medium, such as sculpting, whether or not you have a natural talent for it.
3. Make periodic changes in your daily or weekly routine to give yourself the opportunity to view things from a different perspective.
4. Practice reframing your negative thoughts in order to identify the positive outcomes that may result from challenging situations.
5. Continuously engage yourself in learning something new: new hobbies, skills, etc.
6. Change your regular routines. If you always take the same route to work, vary it. Put your belt on the other way, alter your clothing sequence-put on the right shoe first, do things with your opposite hand, drive a different route to work, etc.

Exercises and General Development Ideas:

1. Maintain mental flexibility when others are expressing ideas with which you disagree. Listen and learn more about them.
2. Allow your mind to stay open to new thoughts or ways of doing things.
3. Ask others in the same situation how they view it and how they are responding.
4. Consider alternate scenarios for the situations and "try on" your feelings for each.
5. Expand your comfort zone by challenging yourself.
6. Surround yourself with people whose lifestyle, goals, and viewpoints are different than your own.
7. Consider traveling to unfamiliar places as an exercise in developing your flexibility.
8. Do a search on the article The Neuroscience of Change by David Rock and Jeffrey Schwartz.

Books/Plays/Operas/Fables/CDs/Magazines:

1. Read Too Perfect by A. Mallinger.
2. If you are a manager, read about the psychology of change; e.g. Transitions by William Bridges.
3. Read any books on resilience; e.g. Resilience; the Power to Bounce Back When the Going Gets Tough by Frederic Flach.
4. Read Who Moved My Cheese? By Spencer Johnson, M.D..
5. Read Change Anything by Patterson, Kerry, and Grenny.

Movies/TV/Videos:

1. Lilies of the Field-Sidney Poitier's character learns what it is to be truly flexible when a group of nuns convinces him to build them a church.
2. Zelig-Zelig is the most flexible man on earth, so much so that he changes his physical characteristics to match the people around him.
3. Dr. Zhivago-Omar Sharif's character learns to be flexible and take what comes in this epic family drama.
4. Tootsie-Dustin Hoffman's character is a paradox of flexibility. Very flexible in some ways, Hoffman's character is inflexible in others.
5. Easy Rider-Two motorcycle riders search for the real America and takes what comes.
6. The Great Santini-Watch how Bull Meacham's rigid philosophies pushes his family away.

Websites/Apps:

1. Google perfectionist and see tons of articles and blogs.
2. Calm app
3. Gratitude Journal app
4. Noisli app

Inspirational Quotes:

1. "Thanks to impermanence everything possible." Thich Nhat Hanh
2. "New ideas stir from every corner. They show up disguised innocently as interruptions, contradictions and embarrassing dilemmas. Beware of total strangers and friends alike who shower you with comfortable sameness, and remain open to those who make you uneasy, for they are the true messengers of the future." Rob Lebow.

3. "The bend in the road is not the end of the road unless you refuse to take the turn." –Anon
4. "Prepare yourself for the world, as the athletes used to do for their exercise; oil your mind and your manners, to give them the necessary suppleness and flexibility; strength alone will not do." Lord Chesterfield
5. "Life belongs to the living and he who lives must be prepared for changes." Goethe
6. "If you want to make enemies, try to change something." Woodrow Wilson
7. "The thing that is really hard, and really amazing, is giving up on being perfect and beginning the work of becoming yourself." Anna Quindlen
8. "Without deviation from the norm, there is no progress." Frank Zappa
9. "An obstinate man does not hold opinions, they hold him." Samuel Butler
10. "Habit and routine have an unbelievable power to destroy." Henri De Lubac, Paradoxes
11. "Courage is the power to let go of the familiar." Raymond Liquist

To decrease Flexibility:

If you are overly flexible, you are likely one of those people who have trouble saying no, who take on too much, who float about on the wind. To decrease flexibility, work on increasing your assertiveness and emotional self-awareness. Stand up for yourself at appropriate times.

Stress Tolerance:

involves coping with stressful or difficult situations and believing that one can manage or influence situations in a positive manner.

NOTE: If you believe you are having mental health issues such as anxiety, depression and/or suicidal thoughts, please reach out to the suicide prevention hotline at 1-800-273-8255 or visit: preventconstructionsuicide.com for information, risk assessments, and support material.

Practical Daily Application:

All of the following are good steps to reduce blood pressure and stop tobacco.

1. Avoid leaving things to the last minute. Schedule your days, weeks and months. Don't keep it in your head. Write it down and keep it portable.
2. Eat breakfast every day with a protein and not too many carbs.
3. Eat regularly and nutritiously throughout the day. Eat or drink something at least every two hours.
4. Recognize when you are approaching burnout and take proactive steps to avoid it.
5. Develop an exercise routine even if it is just walking 10 minutes per day. Start off slowly and simply and build on it. Love your exercise and get a partner to make you accountable.
6. When you feel overwhelmed, just take one small step.
7. When you feel overwhelmed, take a break and walk away from it for a while.
8. Build in brief recovery times throughout the day. It can be as simple as taking three deep breaths or getting away from work to have a leisurely, unhurried lunch.
9. Cut down or cut out caffeine.
10. Cut down or cut out simple sugars.
11. Cut down or cut out cigarettes.
12. Cut down your TV watching and replace it with restorative activities such as reading, spending time with family, focusing on self-development, listening to music, or some type of physical activity.

13. Take a brief walk every day.
14. Practice visualization in advance of stressful situations. Picture the positive outcome in your mind.
15. Keep your body hydrated at all times.
16. Leverage your social support system to help manage stress.
17. Set reasonable daily objectives for yourself and keep them.
18. Play more! Recreation means re-create.
19. Share your feelings with someone you trust.
20. Express gratitude to others. You will feel better and so will they. It is physiologically impossible to feel stressed and grateful at the same time. Commit with your accountability partner to email a gratitude list to each other every day.
21. When you start to feel stressed, take ten deep breaths and on each exhale, think about a blessing in your life.
22. Improve your laughter quotient. Laughing releases health-promoting chemicals.
23. Get enough sleep and have a regular schedule for getting to bed and getting up.
24. Smile in order to shift your mood.
25. Develop a daily habit of meditation, relaxation, or prayer.
26. Start a laugh club. Set up a time to laugh each day.

Exercises and General Development Ideas:

1. Learn deep breathing techniques.
2. Learn basic meditation techniques. You can meditate yourself or buy guided meditation tapes or CD's.
3. Take a yoga class. Learn yoga, tai chi or other eastern techniques that will help with stress management.
4. Learn progressive relaxation techniques.
5. Make a plan to renew your body, mind and spirit and implement it.
6. Focus on the things within your realm of control. Don't sweat the small stuff.
7. Tell your doctor if you are feeling especially stressed, anxious, or depressed.
8. Maintain perspective; learn to step back, learn to say "no".
9. Learn to set proper boundaries.
10. Take your earned vacations.
11. Complete a stress assessment instrument to evaluate how vulnerable you are to stress.
12. Check out Mindmap software for planning your work and your life.
13. Check out Mind Manager software for getting things done.
14. Determine if you have stress related symptoms such as fatigue, trouble sleeping, stomach problems, headaches and other chronic pains, decreased libido, decreased immunity, sinus/allergies/asthma, skin problems, or irritability. These symptoms are your body's way of telling you that you are under too much stress and that something is wrong. Don't cover up these symptoms with drugs, but address the root cause, which is stress.
15. Learn visualization and centering techniques.

Books/Plays/Operas/Fables/CDs/Magazines:

1. Read <u>The Tough Guy Survival Kit</u> by Brent Darnell.
2. Read <u>Getting Things Done</u> by David Allen.
3. Read <u>The 4 Hour Work Week</u> by Tim Ferriss.
4. Read <u>Why Zebras Don't Get Ulcers</u> by Robert M. Sapolsky

5. Read <u>The Relaxation Response</u> by Herbert Benson.
6. Read <u>Learning to Live in the Now</u> by Ruth Fishel.
7. Read <u>Coming to Our Senses</u> by Jon Kabat-Zinn.
8. Complete the exercises in <u>The Relaxation and Stress Reduction Workbook</u> by Martha Davis, Elizabeth Robbins Eshelman, and Matther McKay.
9. Learn about good stress vs. bad stress; e.g. in <u>Stress for Success</u> by Jim Loeher.
10. Read <u>The Lemming Conspiracy</u> by Bob D. McDonald and Don Hutcheson.
11. Read <u>Real Men Do Yoga</u> by John Capouya. Professional athletes increase performance with yoga.
12. Read <u>Richard Hittleman's 28 Day Yoga Exercise Plan</u> by Richard Hittleman and follow the exercise plan.
13. Read <u>The Breathing Book</u> by Donna Farhi.
14. Read <u>Beyond Juggling</u> by Sandholtz, Derr, Buckner, and Carlson.
15. Read <u>The Book of Yoga</u> by Christina Brown.
16. Read <u>Learn to Relax</u> by Mike George.
17. Read <u>If You Haven't Got Time To Do It Right, When Will You Find the Time To Do It Over?</u> By Jeffrey J. Mayer.
18. Read <u>Wherever You Go There You Are</u> by Jon Kabat-Zinn and practice the mindfulness exercises he offers.
19. Read <u>The Time Trap</u> by Alec Mackenzie.
20. Read <u>Babar's Yoga for Elephants</u> by Laurent De Brunhoff and do some yoga with your kids.
21. Read <u>Energy Addict</u> by Jon Gordon.
22. Read <u>The Energy Bus</u> by Jon Gordon.
23. Read <u>Peak-Performance Living</u> by Dr. Joel Robertson with Tom Monte.
24. Read <u>Life without Stress, The Far Eastern Antidote to Tension and Anxiety</u> by Dr. Arthur Sokoloff.
25. Read <u>The Art of the Possible</u> by Alexandra Stoddard.
26. Read <u>Shattered Dreams</u> by Larry Crabb.
27. Read <u>The Grasshopper and the Ants</u> by Aesop.
28. Read The Appreciative Heart (e-book) available on www.heartmath.com .
29. Read <u>Wenn Due s eilig hast, gehe langsam</u> by Lothar J. Seiwert
30. Read <u>Time Management for Unmanageable People</u> by Ann McGee-Cooper.
31. Listen to the CD The Art of Meditation by Daniel Goleman.
32. Read <u>Easier Than You Think . . . The Small Changes That Add Up to a World of Difference</u> by Sylvia Boorstein.
33. Read <u>The Little Red Book of Wisdom</u> by Mark Demoss.
34. Read <u>A Perfect Mess</u> by Eric Abrahamson and David H. Freedman.
35. Read Ecclesiastes in the Bible.

Movies/TV/Videos:

1. The Negotiator-Roman uses humor to reduce the stress of the hostage taker and buy him time to figure things out.
2. Dog Day Afternoon-Sal eventually cracks under pressure, not being able to handle the stress.
3. Double Indemnity-Fred MacMurray's character handles his stress despite being pursued by an insurance claims adjuster.
4. Raiders of the Lost Ark-Indiana Jones stays cool and calm under the worst of circumstances.
5. High Noon-Despite impending peril, Gary Cooper's character remains calm.
6. Taxi Driver-Watch how the stress of the modern world drives this taxi driver to madness.

Websites/Apps:

1. Learn and practice the Freeze-Frame technique from HeartMath (www.heartmath.com)
2. Get on an e-mail distribution list to receive daily positive quotes and tips; e.g. Cyber Quotes from www.cyber-nation.com or Heart Quotes from www.heartmath.com
3. Visit www.growthcentral.com .
4. Visit www.stresscenter.com for stress and anxiety issues.
5. Visit www.coping.org for stress issues.
6. Visit www.seiwert.de (German)
7. Visit www.mindtools.com
8. Visit www.gratefulness.org
9. Visit www.realage.com
10. Visit www.workyourlife.com
11. Visit www.naturallybalanced.com for weight loss, detoxification, smoking cessation, and nutritional wellness advice.
12. Download the app: Stress Check
13. Download the app: Stress Stopper
14. Download the app: iStress
15. Download the app: Stress Tracker

Inspirational Quotes:

1. "Do not anxiously hope for what is not yet come; do not vainly regret what is already past." Chinese Proverb
2. "Adopting the right attitude can convert a negative stress into a positive one." Dr. Hans Selve
3. "Stress is basically a disconnection from the earth, a forgetting of the breath. Stress is an ignorant state. It believes that everything is an emergency. Nothing is that important. Just lie down." Natalie Goldberg
4. "A careless word may kindle strife. A cruel word may wreck a life. A timely word may level stress. A loving word may heal and bless." Unknown
5. "Stress is when you wake up screaming and you realize you haven't fallen asleep yet." Unknown
6. "Worry and stress affects the circulation, the heart, the glands, the whole nervous system, and profoundly affects heart action." Dr. Charles W. Mayo

Optimism:

is an indicator of one's positive attitude and outlook on life. It involves remaining hopeful and resilient, despite occasional setbacks.

Practical Daily Application:

1. Practice seeing things from other people's perspectives.
2. Challenge your negative thoughts. Use a mental or physical technique to make yourself stop: use an elastic band to snap when you think pessimistically or put a loved one's photo as the wallpaper on your computer or phone and focus on that.
3. Maintain a positive attitude.
4. Recognize that your negative self-talk is usually just an interpretation of an event, not the reality of the event.
5. Carry a clicker for a day to record the number of times you use negative self-talk.
6. Identify the "silver lining" in adverse events.
7. Develop a daily habit of meditation, relaxation or prayer.
8. Practice daily positive affirmations.

Exercises and General Development Ideas:

1. Surround yourself with optimistic people.
2. Recognize the impact negative people have on you.
3. Be hopeful when dealing with problems and difficult situations.
4. Set a positive example for others and you will feel more positive yourself.
5. When faced with adversity, release your negative emotions, then move on.
6. Don't dwell on the past or fret about the future. Practice mindfulness and be in the moment as much as possible.
7. Learn the difference between hopefulness the helplessness and adopt a hopeful attitude as much as possible.
8. Search on "the law of attraction" and investigate the concept of like attracting like. Positive attracts positive and negative attracts negative. Don't come from a place of lack.

Books/Plays/Operas/Fables/CDs/Magazines:

1. Read the book The Power of Positive Thinking by Norman Vincent Peale.
2. Read the book Spontaneous Optimism by Dr. Michael Mercer and Dr. Maryann Troiani.
3. Read the book Learned Optimism by Martin Seligman.
4. Read the book or see or read the play The Diary of Anne Frank.
5. Read How Full is Your Bucket? by Tom Rath and Donald O. Clifton, Ph.D.
6. Read Joy Comes in the Morning by Bob Gass.
7. Read Learn to be an Optimist by Lucy Macdonald.
8. Read Authentic Happiness by Martin Seligman.
9. Read Tough-Minded Optimist by Norman Vincent Peale.
10. Read Thoughts of a Christian Optimist by Arthur Ward.
11. Read the book of Job in the Bible. Despite many setbacks, Job remains faithful and optimistic even though he gripes about his present situation.
12. Read Your Best Life Now by Joel Osteen.
13. Read Shattered Dreams by Larry Crabb.

14. Read The Appreciative Heart (e-book) available on www.heartmath.com.
15. Read Excuse Me Your Life is Waiting by Lynn Grabhorn.
16. Read Gung Ho by Ken Blanchard.
17. Read Energy Addict by Jon Gordon.
18. Read The Energy Bus by Jon Gordon.
19. Read Man's Search for Meaning by Viktor Frankl.
20. Subscribe to The Intelligent Optimist magazine.

Movies/TV/Videos:

1. The Wizard of Oz –Although their worlds are destroyed and they should have little hope, Dorothy, The Scarecrow, The Tin Man, and the Cowardly Lion go forward with optimism in the hope that their dreams will come true.
2. Castaway-Tom Hanks stays optimistic despite many setbacks.
3. The Diary of Anne Frank-The Franks stay positive despite horrible conditions and constant fear.
4. Rocky-An underdog fighter finds his optimism.
5. Cool Hand Luke-Despite the odds, Paul Newman's character remains optimistic.
6. The African Queen-Two people never give up despite the circumstances.
7. The World's Greatest Indian. See one man fulfill his destiny through a positive outlook.
8. The Karate Kid-A kid triumphs with the help of a master.
9. Drumline-Tap into positive passion.
10. Watch The Cooler and see how a negative person can change the energy. Also see what happens after he changes his energy from negative to positive.
11. Watch any of Martin Seligman's Ted Talks.

Websites/Apps:

1. Visit www.happiness.com
2. Visit www.thewaytohappiness.org
3. Visit www.drkenner.com
4. Visit www.authentichappiness.org
5. Download the app: Optimism
6. Download the app: Optimism by Dr. Milne
7. Download the app: Spontaneous Optimism (Audio Book)

Inspirational Quotes:

1. "An optimist is a guy who has never had much experience." Don Marquis
2. "Positive thinking is the key to success in business, education, pro football, anything that you can mention. I go out there thinking that I'm going to complete every pass." Ron Jaworski
3. "I am optimistic and confident in all that I do. I affirm only the best for myself and others. I am the creator of my life and my world. I meet daily challenges gracefully and with complete confidence. I fill my mind with positive, nurturing, and healing thoughts." Alice Potter
4. "Few things in the world are more powerful than a positive push. A smile. A word of optimism and hope. A "you can do it" when things are tough." Richard M. DeVos
5. "You can do anything you think you can. This knowledge is literally the gift of the gods, for through it you can solve every human problem. It should make of you an incurable optimist. It is the open door." Robert Collier
6. "For myself I am an optimist--it does not seem to be much use being anything else." Winston Churchill

7. "Live each day as it comes, and not to borrow trouble by dreading tomorrow. It is the dark menace of the future that makes cowards of us." Dorothy Dix
8. "Optimism is true moral courage." Sir Ernest Shackleton, whose Antarctic expedition was stranded for almost two years.
9. "A positive attitude may not solve all your problems, but it will annoy enough people to make it worth the effort." Herm Albright
10. "I have never seen a monument erected to a pessimist." Paul Harvey
11. "Things are only impossible until they're not." Jean Luc Picard
12. "In the long run, the pessimist may be proved right, but the optimist has a better time on the trip." Daniel L. Reardon
13. "With optimism, you look upon the sunny side of things. People say, 'Studs, you're an optimist.' I never said I was an optimist. I have hope because what's the alternative to hope? Despair? If you have despair, you might as well put your head in the oven." Studs Terkel

To decrease Optimism: If you have a tendency to be overly optimistic, you may not take action on pending problems until it is too late. To decrease optimism, work on the strategies in Reality Testing.

Happiness:

is the ability to feel satisfied with one's life, to enjoy oneself and others, and to have fun.

Practical Daily Application:

1. Smile often and sincerely make eye contact with others.
2. Decrease the time you spend watching violent or upsetting television.
3. Practice forgiveness daily.
4. Laugh - at yourself, at life, and with others.
5. Pamper yourself.
6. Create good life balance.
7. Create good health by eating properly, exercising, and watching your stress levels.
8. Watch uplifting movies
9. Read inspiring literature.
10. Listen to inspiring music.
11. Focus on what others are thinking and feeling rather than on your own needs.
12. Decrease the amount of time you spend complaining, no matter how legitimate the complaint.
13. Set aside time for leisure.
14. Develop a daily habit of meditation, relaxation or prayer.
15. Create celebration traditions for you and your loved ones.
16. Celebrate your accomplishments.
17. Cheer up others who may be blue. You will feel good as well.
18. Spend one week observing in yourself the differences in your energy when you are feeling optimistic or pessimistic.
19. Create "best case scenarios" to help you see things optimistically.
20. Don't generalize from one bad situation to all similar situations.
21. Recognize that realism is a good thing. Being realistic is not the same as being negative.
22. End each day by creating your own "gratitude list."
23. Decrease desire, especially for "things". Focus on what is really important in your life.

Exercises and General Development Ideas:

1. Learn what gives you joy and vow to have more of it in your life.
2. If you cannot eliminate things that make you sad, avoid those people and situations that have that effect on you.
3. Spend more time with people who make you happy and who make you laugh. It rubs off!
4. Take responsibility for making yourself happy instead of expecting someone else to do so.
5. Treat setbacks as opportunities for change rather than as failures.
6. Create positive affirmations on index cards and read them to yourself several times a day.
7. Develop a spiritual practice.
8. Read about the mind/body connection to learn about the health consequences of negativity.
9. Read biographies of inspiring, optimistic people.

Books/Plays/Operas/Fables/CDs/Magazines:

1. Read Happiness: The Nature and Nurture of Joy and Contentment by Dr. David Lykken.
2. Read The Art of Happiness by the Dalai Lama.
3. Read The Feeling Good Handbook by David G. Meyers, PhD.
4. Read The Pursuit of Happiness by David G. Meyers, PhD.
5. Read When Am I Going to Be Happy? By Penelope Russianhoff, PhD
6. Read You Can be Happy No Matter What or Don't Sweat the Small Stuff by Richard Carlson, PhD.
7. Read Learned Optimism by Martin Seligman.
8. Read Authentic Happiness by Martin Seligman.
9. For an academic understanding of the nature of optimism, read The Science of Optimism and Hope by Jane Gillham.
10. Read about the power of hopefulness in Man's Search for Meaning by Victor Frankl.
11. Read Your Best Life Now by Joel Osteen.
12. Read Shattered Dreams by Larry Crabb.
13. Read What's so Amazing About Grace? By Philip Yancey.
14. Read any books by Stephen Covey.
15. Read Life's 2% Solution by Marcia Hughes.
16. Read Excuse Me Your Life is Waiting by Lynn Grabhorn.
17. Read Stumbling on Happiness by Daniel Gilbert.
18. Read Energy Addict by Jon Gordon.
19. Read The Energy Bus by Jon Gordon.
20. Read The Happiness Trap by Russ Harris.
21. Read The Happiness Advantage by Achor.

Movies/TV/Videos:

1. Love, Actually-This movie demonstrates choosing happiness through love.
2. It's a Wonderful Life-George Bailey finds out what happiness is all about.
3. Pee Wee's Big Adventure-Pee Wee stays happy despite setbacks on his adventure to find his bike.
4. Willie Wonka and The Chocolate Factory-A boy finds happiness.
5. Being There-Chance, the gardener, is always happy.
6. The Wizard of Oz-there's no place like home.
7. The African Queen-Two people find happiness despite the circumstances.

Websites/Apps:

1. Visit www.happiness.com
2. Visit www.thewaytohappiness.org
3. Visit www.drkenner.com
4. Visit www.authentichappiness.org
5. Visit www.theartofhappiness.net
6. Download the app: Stay Happy
7. Download the app: How to be Happy

Inspirational Quotes:

1. "In dealings between man and man, truth, sincerity, and integrity are of the utmost importance to the felicity of life." Benjamin Franklin
2. "It is not in doing what you like, but liking what you do that is the secret of happiness." James M. Barrie
3. "The happiness of your life depends on the quality of your thoughts." Marcus Aurelius Antoninus
4. "We are about as happy as we make up our minds to be." Abraham Lincoln
5. "Happiness is the only good. The time to be happy is now. The place to be happy is here. The way to be happy is to make others so." Robert Green Ingersoll
6. "There are three sureties of happiness: good habits, amiability, and forbearance." Welsh Proverb
7. "The happiness of this life depends less on what befalls you than the way in which you take it." Elbert Hubbard
8. "Success is getting what you want. Happiness is wanting what you get." Dave Gardner
9. "How simple . . . a thing is happiness: a glass of wine, a roast chestnut, a wretched little brazier, the sound of the sea . . . All that is required to feel that here and now is happiness is a simple . . . heart." Nikos Kazantzakis from Zorba the Greek.
10. "The most certain sign of wisdom is cheerfulness." Michel de Montaigne
11. "If you want others to be happy, practice compassion. If you want to be happy, practice compassion." The Dalai Lama
12. "I am still determined to be cheerful and happy, in whatever situation I may be; for I have also learned from experience that the greater part of our happiness or misery depends on our disposition and not upon our circumstances." Martha Washington
13. "When one door of happiness closes, another opens, but often we look so long at the closed door that we do not see the one that has been opened for us." Helen Keller
14. "The basic thing is that everyone wants happiness, no one wants suffering. And happiness mainly comes from our own attitude, rather than from external factors. If your own mental attitude is correct, even if you remain in a hostile atmosphere, you feel happy." The Dalai Lama
15. "Exude Happiness and you will feel it back a thousand times." Oscar Wilde

Biliary and Liver

The liver is the industrial center of the body. It's a chemical factory making new body chemistry and breaking down toxic waste. The gallbladder (biliary) handles fat, and fat is necessary to make hormones. The liver is responsible for the breakdown of all non-food substances such as food preservatives and colorings, medicines, caffeine and alcohol.

Practical Daily Application:

1. The best results for the least effort. Take a nutritional supplement. The listed supplements are intended to be recommended by a physician. But they can sometimes be found by googling the brand and name. If you can't find them, contact us and we can help. Metagenics UltraClear. This is a medical food designed to support liver detoxification and reduce chronic fatigue. Ask your pharmacist if it is OK to take with your medications. Don't take if you are pregnant or nursing. Do this for three weeks and re-take the symptom survey. Use your same log in and password. Blood Pressure, Body Mass Index, Cholesterol, Glucose, Tobacco

2. Keep a food log. My fitness Pal is a good app. Blood Pressure, Body Mass Index, Cholesterol, Glucose, Tobacco

3. Limit fast food Blood Pressure, Body Mass Index, Cholesterol, Glucose, Tobacco

General Improvement Ideas:

1. Read, "The Principles of Fat Burning," by Dr. Eric Berg. Order from www.drberg.com. Do Chapter 10 for two to three weeks and re-take the symptom survey. Use your same log in and password. Blood Pressure, Body Mass Index, Cholesterol, Glucose, Tobacco
2. Get rid of all toxic cleaners and products in your home. Cholesterol
3. Get a good water filter.
4. Start eating more organic food; especially meat and dairy. Cholesterol
5. Eliminate plastic containers, especially if you heat them.
6. Go to www.drberg.com for ideas on nutrition, exercise, shopping and much more.
7. Limit fast food.
8. Non-Toxic Home Cleaning: www.eartheasy.com/live_nontoxic_solutions.htm
9. "10 Quick Tips to Save the Planet and Your Health" by Cynthia Perkins: www.naturalfamilyonline.com/2-h&w/49-save-the-planet.htm
10. Natural herbicides and pesticides (you can either use the website below or do a Google search: www.gardensalive.com
11. 33 Secrets to a Good Night's Sleep: www.mercola.com/article/sleep.htm

12. Tips to relax, eat in a calm environment, practice yoga and proper breathing: www.banyanbotanicals.com/nl/611.html
13. The Mediterranean diet has been called the stressed out person's diet. It contains healthy foods and good fats. Blood Pressure, Body Mass Index, Cholesterol, Glucose, Tobacco
14. Great search engine that you can enter any food and see glycemic index, and much, much more: www.nutritiondata.com/facts/snacks/5356/2 Blood Pressure, Body Mass Index, Cholesterol, Glucose, Tobacco
15. A good way to learn better portions and food choices, and still be able to eat anything you want. A great diet for balanced living!!! You can get a free month: www.weightwatchers.com/index.aspx. They have apps too. Body Mass Index
16. This website compares the popular low carb diets and has recipes: www.low-carb-diet-recipes.com/ Glucose
17. This is a great search engine that you can enter any food and see amounts of carbs, protein, fat, glycemic index, etc! Calculate your daily needs for nutrition – www.nutritiondata.com/facts/snacks/5356/2
18. Read, "Lose it for Life" by Steve Arterburn:
    - The book explores the underlying cause of why you eat the way you eat and helps you to change. Body Mass Index

19. Look at calming and restorative strategies especially related to the way you eat in the Stress Handling section. Stress slows gut activity and delays digestion. This is very important; even more so than changing your actual diet. There are books, CD's, and activities in that part of the workbook for you to review.

Movies/T.V.:

1. Watch the movie "Supersize Me" to see how sick you can get and how quickly, eating poor quality foods. Blood Pressure, Body Mass Index, Cholesterol, Glucose, Tobacco
2. Watch the movie "Fast Food Nation." Blood Pressure, Body Mass Index, Cholesterol, Glucose, Tobacco

Exercise

1. Find an exercise you LOVE. That's the best way to stick to it. Keep looking and trying until you find something you love. Blood Pressure, Body Mass Index, Cholesterol, Glucose, Tobacco
2. A nice walk can be done ANYWHERE, and requires no special toys or clothes, other than some good shoes. Start by wearing your pedometer and increasing the number of steps each day. See the following website for more information about walking: www.walking.about.com. Sign up for a daily newsletter that is excellent and encouraging, if a bit overwhelming. Even if you do 5 minutes a day, it is a great start. Blood Pressure, Body Mass Index, Cholesterol, Glucose, Tobacco
3. Stick with it!! For those who don't exercise, it's about finding the motivation to start – and stay – on a program. We now have techniques like EFT – a form of psychological acupressure – to help us successfully stick with a long-term exercise program. Go to www.emofree.com. Sign up for the newsletter. You can use EFT to help with your emotional development. Blood Pressure, Body Mass Index, Cholesterol, Glucose, Tobacco
4. Search "Exercise"!! You might be surprised by what you find! The world's largest directory of sports and recreational activities, facilities, venues and classes, which includes more than 66,000 races, leagues, tournaments, camps and other recreational listings in over 80 sports and 5,000 cities all at: www.active.com/ Blood Pressure, Body Mass Index, Cholesterol, Glucose, Tobacco

Sugar Handling: Food to Fuel

All sugars and carbohydrates are converted to glucose in the blood. If the body doesn't do this well or you overeat these foods, you'll have shifts in energy and mood; sometimes dramatic shifts. These shifts also weaken the adrenals and the nervous systems.

Practical Daily Application:

1. The best results for the least effort. Take a nutritional supplement. The listed supplements are intended to be recommended by a physician. But they can sometimes be found by googling the brand and name. If you can't find them, contact us and we can help. Metagenics UltraMeal. This is a medical food with low glycemic index designed to support sugar handling and conditions associated with metabolic syndrome, obesity, altered body composition, and insulin resistance Ask your pharmacist if it is OK to take with your medications. Don't take if you are pregnant or nursing. Do this for three weeks and re-take the symptom survey. Use your same log in and password. Blood Pressure, Body Mass Index, Cholesterol, Glucose, Tobacco

2. Keep a food log. My fitnesspal is a good app. Blood Pressure, Body Mass Index, Cholesterol, Glucose, Tobacco

3. Start reading labels. Watch for sugar, syrups, words ending in "ose" or "ol". Blood Pressure, Body Mass Index, Cholesterol, Glucose, Tobacco

4. Stop drinking any sweet drinks including sodas, sweet teas and fruit juices. Blood Pressure, Body Mass Index, Cholesterol, Glucose, Tobacco

5. Stop eating sweets unless it is after a meal. Blood Pressure, Body Mass Index, Cholesterol, Glucose, Tobacco

6. Limit fast food Blood Pressure, Body Mass Index, Cholesterol, Glucose, Tobacco

General Improvement Ideas:

1. Read, "The Principles of Fat Burning," by Dr. Eric Berg. Order from www.drberg.com. Do Chapter 10 WITH ADDED PROTEIN for two to three weeks and re-take the system survey. Use you same login and password. Blood Pressure, Body Mass Index, Cholesterol, Glucose, Tobacco
2. Go to www.drberg.com for ideas on nutrition, exercise, shopping and much more. Blood Pressure, Body Mass Index, Cholesterol, Glucose, Tobacco
3. Read "The Paleo Solution" by Robb Woff Do the program for 30 days. Body Mass Index, Glucose
4. Google "paleo" recipes. Glucose
5. Google "high protein recipes" and "low glycemic recipes" Glucose
6. The Mediterranean diet has a low glycemic index and has been called the stressed out person's diet. This website has information on it and sources of foods. For those in major cities, you can find most foods at regular or specialty groceries. Blood Pressure, Body Mass Index, Cholesterol, Glucose, Tobacco
7. Great search engine that you can enter any food and see glycemic index, and much, much more: www.nutritiondata.com/facts/snacks/5356/2 Blood Pressure, Body Mass Index, Cholesterol, Glucose, Tobacco
8. Website for glycemic index: http://www.glycemicindex.com/ Blood Pressure, Body Mass Index, Cholesterol, Glucose, Tobacco
9. List of high-protein foods and amount of protein in each: http://lowcarbdiets.about.com/od/whattoeat/a/highproteinfood.htm Blood Pressure, Body Mass Index, Cholesterol, Glucose, Tobacco
10. A good way to learn better portions and food choices, and still be able to eat anything you want. A great diet for balanced living!!! You can get a free month: www.weightwatchers.com/index.aspx. They have apps too. Blood Pressure, Body Mass Index, Cholesterol, Glucose, Tobacco
11. 33 Secrets to a Good Night's Sleep: www.mercola.com/article/sleep.htm
12. Look at calming and restorative strategies especially related to the way you eat in the Stress Tolerance section. Stress slows gut activity and delays digestion. This is very important; even more so than changing your actual diet. There are books, CD's, and activities in that part of the workbook for you to review.
13. This is the definitive table for both the glycemic index and the glycemic load. Very comprehensive, but can't search: www.mendosa.com/gilists.htm
14. Read "Lose it for Life" by Steve Arterburn:
    - The book explores the underlying cause of why you eat the way you eat and helps you to change. Body Mass Index
15. Read Dr. Atkins', "New Diet Revolution." The book will help you to see different ways to get more protein in your diet. Glucose
16. Read "Beat Sugar Addiction Now" by Jacob Teitelbaum. Glucose
17. Tips to relax, eat in a calm environment, practice yoga and proper breathing: www.banyanbotanicals.com/nl/611.html

Movies/T.V.:

1. Watch the movie "Supersize Me" to see how sick you can get and how quickly, eating poor quality foods. Blood Pressure, Body Mass Index, Cholesterol, Glucose, Tobacco
2. Watch the movie "Fast Food Nation." Blood Pressure, Body Mass Index, Cholesterol, Glucose, Tobacco

Exercise

1. Find an exercise you LOVE. That's the best way to stick to it. Keep looking and trying until you find something you love. Blood Pressure, Body Mass Index, Cholesterol, Glucose, Tobacco
2. A nice walk can be done ANYWHERE, and requires no special toys or clothes, other than some good shoes. Start by wearing your pedometer and increasing the number of steps each day. See the following website for more information about walking: www.walking.about.com. Sign up for a daily newsletter that is excellent and encouraging, if a bit overwhelming. Even if you do 5 minutes a day, it is a great start. Blood Pressure, Body Mass Index, Cholesterol, Glucose, Tobacco
3. Stick with it!! For those who don't exercise, it's about finding the motivation to start – and stay – on a program. We now have techniques like EFT – a form of psychological acupressure – to help us successfully stick with a long-term exercise program. Go to www.emofree.com. Sign up for the newsletter. You can use EFT to help with your emotional development. Blood Pressure, Body Mass Index, Cholesterol, Glucose, Tobacco
4. Search "Exercise"!! You might be surprised by what you find! The world's largest directory of sports and recreational activities, facilities, venues and classes, which includes more than 66,000 races, leagues, tournaments, camps and other recreational listings in over 80 sports and 5,000 cities all at: www.active.com/ Blood Pressure, Body Mass Index, Cholesterol, Glucose, Tobacco

Digestive

Deals with the breakdown of protein. Protein is necessary to heal and repair of the body, and hence keeps you from aging too rapidly. Protein transports the minerals that are the 'spark plugs' for every action in the body.

Practical Daily Application:

1. The best results for the least effort. Take a nutritional supplement. The listed supplements are intended to be recommended by a physician. But they can sometimes be found by googling the brand and name. If you can't find them, contact us and we can help. Standard Process Zypan. This is a comprehensive enzyme that breaks down carbohydrates, protein and fat. Ask your pharmacist if it is OK to take with your medications. Don't take if you are pregnant or nursing.
2. Keep a food log. My Fitness Pal is a good app. Blood Pressure, Body Mass Index, Cholesterol, Glucose, Tobacco
3. If you are over 50 years old, you may lack the specific enzymes need to break down protein.
4. Do NOT eat a high protein diet.
5. Limit fast food. Blood Pressure, Body Mass Index, Cholesterol, Glucose, Tobacco

General Improvement Ideas:

1. Read, "The Principles of Fat Burning," by Dr. Eric Berg. Order from www.drberg.com. Do Chapter 10 for two to three weeks. Blood Pressure, Body Mass Index, Cholesterol, Glucose, Tobacco
2. Read "Lose it for Life" by Steve Arterburn:
   - The book explores the underlying cause of why you eat the way you eat and helps you to change. Blood Pressure, Body Mass Index, Cholesterol, Glucose, Tobacco
3. Go to www.drberg.com for ideas on nutrition, exercise, shopping and much more. Blood Pressure, Body Mass Index, Cholesterol, Glucose, Tobacco
4. A good way to learn better portions and food choices, and still be able to eat anything you want. A great diet for balanced living!!! You can get a free month: www.weightwatchers.com/index.aspx. This is a great diet for you. There are also apps. Blood Pressure, Body Mass Index, Cholesterol, Glucose, Tobacco
5. 33 Secrets to a Good Night's Sleep: www.mercola.com/article/sleep.htm

6. Look at calming and restorative strategies especially related to the way you eat in the Stress Handling section. Stress slows gut activity and delays digestion. This is very important; even more so than changing your actual diet. There are books, CD's, and activities in that part of the workbook for you to review.
7. The Mediterranean diet has been called the stressed out person's diet. It will not contain too much protein for you. This website has information on it and sources of foods. For those in major cities, you can find most foods at regular or specialty groceries. Blood Pressure, Body Mass Index, Cholesterol, Glucose, Tobacco
8. Enter your vitals and get your BMI plus further instructions for calories. Sign up to use the pantry and keep information, recipes and track foods for weight loss: www.nutritiondata.com/tools/calories-burned Blood Pressure, Body Mass Index, Cholesterol, Glucose, Tobacco
9. Tips to relax, eat in a calm environment, practice yoga and proper breathing: www.banyanbotanicals.com/nl/611.html
10. Conscious eating: http://ezinearticles.com/?Balanced-When-Busy&id=825842

Movies/T.V.:

1. Watch the movie "Supersize Me" to see how sick you can get and how quickly, eating poor quality foods. Blood Pressure, Body Mass Index, Cholesterol, Glucose, Tobacco
2. Watch the movie "Fast Food Nation." Blood Pressure, Body Mass Index, Cholesterol, Glucose, Tobacco

Exercise

1. Find an exercise you LOVE. That's the best way to stick to it. Keep looking and trying until you find something you love. Blood Pressure, Body Mass Index, Cholesterol, Glucose, Tobacco

2. A nice walk can be done ANYWHERE, and requires no special toys or clothes, other than some good shoes. Start by wearing your pedometer and increasing the number of steps each day. See the following website for more information about walking: www.walking.about.com. Sign up for a daily newsletter that is excellent and encouraging, if a bit overwhelming. Even if you do 5 minutes a day, it is a great start. Blood Pressure, Body Mass Index, Cholesterol, Glucose, Tobacco

3. Stick with it!! For those who don't exercise, it's about finding the motivation to start – and stay – on a program. We now have techniques like EFT – a form of psychological acupressure – to help us successfully stick with a long-term exercise program. Go to www.emofree.com. Sign up for the newsletter. You can use EFT to help with your emotional development. Blood Pressure, Body Mass Index, Cholesterol, Glucose, Tobacco

4. BMI and calorie calculator, articles on weight loss: www.projectweightloss.com Blood Pressure, Body Mass Index, Cholesterol, Glucose, Tobacco

Foundation

Relates to nerve and muscle function, including heart function and brain chemistry. Heavily reliant on B vitamins. Stress depletes vitamin B; and adding it helps you handle stress better. B vitamins are especially important to weak adrenals or nervous system weakness.

Practical Daily Application:

1. The best results for the least effort. Take a nutritional supplement. The listed supplements are intended to be recommended by a physician. But they can sometimes be found by googling the brand and name. If you can't find them, contact us and we can help. Go to a health food store and get a FOOD BASED B Complex. If the % RDA is in the 1,000 % it is likely NOT food based.
2. To determine your correct dosage of vitamin B: Take a whole food, B vitamin at the recommended daily dose and check to see if your urine is bright yellow. If not, continue to increase the dosage until it is. Take that dose for three days. Back down slowly one or two pills per day until your urine is clear. Then increase two pills and that is your perfect dosage. Your urine should stay yellow throughout the day so you may need to spread your dosage out throughout your day.
3. I don't mean to minimize the importance of creating better balance in your life by developing a healthy lifestyle, adding exercise to your routine and working on emotional competencies. However, if you do all those things, and Vitamin B is not added by supplement and/or food, the results will still be less than good. If supplementation is added, and these other things are done, the results will be excellent.
4. Keep a food log. My Fitness Pal is a good app.
5. Google Vitamin B foods
6. Eat unprocessed foods
7. Limit fast food

General Improvement Ideas

1. Refer to the 'Stress Tolerance' section – Stress *depletes* Vitamin B. The converse is true if Vitamin B is added; it helps one *handle* stress better.
2. Read "Lose it for Life" by Steve Arterburn:
   - The book explores the underlying cause of why you eat the way you eat and helps you to change.
3. The Mediterranean diet has been called the stressed out person's diet. It is heavy in vitamin B.
4. Great search engine that you can enter any food and see Vitamin B content, and much, much more: www.nutritiondata.com/facts/snacks/5356/2

5. Tips to relax, eat in a calm environment, practice yoga and proper breathing: www.banyanbotanicals.com/nl/611.html
6. Conscious eating: http://ezinearticles.com/?Balanced-When-Busy&id=825842

Movies/T.V.:

1. Watch the movie "Supersize Me" to see how sick you can get and how quickly, eating poor quality foods.
2. Watch the movie "Fast Food Nation."

Exercise

1. Find an exercise you LOVE. That's the best way to stick to it. Keep looking and trying until you find something you love.
2. A nice walk can be done ANYWHERE, and requires no special toys or clothes, other than some good shoes. Start by wearing your pedometer and increasing the number of steps each day. See the following website for more information about walking: www.walking.about.com. Sign up for a daily newsletter that is excellent and encouraging, if a bit overwhelming. Even if you do 5 minutes a day, it is a great start.
3. Stick with it!! For those who don't exercise, it's about finding the motivation to start – and stay – on a program. We now have techniques like EFT – a form of psychological acupressure – to help us successfully stick with a long-term exercise program. Go to www.emofree.com. Sign up for the newsletter. You can use EFT to help with your emotional development.

Sympathetic Dominance (The Gas)

The part of the nervous system that responds to stress. It's the gas pedal; the fight/flight mode. If it's weak, we see anxiety, revved up mind, loose bowels and the many other signs of stress.

Practical Daily Application:

Sympathetic dominance is stress on the nervous system so to help it we support the nervous system and the adrenal glands that are the stress glands.

1. The best results for the least effort. Take a nutritional supplement. The listed supplements are intended to be recommended by a physician. But they can sometimes be found by googling the brand and name. If you can't find them, contact us and we can help. Standard Process Min Tran is an herbal stress management formula to nourish and quiet the heart, ideal for those that are stressed and wired. Ask your pharmacist if it is OK to take with your medications. Don't take if you are pregnant or nursing.
2. To determine your correct dosage of vitamin B: Take a whole food, B vitamin at the recommended daily dose and check to see if your urine is bright yellow. If not, continue to increase the dosage until it is. Take that dose for three days. Back down slowly one or two pills per day until your urine is clear. Then increase two pills and that is your perfect dosage. Your urine should stay yellow throughout the day so you may need to spread your dosage out throughout your day.
3. Avoid caffeine
4. Refer to *Stress Tolerance Section* for Practical Daily applications there.
5. Sugar is very detrimental to the nervous system. Do strategies in the sugar handling section.

General Improvement Ideas:

1. In the 'Stress Tolerance' section, you can review strategies to relax, calm, and restore you. See the information about sleep and meditation. More important than what you eat is the way in which you eat. Choose recovery activities regarding eating habits rather than specific foods.
2. Google Desk Yoga
3. Read, "Eat, Pray, Love," by Elizabeth Gilbert.
4. Read, "Lose it for Life" by Steve Arterburn:
   - The book explores the underlying cause of why you eat the way you eat and helps you to change.

5. Read, "Getting Things Done" by David Allen for time management tips.
6. Read, "The Four Hour Work Week" by Timothy Ferriss for time management tips.
7. Read, "Excuse Me, Your Life is Waiting" by Lynn Grabhorn.
8. Do the workbook, "Excuse Me, Your Life is Waiting Playbook" by Lynn Grabhorn.
9. Read, "Don't Bite the Hook" by Pema Chodron.
10. 33 Secrets to a Good Night's Sleep: www.mercola.com/article/sleep.htm
11. Free introductory CD on how to recover from stress, anxiety and depression. 12-week CD set for 8 payments of $59.95 – call 800-611-0857 or visit www.stresscenter.com.
12. Tips to relax, eat in a calm environment, practice yoga and proper breathing: www.banyanbotanicals.com/nl/611.html
13. Conscious eating: http://ezinearticles.com/?Balanced-When-Busy&id=825842
14. In the 'Stress Tolerance' section, you can review strategies to relax. Calm, and restore you. See the information about sleep and meditation. More important than what you eat is the way in which you eat. Choose recovery activities regarding eating habits rather than specific foods.

Movies/T.V.:

1. Any comedy movie. Laughter decreases stress.

Exercise

1. Find an exercise you LOVE. That's the best way to stick to it. Keep looking and trying until you find something you love. Exercise EVERY SINGLE DAY. You are encouraged to do "hard exercise" such as cycling, weights, boxing, martial arts, or running.

2. A nice walk can be done ANYWHERE, and requires no special toys or clothes, other than some good shoes. Start by wearing your pedometer and increasing the number of steps each day. See the following website for more information about walking: www.walking.about.com. Sign up for a daily newsletter that is excellent and encouraging, if a bit overwhelming. Even if you do 5 minutes a day, it is a great start.

3. Stick with it!! For those who don't exercise, it's about finding the motivation to start – and stay – on a program. We now have techniques like EFT – a form of psychological acupressure – to help us successfully stick with a long-term exercise program. Go to www.emofree.com. Sign up for the newsletter. You can use EFT to help with your emotional development.

Parasympathetic Dominance (The Brakes)

Parasympathetic Dominance is the resting side of the nervous system. Things we don't have to think about like digestion, breathing, and blood pressure. If weak, we see low energy and motivation, depression, poor coping and other issues.

Practical Daily Application:

Para Sympathetic dominance is stress on the nervous system so to help it we support the nervous system and the adrenal glands that are the stress glands.

1. The best results for the least effort. Take a nutritional supplement. The listed supplements are intended to be recommended by a physician. but they can sometimes be found by googling the brand and name. If you can't find them, contact us and we can help. Standard Process Phosfood Liquid. It tastes bad to some people but is totally worth it. It provides nutritional support for healthy nervous system and adrenals by combining a select blend of B vitamins especially those that are involved in hormone regulation. Ask your pharmacist if it is OK to take with your medications. Don't take if you are pregnant or nursing.

2. Take vitamin B. To determine your correct dosage of vitamin B: Take a whole food, B vitamin at the recommended daily dose and check to see if your urine is bright yellow. If not, continue to increase the dosage until it is. Take that dose for three days. Back down slowly one or two pills per day until your urine is clear. Then increase two pills and that is your perfect dosage. Your urine should stay yellow throughout the day so you may need to spread your dosage out throughout your day.

3. Refer to *Stress Tolerance Section* for Practical Daily applications there.

4. Avoid caffeine

General Improvement Ideas

1. 33 Secrets to a Good Night's Sleep: www.mercola.com/article/sleep.htm
2. Free introductory CD on how to recover from stress, anxiety and depression. 12-week CD set for 8 payments of $59.95 – call 800-611-0857 or visit www.stresscenter.com
3. In the 'Stress Tolerance' section, you can review strategies to relax. Calm, and restore you. See the information about sleep and meditation. More important than what you eat is the way in which you eat. Choose recovery activities regarding eating habits rather than specific foods.
4. Google Desk Yoga

5. Read, "Eat, Pray, Love," by Elizabeth Gilbert
6. Read, "Getting Things Done" by David Allen for time management tips.
7. Read, "The Four Hour Work Week" by Timothy Ferriss. for time management tips.
8. Read, "Excuse Me, Your Life is Waiting" by Lynn Grabhorn
9. Do the workbook, "Excuse Me, Your Life is Waiting Playbook" by Lynn Grabhorn.
10. The Mediterranean diet has been called the stressed out person's diet. This website has information on it and sources of foods. For those in major cities, you can find most foods at regular or specialty groceries.
11. Tips to relax, eat in a calm environment, practice yoga and proper breathing: www.banyanbotanicals.com/nl/611.html
12. Conscious eating: http://ezinearticles.com/?Balanced-When-Busy&id=825842
13. And more information on yoga: www.articlehealthandfitness.com
14. Martial Arts – especially Chi Gung and Tai Chi Chuan – are done for health benefits. In fact, Chi Gung means 'energy practice': www.youtube.com/watch?v=bSZq78t4WMg

Movies/T.V.:

1. Watch any Comedy movie

Exercise

1. Find an exercise you LOVE. That's the best way to stick to it. Keep looking and trying until you find something you love. Exercise EVERY OTHER DAY. You are discouraged to do "hard exercise" such as cycling, weights, boxing, martial arts, or running. See below and/ or choose gentle walking, Tai Chi, gentle yoga.

2. A nice walk can be done ANYWHERE, and requires no special toys or clothes, other than some good shoes. Start by wearing your pedometer and increasing the number of steps each day. See the following website for more information about walking: www.walking.about.com. Sign up for a daily newsletter that is excellent and encouraging, if a bit overwhelming. Even if you do 5 minutes a day, it is a great start.

3. Stick with it!! For those who don't exercise, it's about finding the motivation to start – and stay – on a program. We now have techniques like EFT – a form of psychological acupressure – to help us successfully stick with a long-term exercise program. Go to www.emofree.com. Sign up for the newsletter. You can use EFT to help with your emotional development.

Cardiovascular Stress

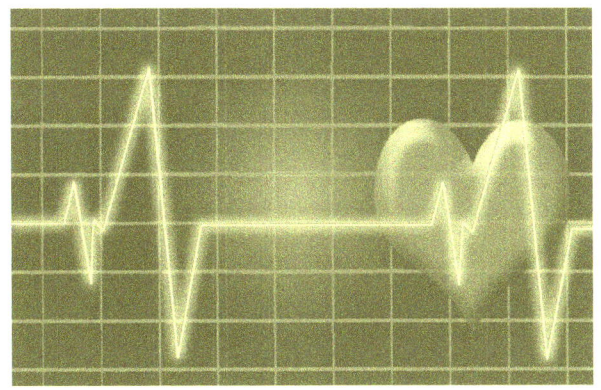

Stress has noticeable effects on the cardiovascular system. Who hasn't felt their heart beat faster because of stress or anxiety? Chronic stress can result in high blood pressure, atherosclerosis, strokes, heart attacks, and other cardiovascular system disorders.

Practical Daily Application:

1. The best results for the least effort. Take a nutritional supplement. The listed supplements are intended to be recommended by a physician. But they can sometimes be found by googling the brand and name. If you can't find them, contact us and we can help. Standard Process Cardio Plus. Also, Metagenics Ultra Meal if you have metabolic syndrome, obesity, altered body composition, and insulin resistance. Ask your pharmacist if it is OK to take with your medications. Don't take if you are pregnant or nursing. Blood Pressure, Body Mass Index, Cholesterol, Glucose, Tobacco
2. Keep a food log. My fitnesspal is a good app. Blood Pressure, Body Mass Index, Cholesterol, Glucose, Tobacco
3. Read the section of the workbook on stress tolerance for other development strategies. Blood Pressure
4. In the 'Stress Tolerance' section, look for activities that are calming and restorative. Blood Pressure
5. Choose activities to support the way in which you eat your food. Blood Pressure
6. Eat in a relaxed and calm environment. Blood Pressure
7. Avoid caffeine Blood Pressure

General Improvement Ideas:

1. Research shows that poor sugar metabolism may be a bigger risk factor in cardiovascular disease than fat intake. See the websites and books below for the Mediterranean diet. It is a perfect choice as it contains low glycemic foods and foods with good fats. Blood Pressure, Body Mass Index, Cholesterol, Glucose, Tobacco
2. Ask your medical doctor about a C Reactive Protein blood test to evaluate your risk for cardiovascular disease. Blood Pressure
3. Google Desk Yoga Blood Pressure
4. Free introductory CD on how to recover from stress, anxiety and depression. 12-week CD set for 8 payments of $59.95 – call 800-611-0857 or visit www.stresscenter.com. Blood Pressure
5. Read "Lose it for Life" by Steve Arterburn:
   - The book explores the underlying cause of why you eat the way you eat and helps you to change. Blood Pressure

6. Read, "Getting Things Done" by David Allen.
7. Read, "The Four Hour Work Week" by Timothy Ferriss.
8. Read, "Excuse Me, Your Life is Waiting" by Lynn Grabhorn.
9. Do the workbook, "Excuse Me, Your Life is Waiting Playbook" by Lynn Grabhorn.
10. Read, "Don't Bite the Hook" by Pema Chodron. Blood Pressure

Movies/T.V.:

1. Watch the movie "Supersize Me" to see how sick you can get and how quickly, eating poor quality foods. Blood Pressure, Body Mass Index, Cholesterol, Glucose, Tobacco

Exercise

1. Before beginning any exercise program, get cleared by a doctor. If you are a beginner to exercise, start with walking, Tai Chi, Chuan or Yoga, then move up to cardiovascular exercises. Blood Pressure, Body Mass Index, Cholesterol, Glucose, Tobacco

2. Find an exercise you LOVE. That's the best way to stick to it. Keep looking and trying until you find something you love. Exercise EVERY OTHER DAY. You are discouraged to do "hard exercise" such as cycling, weights, boxing, martial arts, or running. See below and/ or choose gentle walking, Tai Chi, gentle yoga. Blood Pressure, Body Mass Index, Cholesterol, Glucose, Tobacco

3. A nice walk can be done ANYWHERE, and requires no special toys or clothes, other than some good shoes. Start by wearing your pedometer and increasing the number of steps each day. See the following website for more information about walking: www.walking.about.com. Sign up for a daily newsletter that is excellent and encouraging, if a bit overwhelming. Even if you do 5 minutes a day, it is a great start. Blood Pressure, Body Mass Index, Cholesterol, Glucose, Tobacco

4. Stick with it!! For those who don't exercise, it's about finding the motivation to start – and stay – on a program. We now have techniques like EFT – a form of psychological acupressure – to help us successfully stick with a long-term exercise program. Go to www.emofree.com. Sign up for the newsletter. You can use EFT to help with your emotional development. Blood Pressure, Body Mass Index, Cholesterol, Glucose, Tobacco

5. Weight Training is actually safer than aerobic exercise for cardiac patients. Professional Fitness and Cardiovascular exercises for the heart and lungs all free from netfit! Improve your fitness on-line: www.netfit.co.uk/hrlmen.htm. Blood Pressure

6. Using resistance bands – resistance band workout for beginners: http://exercise.about.com/library/bltotalresistancebeginners.htm. Blood Pressure

7. Information on yoga: www.yogawiz.com. Blood Pressure

Adrenals

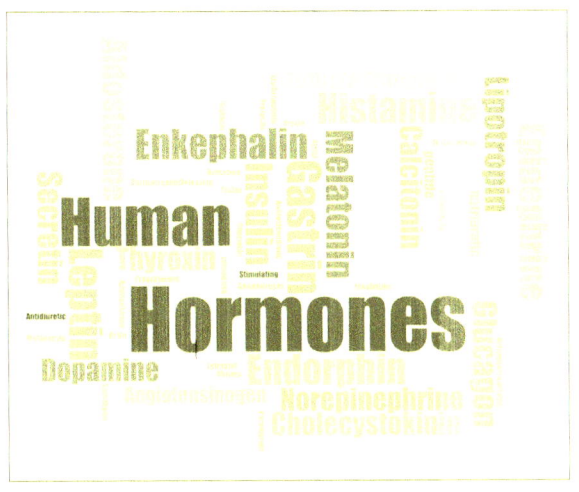

Adrenals are the emergency back-up system of the body that jumps in when you need a boost. They are the jumper cable and the battery, but they are greatly affected by stress. They aid in sugar handling and are weakened by too much sugar. If they are tired, they are tired, they are priority. Caffeine to adrenals is like taking a whip to an exhausted horse.

Practical Daily Application:

1. The best results for the least effort. Take a nutritional supplement. The listed supplements are intended to be recommended by a physician. But they can sometimes be found by googling the brand and name. If you can't find them, contact us and we can help. One bottle of Standard Process Dessicated Adrenal 3 X per day, then ongoing Standard Process Drenamin. It provides nutritional support for healthy adrenal function by combining a select blend of B vitamins that are involved in hormone regulation. Ask your pharmacist if it is OK to take with your medications. Don't take if you are pregnant or nursing.

2. Refer to *Stress Tolerance Section* for Practical Daily applications there.

3. Avoid caffeine

General Improvement Ideas:

1. General Guidelines for all Hormone Systems:
   - Choose exercise such as Tai Chi Chuan, Yoga, walking, belly dancing, and Pilates.
   - In the 'Stress Tolerance' section, you can review strategies to calm and restore you such as meditation, eating in a calm environment and tips for sleep.
   - Read the section on impulse control for development strategies.

2. Read the section of the workbook on stress tolerance for development strategies.
3. Meditation: go to www.brentdarnell.com and get a free guided meditation CD.
4. Too much sugar is stressful to the body. Look at the sugar handling section.
5. The Mediterranean diet has been called the stressed out person's diet. This website has information on it and sources of foods. For those in major cities, you can find most foods at regular or specialty groceries.
6. Google Desk Yoga.

7. Read, "The 7 Secrets to Fat Burning," by Dr. Eric Berg.
8. Read "Lose it for Life" by Steve Arterburn:
9. The book explores the underlying cause of why you eat the way you eat and helps you to change.
10. Read, "Getting Things Done" by David Allen for time management tips.
11. Read, "The Four Hour Work Week" by Timothy Ferriss for time management tips.
12. Read, "Excuse Me, Your Life is Waiting" by Lynn Grabhorn.
13. Do the workbook, "Excuse Me, Your Life is Waiting Playbook" by Lynn Grabhorn.
14. Free introductory CD on how to recover from stress, anxiety and depression. 12-week CD set for 8 payments of $59.95 – call 800-611-0857 or visit www.stresscenter.com.

Movies/T.V.:

1. Watch the movie "Supersize Me" to see how sick you can get and how quickly, eating poor quality foods.
2. Watch the movie "Fast Food Nation."
3. Watch any comedy T.V. or movie.

Exercise

1. Find an exercise you LOVE. That's the best way to stick to it. Keep looking and trying until you find something you love. Exercise EVERY OTHER DAY. You are discouraged to do "hard exercise" such as cycling, weights, boxing, martial arts, or running. See below and/ or choose gentle walking, Tai Chi, gentle yoga.

2. A nice walk can be done ANYWHERE, and requires no special toys or clothes, other than some good shoes. Start by wearing your pedometer and increasing the number of steps each day. See the following website for more information about walking: www.walking.about.com. Sign up for a daily newsletter that is excellent and encouraging, if a bit overwhelming. Even if you do 5 minutes a day, it is a great start.

3. Stick with it!! For those who don't exercise, it's about finding the motivation to start – and stay – on a program. We now have techniques like EFT – a form of psychological acupressure – to help us successfully stick with a long-term exercise program. Go to www.emofree.com. Sign up for the newsletter. You can use EFT to help with your emotional development.

How to Create Lifelong Learning Review:

Here are a few tips to create lifelong learning and not let this powerful work go away in time.

1. Create a future vision for yourself. Sit with your eyes closed and imagine your perfect future life. Then write down what you imagined.

2. Write down a few affirmations to put into words what your future vision is. Put them in present tense as if you have already attained this vision.

3. Another great way to change those old tapes in your subconscious (I'm not good enough, I'm a failure, I'm fat, I don't deserve to be successful or happy, I'm a bad father or mother, etc) is self-hypnosis (www.instant-hypnosis.com or www.innertalk.com). There are many websites that have hypnosis audios that will reprogram your subconscious with positive thoughts. Find the ones that are applicable to what you are trying to accomplish or overcome. This accomplishes a lot of things. Even if you aren't consciously thinking about it, your subconscious is and creating your future.

4. Have a plan. This could be your EI development plan or your personal mission statement or some type of weekly worksheet with your roles and goals that you have for your life. IT MUST BE WRITTEN! Don't keep it in your head. Make it easy and simple and portable. Carry it with you always. Put it in your day timer or electronically in your Smartphone.

5. Work your plan. You must make a commitment to be proactive and work your plan. Always have a plan A, B, and C. Plan A is the best (exercise five times a week), Plan B is for when you get busy (exercise two times per week), Plan C is for when things get insane (walk for 20 minutes during lunch).

6. You must continually measure your progress. How will you tell if you are attaining your goals? You can re-take the EQi or the Ghyst EI Test, but there are many other ways to measure success and change.

7. Build in accountability. Find an accountability partner or several partners. Let them know what you are working on and have them hold you accountable. You can help each other to stay focused. Roll this into your review process at work. Let your boss know what you are working on.

8. Write a letter to yourself dated one year from the date you begin your plan. Or you can create a mind movie that is a future diary in video format. This plants these future visions in your subconscious so that you are working on them even when you aren't consciously thinking about them.

9. Example: Dear Brent, Congratulations for losing that last 20 pounds and for improving your empathy and impulse control. You have better relationships with your colleagues and your family and friends. Also, congratulations for your recent promotion and for winning the President's Award. You are firing on all cylinders. Keep up the great work! All the best, Brent

10. If you are in a group, listen to your music on your playlist. If you are working on your own, listen to the music that inspires you. The same goes for books and movies. Go to the sources that motivate you.

11. You will have setbacks. Don't beat yourself up. Be kind to yourself and get back on track. Go to the places and people and sources that give you encouragement.

12. Pay attention to your measurements, then follow up continuously and make adjustments. Ask people how you are doing. Continually look for ways to improve-read books, take classes, discuss this work with others. Revisit your EI Roadmap and look for more development strategies.

13. Check in at least once a year and take the EQi or Ghyst EI Test every year to two years. Revisit your development plans, see what has changed in your life and revise, as necessary.

14. <u>You MUST HAVE reflection time</u> every day if possible-call it meditation time, prayer time, quiet time, visualization time or whatever you want to call it. Be alone with your thoughts and start seeing yourself as you want to be. This is the <u>single most important thing</u> you can do.

THE TOUGH GUY
SURVIVAL KIT

By

G. Brent Darnell

INTRODUCTION

This book was written for tough guys. And make no mistake. The term "guy" is not gender specific. You know who you are. You are the ones who get things done. You are the alphas, the ones who make things happen, the grease that keeps things moving. You are the ones with calluses on your hands and mud on your boots. You are the tough guys. But did you know that same get- r-done attitude that you possess may be holding you back in some ways. How can that be possible?

Think of someone you look up to, someone you admire, a mentor, a leader in your field. Think of someone who is the best of the best. Now ask yourself, "What makes this person who they are? What are the characteristics that make this person the best of the best?" You will likely come up with a long list of characteristics. They are passionate and assertive. They are empathetic. They are motivators. They make people feel special. They have great relationship skills, a sense of humor, a drive. It is always a list of intangibles and the so-called "soft" skills. No one ever says, "They have an IQ of 160" or "They have two PhDs." There is nothing soft about soft skills. It's what makes us who we are. And it is those critical people skills that separate the great from the good. You need these skills to be successful.

That is my business, teaching critical people skills to the AEC Industry using emotional intelligence. Emotional intelligence can be defined as social competence or the ability to deal with people. I mostly work with construction folks and engineers. When I told my wife that I was going to teach emotional intelligence to technical people, she laughed. How could I teach these folks all these critical people skills that I know they needed to become successful? Even I had my doubts.

How would they react to learning about their own emotions and the emotions of others? The initial reactions, which are now predictable, were apprehension, skepticism, and resistance. But once these initial reactions were overcome, and participants realized that emotional intelligence was something that could be quite important for their career development and personal lives, virtually all of them embraced the concept. And once they embraced the concept and worked on their emotional intelligence, the results were nothing short of remarkable. Then, we added a peak performance component to the mix where we focus on nutrition, stress, sleep, exercise, and lifestyle choices. We began treating our program participants like athletes to create peak levels of mental, physical, and emotional performance. That's when the results became life changing.

This book is divided into three parts.

The first part of this book is all about communication and presentation skills, an area where most tough guys do not excel. First, we cover killer communication skills that will give you great confidence and will allow you to communicate effectively with just about anyone. Then we go through presentation skills and cover not only how to get up and speak in front of any audience, but we also dive into how people perceive you. There are five basic elements that create how you are being perceived by others. You will learn how to utilize these elements to always create the impression you want.

As most of you know, communicating your ideas and motivating others is the key to success. How many of you are not comfortable speaking in front of a crowd? How many of you freeze up when you must carry on a conversation with a stranger? How about running meetings or those critical one-on-one conversations? This part of the book will give you the confidence to be able to master all of these with ease.

The second part of this book is on the 12 steps to Great Relationships followed by a section called Common Courtesy. These tools and ideas will give you the confidence to be able to establish and maintain relationship both personally and professionally.

The third part of this book is on Stress Management, Time Management, and Life Balance. This part of the book will give you specific tools so that you can better manage your stress and time and create more balance in your life. In the Appendix, we have included some evaluations and worksheets to help you with the process. There is an emotional intelligence evaluation, which will give you a good baseline to work from and see how well you navigate relationships, communication and presentation skills as well as stress management and time management. We have also included our Body Battery Inventory, which measures stressors versus recovery activities, our Time Log Exercise, a Time Management Worksheet, and Holy Crap Meetinig Bingo. More on that later.

These invaluable concepts and resources along with a little bit of application and repetition, will give you the skills you need to be wildly successful in your life and work.

CHAPTER 1

Killer Communication Skills

"Listen with curiosity. Speak with honesty. Act with integrity. The greatest problem with communication is we don't listen to understand. We listen to reply. When we listen with curiosity, we don't listen with the intent to reply. We listen for what's behind the words."

~ **Roy T. Bennett,**
The Light in the Heart

"In times of stress, the best thing we can do for each other is to listen with our ears and our hearts and to be assured that our questions are just as important as our answers."

~ **Fred Rogers,**
The World According to Mister Rogers:
Important Things to Remember

Introduction:

Why are tough guys poor communicators? We have done much work with tough guys, and there is a typical emotional intelligence profile that most tough guys have that prevent them from being great communicators. They tend to have high self-regard, assertiveness, and independence, but low emotional self-awareness, empathy, social responsibility, relationship skills and emotional expression, which is usually the lowest score for any group. This is a recipe for communication disaster. They tend to be poor listeners and come across as aggressive and somewhat dismissive. How do we fix that? The first thing to do is take the emotional intelligence test to see how it affects your communication skills. The second thing is to learn and practice these methods on how to improve them.

1. Listen, listen, listen.

Keep your mouth shut and listen to what people are saying. Don't just hear the words, understand the words. Use paraphrase listening. Repeat what they say in your own words to be sure you understood them. Tell them, "What you're saying is . . .". God gave us one mouth and two ears. Your question to statement ratio should be three to one. If you are talking too much, close your mouth. You will be amazed at how well this works. For those of you who are nervous about talking to people that you have just met, and you feel like you don't have anything to say, get them to talk about themselves. Generally, people love to talk about themselves. Once you get them talking, you will find that it will be hard to get a word in. And at the end of the conversation, they will probably tell others what a great conversationalist you are. And you made that impression by saying practically nothing.

Be fully present. Get rid of any distractions and focus on the person in front of you. There is the story of the mom who went to the park with her two children. While the neighborhood children played, the moms sat on the benches looking at their phones. One day, this mom's phone was broken. She watched her children play. She counted over 100 times in an hour that her kids looked toward her to see if she was watching. They were watching her for safety, for approval, for connection, and just to say, "Hey mom, look at me!" She never took her phone out again while her children played.

2. Verify your understanding.

We do an exercise where you get a partner and think of a popular song that everyone would know like an anniversary song or anthem. Then each person taps out their song on the table and the other person tries to guess the song. Prior to this exercise, they think that this will be quite easy. But as it turns out, they get the right song less than half the time. Why is that? In your mind the song, such as Happy Birthday, is so clear. Why doesn't this other person get it?

Communication doesn't happen until each person understands what the other person is communicating. This takes verification. You can't verify enough. Ask questions and verify the information. Offer to verify your own information. Say it several different ways and ask the person what they heard.

3. Increase your vocabulary and use proper volume and enunciation.

You can sign up for emails that send you a new word each day. There is a thesaurus in Word so that you can make different word choices. Don't go overboard on this. Don't use a long word when a short one will do, but in general, a better command of the English language will help you be more precise and more persuasive with your communication.

One of the most common forms of miscommunication is when we don't use proper volume or enunciation. I've seen it a hundred times. People in the construction business tend to talk in low volumes and tend to not enunciate as clearly as they could. Focus on these two things and increase your communication dramatically!

4. Find the best ways to communicate.

If you want to be a good communicator, practice the following forms of communication in order, the most effective to least effective:

- Face-to-face
- Video conference/Telephone
- Voicemail
- Written (email, text message, social media, letters, memos)

A word on emails. Emails are probably one of the worst forms of communication there is. And we tend to use it way too much. Why is it so ineffective? Although there is much debate over this, everyone can agree that a large percentage of your communication is non-verbal. Most of what you convey to others is through body language, facial expressions, and tone of voice. That means you are only working with a small percentage of your communication. How many times does email get misconstrued because there is no way to tell where the emphasis is, there is no way to tell if they are being ironic. If the communication is important, ditch the email and either meet the other person or pick up the phone and call them.

Here is an example of how emphasis on a word can completely change the meaning of the sentence: He isn't visiting the job tomorrow.

He isn't visiting the job tomorrow.
He **isn't** visiting the job tomorrow.

He isn't **visiting** the job tomorrow.
He isn't visiting **the** job tomorrow.
He isn't visiting the **job** tomorrow.
He isn't visiting the job **tomorrow**.

By the way, several recent studies indicate that emojis can increase comprehension. If you write an email that pokes fun at something, it might be wise to include a "wink" emoji.

Email is no different than any other communication. Be nice. Use please and thank you. If appropriate, write on your email that there is no need to send a reply or thank you. Don't forward emails to long lists of people. If you want to forward something to an individual because you think they might enjoy it, that is courteous, but don't overdo it. Don't tell jokes and don't use irony. When you can't hear the tone of voice, emails can be misconstrued. We've all done it. We've all sent that email full of anger or sarcasm. We've all wished that we could take back hitting that send button.

If you want to put the best face on your email and increase the chances of someone reading it, try the following:

Put something interesting in the subject line. If possible, put your entire message in the subject line. If you cannot put the entire message in the subject line, make the email short enough so they can read the entire email without scrolling down. Don't add attachments unless necessary or if an attachment is expected.

People will appreciate this cyber courtesy. In addition, there is a greater probability that your emails will be read. Let me share with you an email I received from a company where I purchased something online: "We're just checking in to see if you received your order from Better World Books. If your order hasn't blessed your mailbox just yet, heads are gonna roll in the Mishawaka warehouse! Seriously though, if you haven't received your order or are less than 108.8% satisfied, please reply to this message. Let us know what we can do to flabbergast you with service. Thanks again for your support! Humbly Yours, Indaba (our super-cool email robot)"

Now that is a cool email that is read and much appreciated.

A word on writing letters: The same thing for emails holds true for letters. You are only conveying a small percentage of the communication, so make it short, sweet, and to the point. Keep it simple and use concrete language.

5. The Art of Storytelling

Storytelling is an ancient way of communicating. We naturally crave stories. It's in our DNA. Everyone has a story. And everyone wants to tell their story. Find your stories of your life and work. Write down and learn your hero's journey. We all have overcome something. The hero has a quest and then encounters obstacles. The hero's journey is how she overcomes those obstacles and attains her goal. Companies all have stories as well: not only their company history, but the impossible schedule story, the impossibly small site, the safety save, the incredible outcome that defied all the odds. Learn them all, tell them often.

6. Keep an eye on body language and facial expressions.

If you are not sure what you are conveying, you may be conveying something you don't want to convey. Tough guys, in general, have low emotional self-awareness. If you are one of those guys, I encourage you to take an acting class or a dance class to develop some body awareness.

Know what your face is conveying at all times. For most tough guys, their face is much too serious. This is fine if you are delivering a eulogy, but for true open, honest communication, open your face up to some expression. Some folks have neutral faces. With a neutral face, people tend to assume and the assumptions range from bored, disinterested, and angry to the assumption that you don't like them.

Also pay attention to other's facial expressions and body language. Use your empathy skills and adjust based on their reaction to you. Keep in mind that most tough guys score low in empathy, so this may take some work. One person I coached had this issue. When you asked him a question, his face went into engineering problem solving mode, which looked to me like anger. When I pointed it out to him, he had an epiphany. He said when people ask him questions and he gives them answers, they usually get defensive. He began to practice an alternative. Whenever anyone asked him a question, he would say, "Give me a minute and let me process that." Then, they knew he was processing, not becoming angry over the question. He said this entirely changed his interactions with others.

7. Status:

We work a lot with status and rank levels of status with a deck of playing cards. The ace is the lowest status (say someone with lower socioeconomic status or a child) and the King is the highest status (a president, a CEO, a king, a head of state). You must decide which status to use when you present and when you are face-to-face with individuals. You should deliberately alter your status based on the situation to be the most effective. We will work in more detail on status on the presentation skills chapter.

8. Challenge your mental models.

We all have mental models. An example of mental models is the following riddle. You are going through the woods and you see a cabin in the woods. You open the door, walk in, and find that everyone is seated in rows and they are all dead. How did they die? Try a few guesses. Give up? It's the cabin of an airplane. You had the mental model of a log cabin, and no matter how you tried to reason, that mental model prevented you from coming up with the right answer or even asking the right questions.

We all have these mental models, and many times, it is not conducive to good communication. We have models about other people, other professions, and future encounters with others. The trick is to have the awareness to understand when you are projecting a mental model and challenge it. When you do away with mental models, you open yourself up for open, honest communication.

Always project the best outcome. Always assume positive intent. Your energy going into a situation can affect the outcome. If you go in with a negative attitude, you will likely come out with a negative result. By assuming positive intent, you open the door for a positive encounter.

9. Don't climb up the ladder of inference.

There is something that many of us do often. It's called the ladder of inference. We take information and draw conclusions that may be right or wrong. These conclusions lead to other conclusions that become facts, and before you know it, you have reached a totally erroneous conclusion. One example: A person is late for one meeting, so you assume that he will be late for all meetings. This leads to the conclusion that he is always late. This further leads to the conclusion that he is not a team player. Then you keep climbing up the ladder and decide that he should be fired. How did you get here? You climbed up this ladder and now you are prepared to fire this person. How do you climb back down the ladder? By challenging your assumptions, asking questions, and verifying the information. Why not ask this person why he was late for a meeting? He may have a very good reason. Always challenge and verify and stay off the ladder!

I had an Assistant Project Manager who started being late for every weekly meeting. I assumed he was not interested, not engaged, not motivated. Then I climbed up the ladder. I had in my mind that he is NEVER on time for meetings and ALWAYS late. This was not true, by the way. Whenever you hear someone using ALWAYS and NEVER, there are usually assumptions being made. Over time, he became incompetent, trying to sabotage the project. I called my boss and ask that this Assistant Project Manager be removed. My very wise boss encouraged me to take him to lunch and ask him about it, which I did. He told me that his mother was going through chemotherapy for breast cancer and since his dad passed away and he was an only child, he wanted to be there for her. Sometimes they get backed up at the treatment center and on those days, he comes in late for the meeting. I can't tell you how small I felt. If I had only asked and verified my information, then all of that negative energy could have been avoided. To be fair, perhaps he should have let me know. But as the boss, finding out what is really going on should have been my responsibility.

10. Avoid destructive communication.

When you participate in gossip, when you tear people down, it not only hurts them, it hurts you. Don't tolerate gossip and negative talk about others. Find the good in others and build them up. Gossip can destroy communication and relationships. It creates negative energy that is conveyed whether you are aware of it or not. It can destroy workplace environments like a cancer. Make a commitment right now. Use the THINK acronym. Is it True? Is it Helpful? Is it Inspiring? Is it Necessary? Is it Kind? If the answer is no to any of these, then it is probably best to not say it.

11. Use Compassion to Connect:

Think of someone you are having an issue with, perhaps conflict. Picture that person sitting across from you and go through the following statements with them in mind:

- "Just like me, this person is trying to find happiness and meaning in his/her life."
- "Just like me, this person is trying to avoid pain in his/her life."
- "Just like me, this person has known heartache, loss, loneliness and despair."
- "Just like me, this person wants to be loved and connected with others."
- "Just like me, this person has people in his/her life who care about them."
- "Just like me, this person is trying to get his/her needs met."
- "Just like me, this person is trying his/her best to complete this project, make a profit, etc."
- "Just like me, this person is trying his/her best to make this project successful."
- "Just like me, this person wants to excel and be good at what he/she does."
- "Just like me, this person is learning about how to navigate through this sometimes difficult life/project/work environment."

Does your viewpoint change for this person or this situation?

12. Use the language of diplomacy.

Unless you are working on your assertiveness or need very clear communication, it is wise to use qualifiers where appropriate. Avoid absolutes like don't, can't, never, or always unless very clear communication is needed. Use these instead:

Could be, might be, may have, would be . . .
A bit, a slight, a short, or so, a little . . .
I'm afraid, I'm sorry, I prefer . . .
Not (very) convenient . . .
I was wondering, if it's not too much trouble- . . .
With respect, to be honest, to put it bluntly . . .
"Would like" instead of "need" or "must have" . . .

13. Avoid communication killers.

Try this experiment. Ask someone a question that starts with "why". Then ask them for the same information by using who, what, when, where, or how. Ask them if they feel the difference. Why questions tend to sound like interrogations. They feel like accusations. Avoid them and

see if this creates a better dialogue with the person sitting across from you. One example: Why did you draw that detail that way? If you were asked that, would your immediate response be defensive? What if you the person said this: What was your idea behind this detail?

Avoid "yes, buts", "yes, howevers", or "no buts", especially if someone is bringing you an idea. It will kill the communication. Marshall Goldsmith has an exercise in his book, What Got You Here Won't Get You There. It's called Pay it Forward. You solicit advice from others, and they give it to you. Instead of saying, "I tried it and it didn't work", or "that won't work" or "that's a stupid idea" all you say is, "Thank you." Get used to saying thank you when others bring you ideas. It will maintain the relationship and keep the communication flowing. There is an improvisation concept called "yes, and . . .". It doesn't mean agreement. The concept is to "accept and build". Take that person's idea and figure out how to add to it. You will be amazed how this creates a flow of great ideas. It also sends the message to everyone that they will be heard.

14. Use voicemail wisely.

Voice mail can be a good way to communicate. Keep in mind that it is the first impression many people have of you and your company, so make your outgoing message interesting, full of good information on you and your company, and maybe a little humorous. Smile, speak clearly and distinctly, and make it short. Stand and walk when you record your outgoing message. It totally changes the energy. I have heard many dreadful outgoing messages. You know the ones: Sorry I can't take your call right now, but if you leave your name and a message, I'll get back to you. Beep! And even worse, when you only hear the number: Please leave a message for four oh four two four seven three seven four seven. Beep! I always call those back because I think I dialed wrong. Check your own outgoing message right now or have someone check it for you and give you their impression. When leaving voicemails, make them short and to the point. Make it clear when no callback is needed. Don't just say your name and then tell the person to call you back. If possible, convey the information you want to convey if it doesn't take up too much time. Always leave your number because not everyone carries your number in their head or in their phone.

15. Avoid the use of I and me.

Try this exercise. Ask someone to tell you a problem and then have a discussion with them without using the words "I", "me", "my" or "mine". It is quite difficult for some. Many of us are problem solvers and we want to show how smart we are by telling them, "Here is what I would do." I never knew how much I used the word "I" until a friend of mine from Argentina pointed out that I used the word "I" eleven times in a short email. I didn't believe him, but when I went back and looked, it was true. Even though I wasn't trying to do it, the email sounded very arrogant. Have you counted the number of "I"s in this paragraph? Be conscious of how much you use this. Go on a break from talking about yourself or using the words "I" "me", "my" or "mine" for a day and see how it goes. This will really open your communication with others.

CHAPTER 2

Presentation skills and rhetoric
How to present with power and influence

"Engaging in lifelong learning to improve your public speaking skills is far from drudgery. It can lead to a better job, higher profits, more donations, and public policy objectives. That sounds like fun to me."

~ **Ed Barks,**
The Truth About Public Speaking

Introduction:

As most of you know, speaking in front of an audience is difficult. In fact, in terms of our greatest fears, speaking in front of an audience is always listed near the top. For many, speaking in front of people is a stronger fear than death. Jerry Seinfeld put it this way: "Most people would rather be in the casket than have to stand up and give a eulogy." This is especially true for tough guys.

I am a mechanical engineer by education, but at one point in my career, I quit engineering and became a full-time actor for three years, performing tons of theater, improvisation, and even some standup comedy. My claim to fame was a small role on In the Heat of the Night in which I played a redneck auto mechanic drug dealer. After three years of struggling to become a full-time actor, I resumed my career as an engineer, but I took some wonderful things with me from my training as an actor. Acting helped me to be more comfortable in front of audiences and with people in general.

While facilitating a management development program for a multi-national company in 2001, I hired a professor from the Massachusetts Institute of Technology, one of the most prestigious schools in the country, to teach a segment on rhetoric. He had multiple degrees including a PhD, and he had published hundreds of articles and several books on rhetoric. I talked with him on the phone, and he sounded pleasant and articulate.

He began his presentation by putting a transparency on an overhead projector. Yes. We still used overhead projectors in 2001. The transparency was a typed page, single-spaced, with very small type. This professor said "Uh" every third syllable. His voice cracked. To make matters worse, he leaned against the table where the overhead projector sat and jiggled his leg. This shook the image that was already difficult to read.

Then it hit me how brilliant this man was! He was doing all the things that we should never do. What a great way to teach! The only problem was that he kept going. I finally realized that he was not acting. This was his presentation. I stopped him and took a break. I frankly told him the problems with the presentation. He apologized and vowed to correct his mistakes, but when he resumed his presentation, he did it the same way. I ended up dismissing him and teaching the segment myself.

This experience made me realize that no matter how much you know about a subject, the way you present is vital in order to communicate your message properly. This is especially true for the tough guy engineers and construction folks that I work with. They think that if you give the audience enough information, if you inundate them with data, if you put up a lot of complicated graphs on PowerPoint and show them specific areas with a laser pointer, they will be wowed. This is simply not true. The message is not in the slides. It's in the presentation. And presentations can be very powerful without any visual media. People will be persuaded by you during a job interview or a project presentation because they like and trust you and make a connection with you. The information you are conveying is secondary to that.

I have taken the concepts I learned as an actor and applied them to public speaking and presentation. I hope that it will help you to overcome your fears, even if you believe that you are not proficient at speaking in front of an audience. If you already do well with public speaking there may be some things in this book that will help you, give you a different perspective, or give you a new way to approach your presentations.

Think of your presentation as a theatrical production, a stage play if you will. If you are an actor playing a role, then it is much easier to allow yourself to be creative in your approach to presenting. If you prepare as an actor prepares, using the following guidelines, your presentation should be markedly better, perhaps even spectacular. And you may even receive that actor's dream: a standing ovation from the audience.

More than just giving a speech, these concepts apply to how people perceive you. The first question to ask is how do you want them to perceive you? We will cover five basic areas that can alter how you are perceived: Face, Body/Movement, Voice, Status, and Energy. When you learn these basics and how to project them to others, you will be able to handle any situation with any person on this planet.

I have also included a section that covers a simplified version of rhetoric, the ancient art of persuasion. This will help you to formulate better arguments and motivate your audience to action as well as answer audience questions with ease.

Remember, the first thing to do is take the emotional intelligence test to see how it affects your presentation skills. The second thing is to go through the following steps on how to improve them.

The Production:

A theatrical production has many components that work together to create a unique experience for the audience. Many of these components are the same for presentations. When you create a performance, you tell a story with drama or comedy or both. You move the story along with imagination and emotion. You motivate your audience and shape their reactions based on what is happening on stage. When you do a presentation, you should strive to do the same thing. I have listed a few of these theatrical characteristics below.

1. Audience
2. Character
3. Costume
4. Face
5. Body/Movement
6. Voice
7. Energy
8. Status
9. Script
10. Set
11. Props
12. Technical stuff: lighting, sound and music
13. Rehearsals
14. Opening Night
15. Rhetoric
16. Storytelling
17. The Virtual World
18. Final Thoughts and Tips

1. The Audience:

You must know your audience well. Ask the following questions: Who is your audience? Are they from another country or culture? What is your audience's education level? Have you used any words that they may not understand? Will they understand you if you speak too quickly or use idioms or jargon? Does your audience possess the technical skill that you possess? What are you trying to convey to them? What motivates them? What barriers exist between you and the audience? What do you want to say? What do you want to achieve? What do you want them to leave with?

Once you have asked these questions, you will know your audience better and make any necessary adjustments to your speech. There are too many examples where native English speakers speak far too quickly and use local idioms while addressing international audiences. I saw an American speaking in front of a group of Europeans use the term, "how the cow ate the cabbage". They looked like deer in headlights. I've seen folks use outdated references to television shows. One guy talked incessantly about Gilligan's Island and the various characters and the young audience had no idea what he was talking about.

You can lose your audience very quickly. We engineers tend to get caught up in the delivery of information: technical terms, facts, and figures. This can be boring for a technical audience and a total disaster for a non-technical audience. The audience will "check out" five minutes into the speech. See the section on rhetoric for more information on tailoring your message to match the audience.

2. Character:

Whether you know it or not, you play a character when you speak in front of an audience. Are you the boss, the expert, the specialist, or perhaps, the consultant? Ask the following questions: What is your status? Is it high, medium, or low? See item 8 for more details on status. What role are you playing for the audience? How do you want them to perceive you? This will give you clues as to how to present yourself. Do you want to be the guy from the outside with all the answers or perhaps just one of the guys talking to them as if it were a casual chat?

3. Costume:

Dress appropriately for your audience. Ask the following questions: Should your dress be casual/dressy/a costume? What are your audience's expectations? Do you want to meet their expectations or throw them off by wearing something completely different? Dress appropriately for the message. If you are delivering a humorous message, a humorous costume may be appropriate. If you are delivering a message on how to dress for success, blue jeans or overalls probably wouldn't make much of an impression unless you were making an opposite point. Surprises can be fun.

I was giving a presentation to the sales staff at a resort located in a small town south of Atlanta. Since I arrived in the town early, I decided to eat breakfast in a local diner. I met a man at the door. When he saw me in a suit and tie, he exclaimed, "A suit and tie in Pine Mountain. You must be either a preacher or a bill collector." It made me realize I was overdressed for this presentation. I took off my coat and tie, unbuttoned the top button of my shirt, and rolled up my sleeves.

When I worked for a large contractor in Atlanta, we were presenting to a school board in a small, South Georgia County. We all arrived in our suits and ties. Many on the school board were dressed very casually. One of them, a local farmer, wore overalls. We did our fancy, citified presentation on PowerPoint with a projector. We did not win the project. We would have been much better off if we had dressed casually and presented the information on poster board. What you wear says much about you and your message. Dress appropriately.

4. Face

Be aware of your facial expressions always. Most of the folks we work with tend to have a neutral face, which doesn't convey anything in particular. Smile if it is appropriate to the message and use facial expressions. Don't have a stone face.

Ask yourself the following: What does your face convey when you are not trying to convey anything in particular? If you are unsure, ask someone close to you. I pointed out to one of my clients that he had an angry face. He said that his children approach him all the time and ask him if he is angry. This surprises him each time. He is not an angry person, but he has an angry face.

Do you have a serious face? A bored face? A sad face? Does that look fit with your message? I once watched a presenter with a sad face try to motivate a crowd and convey unbridled enthusiasm, but his face would not let him. If your face does not convey your message, then you must work on it. Practice in the mirror. Are always you conveying the right expression to your audience? Spouses and trusted colleagues are good resources for this. Ask them to let you know what your face is conveying.

5. Body/Movement

Be aware of your body language always. Some people are naturally stiff in their body language. You can see it around their shoulders and neck. For those stiff body language types, some physical warm-up exercises may help. Loosen up before a presentation. Do some stretches and relax your body. You may be a sloucher. If you are, be aware, hold your shoulders back and your head up. If you don't you may come across as uninterested or apologetic.

Do you have nervous ticks and gestures? Be aware of what your body is doing or you may convey to the audience nervousness, ineptitude, or boredom. If you're not sure, you may want to record yourself and study it prior to your presentation. Be sure to separate your speech and your movements. Don't move while you are speaking unless it is for effect. Move to another location, set yourself, then start talking.

Move with ease and grace. Be confident. Be fluid and relaxed. Use gestures. Don't deliver a speech with your hands at your sides. Practice gestures so that they are natural and effective. Practice and work on your proprioception, which is the sense of knowing where your body is in space. We do a warm-up exercise where we all walk across the room with the centers of our bodies in different places.

We put the center of our heads and are transformed into cerebral nerds. Then we put the centers in our chests and become tough guys. Then, it's the stomach and we are big, fat guys. Then, it's the hips and we are all runway models. Then, we try a silly walk. Then, we try something different. I ask the group to imagine themselves as the CEO of a large company walking into a stadium filled with employees. How would you feel? What message would you send? Remember, the way you walk into a room and up to the podium will give the audience impressions which can add to or detract from what you are saying.

If you want to learn how to effectively use your body for incredibly motivating presentations, I would recommend that you study evangelist preachers or rock-and-roll stars. You don't have to emulate them exactly, and you should always develop your own style to fit your personality, but these folks really know how translate their body language into crowd motivation.

Don't let your movement get in the way of a good presentation. Don't do too many things at once. Sometimes, presenters talk, move and change slides at the same time. Remember this rule: Do one thing at a time.

To practice, perform your speech totally still, then highly animated, with gestures, with no gestures, be very big, then very small, loud, then quiet. Record all of these and review them. Determine which segments are the best and why.

6. Voice

If you must constantly clear your throat, it can be quite distracting. Do a vocal warm-up. A good vocal warm-up is making a buzzing sound with your lips, opening and closing your mouth while making sound and massaging your face while making sound. Vary the pitch and tempo of your voice. Avoid monotone. Articulate. You must be understood. Speak slowly and distinctly. Use pauses effectively. Pause . . . for . . . effect. Practice your pauses. Write them in if necessary.

Second Languages:

I have found that presentation skills have very little to do with language. I have taught these skills to Swedish and Spanish speaking participants. They presented in English. When they began to struggle, they wanted to switch to their native language. After the switch, the presentation was the same, only in their native language. Communication is mostly body language, voice intonation, and non-verbal cues. Don't get too wrapped up in the language.

Accents:

If you have a regional accent or an accent from another language, the audience will make assumptions about you that you may or may not want. For instance, in the US, if someone with a deep, Southern accent talks in front of an audience from the North, they tend to make assumptions about this speaker, that he is uneducated and dim witted. For this reason, you may want to consider diminishing or eliminating your accent. It takes time, but it can be done.

I was born in Mobile, Alabama, and had a very strong Southern accent growing up. When I became a full-time actor, I decided to get rid of my accent or be doomed only to play Southern roles. I bought a tape recorder, recorded my voice, listened to it carefully, and worked to eliminate my accent.

A word . . . um . . . about . . . uh . . . uttering . . . uh . . . um:

If you are "um"ing and "uh"ing your way through your presentations, this can be a major distraction to the audience. It can make you come across as hesitant, uninformed, and unprepared. You may not even realize how much you are doing it. This is not a difficult thing to improve upon. Record yourself during your rehearsals to see where these gems lie. You can also have a friend correct you. Some speakers' groups ring a small bell whenever these halting words are said. However you do it, get rid of the "um"s and "uh"s. If you um and uh, the audience will think you are inept. If you use silent pauses, they will think you are brilliant.

A few more tips:

Take a few deep breaths before your presentation to relax. Have room temperature (not cold) water available in case you have a dry throat. Don't drink or eat any dairy products before speaking. They may coat your throat or cause mucous, which may cause problems. Attach an emotion to whatever you are saying. That emotion may change throughout the presentation, but it should be a conscious choice. Visualize what you are thinking. If you have visual aids, this is a bonus, but even if you don't you must be able to see what you are trying to convey in your mind's eye. If you can see it, your audience will be able to see it.

To practice with your voice, do your speech in complete monotone, then do it again, overmodulating your voice and playing with volume. Record yourself and see which elements give you the best presentation.

7. Energy:

Good energy is vital to a great presentation. Most people I work with have low energy and I am constantly giving them the note of higher energy. If it's exciting, make it crazy. If it's big, make it HUGE! Most people feel uncomfortable with this notion. When they do this high energy presentation, I ask them how they feel. They tell me that they feel silly. They feel like clowns. Then I ask the audience how the presentation was. The audience ALWAYS says that it was better. Go in with high energy. You can always pull it back if you need to.

There are exceptions to this rule. There are natural introverts who have a great stage presence and command of the audience. For those folks, being who they are is all that they need to be. And for these folks, it just works.

To practice your energy, do your speech with very low energy, then middle energy, then over top, high energy. Record them and determine which elements work the best.

For low energy folks, I give the coaching note a lot to live life 10% louder. Project 10% more energy, volume, engagement, etc.

8. Status:

The awareness of status and how to adjust yours is vital to how you are perceived and how you connect with others. We rank levels of status with a deck of playing cards. The ace is the lowest status (say someone with lower socioeconomic status or a child) and the King is the highest status (a president, a CEO, a king, a head of state). You must decide which status to use when you present and when you are face-to-face with individuals.

Sometimes you will want to lower your status to make others feel more comfortable and connected. Sometimes you want to raise your status to take command and be in more control.

Once you have this idea of status in your mind you can see this dance of status going on all of the time. People naturally lower their status for small children and people who have relatively lower socioeconomic circumstances and people with disabilities or limitations. There is usually an effort to make the status of two the two people equal. Higher status people will lower theirs and lower status people will raise theirs.

These elements can raise or lower your status.

Posture: (slouching is low, shoulders back is high)

Body: (tense is low, relaxed is high)

Voice: (speaking in the throat, stuttering is low, speaking confidently from the diaphragm is high)

Eye contact: (low contact is low, good eye contact is high). The exception to this is when someone has such high status that they don't even look at you.

Energy: (low energy is usually low status, high energy is high status)

To practice status, be deliberate about your status choice and see how your speech goes. Experiment with low status, medium status and high status. Record them and see which works the best for your audience and speech. Raise and lower your status in different situations and see if it affects the outcome. For teams, have everyone pick a card, then pair up and have a discussion on any topic for three minutes. But you must have the discussion in the status on your card (Ace is low, King is high). Then, guess each other's status. Usually everyone gets within one or two points. Then you can discuss which elements (body, voice, face, eye contact, energy, etc) conveyed the status on their card. You can also do this game by having everyone put their card (they don't look at the card) on their forehead and interact in the room. Then have everyone look at their card. How did people treat them based on their status?

9. Script:

Never read your presentation. It is better to miss a few things and connect with the audience than to look down the whole time reading from a piece of paper. Learn your lines and then have the confidence to speak from your heart, not from the page. Any time you relay a personal story, you should tell it. When you read a personal story, you come across as insincere.

Here are two ways to remember a script. One is called loci (Greek for location, pronounced "low sigh") and the other is called memory chain. For loci, imagine a place you know well, like your own house. If you are giving a speech on how to present, your door might be a podium indicating this is a speech about how to give a speech. You walk into a small office and there are a bunch of people in there giving you a standing ovation. Your first point is audience. You turn into your kitchen and there are tons of cartoon characters of your choice on your counters. The second point of your speech is character. You walk into the dining room and see racks and racks of costumes. The third point of your speech is costume. And so on. You put visual reminders in the rooms you know well, and you know every part of your speech as you walk through your house.

The second way to remember your speech is memory chain. The point of the speech you are thinking about reminds you of the next point of your speech. Example: Picture the podium (this is about giving a speech). Out of the podium pops an entire tiny audience giving you a standing ovation. Each audience member then turns into a cartoon character. Then, each of those characters sprouts a costume and so on, and so on.

10. Set:

Ask the following questions: How is the room laid out? Is it adequate? Should the stage be elevated for better sight lines from the audience? Where are you to stand? Can you be seen by everyone? Is there a podium? Do you need one? Are there any distractions you should be aware of such as local train whistles, announcements over public address systems, bright lights through a window, air conditioning systems going on and off? Where is your audience going to sit? Will you be able to address them properly? Check for any power cords and other trip hazards. Check the location of all tables, podiums, AV equipment, etc. If you need to, relocate them so that you can move without having to think about these potential obstacles. After you ask these questions, you will be better equipped to make some adjustments to make your presentation even better.

11. Props:

Props can be very effective metaphors. Are there things besides PowerPoint slides to show the audience? A picture or physical representation speaks volumes. Do you have a model or a tangible, three dimensional illustration? Use the props effectively. Either show it early for effect or bring it out as a surprise. For an environmental presentation, we showed a physical representation of how much trash our company generates per year. We showed how the trash would fill 1,000 Olympic sized swimming pools. This was a much more effective way of presenting the information than reciting the number of cubic yards.

12. Technical Stuff; Lighting, Sound and Music:

The technical side of a presentation is only noticed when it doesn't work. This is something that is commonly overlooked. Check all audio-visuals before your presentation. Make sure everything is working properly: LCD projectors, microphones, flip charts, white boards, markers, etc. LCD projectors are getting better and better, but older models sometimes have problems with compatibility to laptop computers. Always have alternatives just in case.

Microphones:

Learn a little bit about mic techniques. When you are at a podium mic, make sure you don't move your head around too much or your audience will hear uneven sound. Lavalier mics are great inventions, but make sure the placement is good or your sound will be uneven. It is very annoying when speakers rub their Lavalier mics or tap them with their hands. The sound is annoying and the presentation becomes all about the speaker rubbing the microphone.

If your audio-visual technicians are sophisticated, you may have a monitor so you will hear what the audience hears. If you have this, you can adjust as necessary. Do a microphone check prior to your presentation if possible. You may also test to make sure you can be heard in the back. Ask someone to sit in the back prior to the presentation and make sure you can be heard. Don't ask the audience if they can hear you. This may convey to them that you are not prepared. You will want to prepare your presentation in several formats in case there is a problem. Have it on a thumb drive, but you should also be able to do the presentation without anything. It is better to be prepared. Make sure you are properly lit and make sure you can see your presentation on the podium if there is one.

For flip chart presentations, make sure you have plenty of flip chart paper and make sure your markers are not dry. Also make sure your white board is clean and has a good eraser and that your white board markers are not dry. When you write on a flip chart or white board, make sure you write large enough for everyone to read, even in the back of the room.

PowerPoint slides:

Most presentations can be done without PowerPoint. Many people use it as a crutch. There are also alternative like Prezi as well as some great Mac applications. I use Prezi because the videos consistently play well. Too many audio-visuals may prevent you from truly connecting with the audience. I use PowerPoint only for visuals, graphs, and videos (things I can't convey as well by talking). By the way, be careful about embedded videos. They will not save to a new file if you transfer the PowerPoint to your laptop. You must re-insert the video. Be sure to check volume and size of the video prior to your presentation to make sure they can be seen and heard.

If you must use PowerPoint, don't make your slides too busy. Too many photos and visual images can be overwhelming to an audience. Don't overdo the fly-ins, dissolves, and sound effects. If overused, they can distract from the message. Keep it simple. If you must use words on a slide, use bullet points. Use as large a font as possible and bold them if you can. They should be very easy to read. Use no more than five words per line. Use action verbs instead of passive language. If a bullet point says "increasing the bottom line", change it to "INCREASE THE BOTTOM LINE!". Cartoons and jokes are always a good way to get your point across if they pertain to the message. Pay attention to your audience and make sure your jokes don't offend. Use the fifth slide rule to keep the brain awake and engaged. If you have four slides filled with words, make the fifth slide an image. Then, perhaps four image slides, then words again or a video or an exercise.

Don't read your slides. The Audience can read. In fact, whenever you have words on a slide, that's what they are doing. They are not listening to you. Give them a few seconds to read the slide, then begin speaking. Don't talk while you are advancing slides. Perform the action, then speak. Don't stand in front of your slides. For an LCD projector, point to the projected image on the wall if you need to emphasize something. I personally don't like the use of laser pointers and find them to be annoying. If you have an image that you need to clarify by pointing a laser pointer at it and rotating it in a tight circle, then you need a new image.

Music:

Have some music playing beforehand. Have you ever watched a movie without sound? It's rather boring, isn't it? The same principle applies for people walking into a large, empty room. If the room is silent, the energy is low. This is not a good way to start. I encourage you to have some type of music playing as the audience enters the room. Choose the music to match the mood of your presentation. If you are trying to motivate the audience, choose motivating music. Imagine coming into the room with the theme from Rocky playing in the background. It tends to pump people up and prepare them for your presentation. Prior to a session on the company's environmental initiatives, we had songs like "It's not Easy Being Green" and "What's going on?" playing in the background. It set the proper mood for the presentation.

13. Rehearsals:

Practice your presentation, but don't over-rehearse to the point where it has lost its energy. Be confident. Find the time to practice until you are comfortable. Record your presentation and watch it to improve your performance.

If you are having trouble with your presentation, try these tips to practice:

Give your presentation as if you were giving it to a group of five-year-old children, especially if you tend to talk too fast.

Sit down and practice your presentation. This will allow you to focus on your delivery and content without having to think about all the other elements. Once you have practiced while sitting, stand up as if you were in front of an audience.

Technical Rehearsals:

Be sure to take the time to rehearse how to work your audio visual equipment such laptop computers, LCD projectors, white boards, etc. You should use these items with grace and ease. If your slides have links to websites, make sure you have an internet connection.

Final Dress Rehearsal:

Run through one last time prior to your performance using as many of the elements as possible. This should bring out any problems, weaknesses, and areas that may need a little tweaking and improvement. Directors give actors "notes" after their rehearsals to improve their performances. Find someone you trust and ask them to give you feedback on your presentations.

To practice your speech, prepare a slide deck of random words and images and do your speech with this "improv" slide deck. It's great for increasing creativity and your comfort level with presenting. It's also great for handling those weird situations that pop up as well as answering difficult questions.

14. Opening night:

You are finally ready for opening night, your magnificent performance, your world premiere. If you have prepared properly, opening night is nothing but fun. Take a few deep breaths and let yourself be a little nervous. This will keep you on your toes and give you some energy. Enjoy yourself and have the confidence to know that your presentation will WOW your audience.

15. Rhetoric:

Rhetoric is a systematic approach to creating persuasive arguments. It's also great for answering difficult questions.

Introduction and Thesis: State what you will accomplish or what your argument is. It may be good to start out with a question. Example: " What are we going to accomplish in the coming year?"

Main Points (Argumentation): State 2 to 3 main points to support your argument. Example: "We're going to increase sales, reduce overhead without eliminating jobs and increase our bottom line."

Some types of arguments:

General to specific: Everyone is tightening their belts because we don't know when the economy will turn around. We should do the same.

Specific to general: We're tightening our belts at home. Our trade partners and vendors are tightening their belts. Our competitors are tightening their belts. Every company on the planet is tightening their belts and reducing costs.

Convince using threats: If we don't tighten our belts, we are going to have to lay off a lot of people and face the possibility of going out of business.

Always arrange your argumentation from the weakest to the strongest. End on the strongest. You can also include opposite arguments in your arguments. If you know that someone will be opposing your argument, you can say, "I know that some of you think that belt tightening creates fear and uncertainty. But I believe that by being honest with our present situation and working together, we can get through these tough times." Conclusion: restate your premise and draw a conclusion. Motivate the audience to action or convince them that your argument is sound. Example: "If we work hard and accomplish these three things, it will also increase our bonus pool and profit sharing."

Rhetorical devices:

Metaphor: This is a device that uses comparison for a stark image that the audience can relate to immediately. Jesus used these frequently in his many parables. Example: If we don't make these cuts, it could be the death of our business.

Simile: Comparison using "like" or "as". Example: Not tightening our belts would be like putting a gun to our heads.

Rhetorical question: Example: How many of you want to be looking for a new job? If we don't tighten our belts, that may be the case.

Ethos, Pathos, Logos: These are three basic methods to convince an audience. You must know your audience and choose the right approaches. You may use one, two or all three.

Ethos. This is your credibility and who you are. Do you create trust with your audience? Have you listed your qualifications if you are the expert or a background story that they can relate to?

Pathos. This is the emotional argument. Appeal to the audience's emotions. One example is when we are shown photographs of starving children. This appeals to our emotions and motivates us to action.

Logos. This is the logical argument. When you are dealing with technical people such as scientists and engineers, appeal to their logical side. Give them the facts and figures. Tell them "If we reduce our accidents by 5%, our insurance costs will decrease by 15%." If you choose the wrong approach, the results could be disastrous. If you choose pathos for a group of PhD physicists, your message may not be understood. Using the example of the school board in the small South Georgia County, we tried to give them a very logical approach to building their school, but in the end, we know we should have used more pathos. Their decision wasn't based on logic, but emotions.

16: Storytelling:

There is one other vital device to use during a presentation: storytelling. Tell an impactful story that will elicit an emotional response from your audience, and they will never forget what you say. I'll give you an example.

I do this to show people how weak PowerPoint can be. I show a slide with too many words, giving the audience some statistics on social networking, how many million people log onto Facebook every day, trying to show them the reach and power of social networks. Then I continue with my presentation.

That's when I get into storytelling. I tell them a story of a young couple whose child was dying of leukemia and they were looking for a marrow donor. In desperation, they posted their plea on Facebook and miraculously found a donor. I know of someone who found a job using Linked In. And in other parts of the world, there are revolutions taking place that are being fueled by Facebook and Twitter. Now those are amazing examples of how powerful social networking can be.

At the end of the training session, I ask them if they can remember anything from the PowerPoint slide on social networking. They remember very little. Then I ask them if they remember the stories I told about social networking. They remember them all in detail.

Bring your hero's journey into your speech. The hero starts out on some quest, trying to attain something. Along the way, she encounters obstacles. The bigger the obstacle, the more profound the journey. Then, heroically, she overcomes all those obstacles and gets what she wants. Be sure to relate your story to the audience and involve all the senses. What did your hero see, smell, taste, touch, and hear along the journey?

17. Making it all work with online platforms

In the post COVID-19 world, much of our interactions are on online platforms like Zoom and Go To Meeting. Remember that you are working with fewer tools when you are presenting yourself. It is vital that you light yourself well and use a great microphone or headset. Always stand when you are presenting remotely and jack your energy up 20% to 30% above normal. If you perform with normal energy, it will seem flat. Also, use interactive, experiential techniques. Polls and the chat room are both your friends. Get people interacting, and if breakout rooms are available, use them often for smaller group discussions. If you have longer sessions, be sure to do some desk yoga and take breaks often. Move, dance around and shake things out every 90 to 120 minutes.

18. Final Thoughts and Tips:

a. Believe in what you are saying. Make it more than just information.

b. Speak from the heart.

c. Make eye contact throughout your presentation.

d. Be sincere.

e. Be energetic. Use gestures.

f. Avoid monotone. Vary the pitch and volume of your voice.

g. Read and acknowledge the situation. Adjust if necessary. Be flexible. If there is a noise in the room or a big moth flying around the stage, don't just press on. Acknowledge the problem, make a joke about it, deal with it, then move on.

h. Concentrate and focus. It may help to do a short preparatory meditation before your presentation to increase your focus and concentration. A few rounds of deep breathing can relax you and focus your energy.

i. Rehearse: practice to a level that you feel comfortable, but don't memorize or over-rehearse. It's good to be a little bit nervous. It can keep your energy up. If you are nervous, it is likely that you are focusing on yourself. Take away that focus and put it on the audience and your message.

j. Strike a Power Pose: Amy Cuddy tells us through her research that if we adopt a Power Pose (any powerful pose) for two minutes, it significantly increases our testosterone and significantly decreases our cortisol (the stress hormone). If you are feeling nervous, strike a Power Pose for two minutes to feel calm and assertive.

k. Triptychs are effective!

   "Friends, Romans, countrymen . . ." "I came, I saw, I conquered."

   "of the people, by the people, and for the people"

l. Repetition can be effective.

   Martin Luther King's "I have a dream" speech.

   Another example is John F. Kennedy's inaugural speech. Here is an excerpt. Note the repetition of "let both sides".

"Let both sides explore what problems unite us instead of belaboring those problems which divide us. Let both sides, for the first time, formulate serious and precise proposals for the inspection and control of arms—and bring the absolute power to destroy other nations under the absolute control of all nations. Let both sides seek to invoke the wonders of science instead of its terrors. Together let us explore the stars, conquer the deserts, eradicate disease, tap the ocean depths, and encourage the arts and commerce. Let both sides unite to heed in all corners of the earth the command of Isaiah—to "undo the heavy burdens … and to let the oppressed go free.""

m. Silence . . . can be . . . . very . . . effective. Work on your pauses and don't rush through your presentation. And if you get stuck, use the pause to gather your thoughts.

n. Get some support:

There are many speaking classes and speaking groups and clubs. If you are serious about improving your technique, take a class or join one of many speaking clubs such as Toastmasters www.toastmasters.org. The members will give you feedback and pointers on your presentations.

To recap the process:

a. Audience: Know your audience.

b. Character: Know what role you are playing.

c. Costume: Dress appropriately for the audience.

d. Face, Voice, Body/Movement, Energy, and Status: Watch your body language and facial expressions. Know what you are conveying at all times. Do a vocal warm-up. Be relaxed and do one thing at a time. Speak with HIGH energy! Choose your status carefully and convey it to your audience.

e. Script: Know your material, but don't read or memorize word for word.

f. Set: Check out the stage beforehand.

g. Props: Use visual examples and powerful metaphors.

h. Technical stuff: lighting, sound and music: Check out all audio-visual equipment prior to presenting if possible. Have some music playing as people enter.

i. Rehearsals: Practice and get feedback from trusted colleagues.

j. Opening Night: Relax, take some deep breaths and focus. Be enthusiastic and energetic. Believe in what you are saying.

k. Rhetoric: Use the ancient art of rhetoric to motivate the audience to action.

l. Storytelling: Tell powerful, emotional stories that relate to your audience and your message.

m. Remote Presentations: Have 20% to 30% higher energy.

A word about personal branding:

Your personal brand is vital to your success and it's something many of us don't think about often. Try this exercise. Write down 5 to 10 adjectives that would describe you. How do you want people to perceive you?

Verify your list with those you trust. Now ask yourself if you are conveying your brand (the adjectives). How do you dress, act, communicate, interact with others, and show everyone your personal brand? Examples: Do you want to be known as accurate and precise, yet your dress and grooming are very sloppy? Do you want to be seen as a top leader, but come into the workplace each day in ragged jeans? Do you want to be known as a leader who connects with her team, but your relationship skills are not as good as you want them to be?

In Conclusion:

I wish you the best of luck in your presentations and hope that this part of the book has helped you in your quest to become a better speaker. Also, the more you are more aware of how people are perceiving you, the better you will become at using face, body/movement, voice, status and energy to create the perceptions that you want. Keep in mind, this is a process. The more you present, the better speaker you will become. The more awareness you have of other's perception, the more you will be able to adjust. Be kind to yourself, especially in the beginning. As they say in the theatrical world, break a leg!

CHAPTER 3

12 Steps to Great Relationships

"You can make more friends in two months by becoming interested in other people than you can in two years by trying to get other people interested in you."

~ **Dale Carnegie**

"If you would have your relationships endure, fix your mind on the end that endures."

~ **Wu Wei**

"Negative feedback without a relationship is criticism."

~ **Unknown**

Introduction

This section of the book is all about relationships, something that many tough guys struggle with. There is a step-by-step process that, if followed, will give you great confidence and will allow you to establish and maintain great relationships with just about anyone. And as most of you know, having great relationships is the key to success. Relationships give you ideas, encouragement, and opportunities. It drives business and your personal success.

How many of you are uncomfortable at parties, gatherings, and networking events? These methods will give you the confidence to be able to master those situations with ease. We start with the 12 steps to great relationships. Then, we cover common courtesy, which is the foundation for all great relationships both business and personal. I discuss the tools to use, the situations you will encounter, and the chain of courtesy. I will give you practical information that you can readily apply so that you will become a master of relationships.

In South Africa, they have philosophy known as Ubuntu. When you greet someone, you say, "I see you." They answer by saying, "I am here." In other words, you don't exist until the other person acknowledges you. Imagine the implications of walking past someone in the office because you are preoccupied. You are saying that they don't exist. There is a sense of being connected to every other human being. I think we've lost that sense of being connected to each other, and relationships are all about those connections.

In our classes, we show the first scene from the movie, The Godfather. In it, Bonasera, the funeral director, asks the Godfather to kill some guys who beat up his only daughter. The Godfather's response at first is no. Why does he refuse him? Because, as the Godfather says, "You don't ask with respect. You don't offer friendship." Bonasera had not cultivated a relationship with the Godfather prior to asking him for a favor. How many times do we do that on construction projects? We don't cultivate relationships with other stakeholders. Then, we need something from them. Is it any wonder that more times than not, they refuse to cooperate?

Think about the best project you've ever been on. What were the relationships like? My guess is that they were pretty good. Now think of the worst project you've ever been on. What were those relationships like? My guess is that they weren't so good. There is a correlation there. No one has ever told me, "You know, that was the best job I've ever been on, and we hated each other's guts."

This is an exercise we do often. Think of all your professional relationships (clients, colleagues, trade partners, bosses, direct reports, etc). How would you describe these relationships? What adjectives would you use? You would say they have a lot of blank or they are filled with blank. I usually get a long list like respect, mutual, trust, symbiotic, contentious, difficult, hard, a struggle, and sometimes words like fun. Now think of all your personal relationships (your spouse, children, parents, siblings, family, best friends, etc). How would you describe these relationships? What adjectives would you use? You would say they have a lot of blank or they are filled with blank. There are some of the same words like trust and respect, and we also get words like loving, compassionate, forgiving, caring, and supportive. The question I then ask is, "Should more of the personal descriptions be in your professional relationships? And if not, why not? What is the dividing line? I encourage you to put more of the personal into the professional, as much as your comfort level and your company and project culture will stand. You will find that your business relationships will be better and your projects will be more successful.

The following twelve steps will help you establish and maintain great relationships. There is nothing magic about these twelve steps. You may have more steps or less steps. Apply them to your life and work as you see fit.

Step 1: Know yourself, develop yourself and become more self-aware.

As tough guys, we tend to shun away from self-knowledge. We're just too busy getting things done. But the first step toward great relationships is getting to know yourself better. Generally, tough guys have low emotional self-awareness. Partly, it's just the way our brains are wired. That, plus society has told us, especially males, that we should not let our feelings show. We are not supposed to recognize or share those feelings, so we tend to shut ourselves down.

In order to be good with others, you must first explore yourself. There are many ways to do this. The first thing I recommend is to build in reflection time each day. We tough guys tend to spend about 80% of our time and energy at work and the other 20% on our family. Have you done the math yet? That leaves zero time for ourselves. This must change if you are to become more self-aware. Look for ways to explore who you are, what you are about. This reflection time is crucial for your personal development. You cannot spend this time working, planning, or strategizing. You must use it for total reflection.

Sit down in a quiet place and just reflect and be. We are human BEINGS, not human DOINGS. Most tough guys have this insane notion that you must constantly be DOING something. And by adopting this attitude, you rarely find the time to just BE. Find the time before the family gets up or after they go to bed. But find the time. It is vital for your well-being and success.

There are more ways to tap into who you are. During this reflective time, you can meditate or be prayerful. You can explore your values. You can become more aware and involve all your senses. Sit quietly and note what you see, smell, hear, touch, and taste (if you are eating or drinking at the time).

I recommend taking courses in self-discovery. There are also some great books on the subject. Peter Senge's The Fifth Discipline is one. Stephen Covey's 7 Habits of Highly Effective People is another. Take the EQi 2.0 (emotional intelligence evaluation) or our free emotional intelligence test in the Appendix. You can also take a personality test (DISC, Myers Briggs, 16PF) so that you can know yourself better. These evaluations will give you clues as to your strengths and development needs. Fully explore who you are, and you have taken the first step toward great relationships.

To practice more, try this: Write down 10 things you need, 10 things you want, and 10 things you love. Are there any overlaps? What does this tell you about who you are?

Be relentless in your thirst for knowledge about yourself. Always look for ways to improve. Know your strengths and development needs. Develop the areas that are holding you back. This self-knowledge is the foundation for all great relationships.

Step 2: Develop a compassion and genuine love or at least acceptance of yourself

Be comfortable with yourself. Accept yourself with all your limitations. This may be hard for some of you. We all know our dirty little secrets about ourselves that nobody else knows. Your self-regard may be low. You may have a family history that is not conducive to acceptance. But this step is vital to creating great relationships. We all are human beings. We all have limitations. Some of us try to cover those limitations in a variety of ways. Some wallow in them. If you have completed step one, you know your strengths and development needs. Of course, you can work on your development needs and improve them. That is probably a good thing. But you can accept yourself with all of your limitations, especially those you cannot change. Don't worry so much about your physical appearance or other things that bother you about yourself. If they bother you, that will translate to others.

I'll give you a very practical example: Have you ever tried desperately to get someone to like you, and they wouldn't give you the time of day? Then when you started a relationship with someone else, what happened? Usually the people you were pursuing come out of the woodwork and want to be with you. Why do you think that is? Did all of them change? It is more likely that because you are in a relationship, you feel better about yourself and create a different emotional energy. People are drawn to that energy and want to be around you. This will take some effort, but you can develop a love for yourself. If that's too hard, try accepting yourself. Once you start accepting yourself for who you are with all your limitations, you will draw people to you. And it will be easier to accept others.

To practice: What is your reaction when someone else makes a mistake or is struggling? How do you normally respond? Do you have the same response when it is you who is struggling? Treat yourself with the same compassion with which you treat others.

Approach the people you know well and ask them to make a list of the things they like/love/respect about you. Compile the list. The next time you are beating yourself up, pull the list out and read it out loud. This list is likely closer to reality than the inner critic that is running you down.

To practice, write down three things you are really good at. Was that hard to do? We value humility, but don't forget to celebrate yourself and be comfortable doing it.

Step 3: Expand your knowledge

Learn as much as you can about as many different subjects as you can, even the ones that don't interest you. Know a little bit about a lot of different things. Many technical folks have knowledge that is an inch wide and a mile deep. Develop knowledge that is an inch deep and a mile wide. I've found that the people who can develop relationships quickly have a lot of different interests. You don't have to become an expert. All you must do is have to have a thirst for knowledge. Turn off the television and read more. If you can read a book a week, you will increase your knowledge dramatically. Most of the people you look up to are likely readers and searchers for knowledge. Learn more. Keep up with current events as best you can. Know how things work. Become a trivia hound. Become an observer of people. Notice more. Know about other cultures. Travel more. Develop a sense of wonder about the world. The more you know, the more you will be able to relate to others.

I'm not a NASCAR fan, but I know enough about it to carry on a decent conversation with others about it. And many of my clients are NASCAR fans. They love talking about it. I ask them who their favorite driver is and why. I ask them about the current standings and their favorite tracks. I ask them why someone from California should be allowed to be a driver in NASCAR. My brother, Ben, is a master at this. With his knowledge of so many different things, he would be comfortable talking to just about anyone.

And even if you know nothing about a subject, you can still make this work. Admit to the other person that you know nothing about the subject and ask them to tell you about it. If it is something that they are passionate about, they will certainly fill you in. I use the example of curling. I have many Swedish friends who are fanatical about the sport. All I must do is ask about the sport. What does the broom do? How is this game played? What are the strategies? They are happy to tell you in detail about it.

One caveat here: Don't become a bore with your knowledge. Use your knowledge to make connections, not to show how smart you are.

Step 4: Learn about perspectives on different values and cultures

This also goes for gender differences. Learn about and appreciate the differences while emphasizing the similarities. When it comes down to it, we are all human beings who have a need to love and be loved. Find that common connection. For some difficult people your only connection may be that you are both carbon-based life forms. If you can travel more, this is like getting a PhD in relationships. Find out about different cultures, food, art, music, dance, and language. Learn a language if you can. Learn about cultural differences with greetings, meetings, social situations, and business situations. There are thousands of books on cultural differences.

Also, learn about gender differences and how men and women approach things differently. I recently went on a yoga retreat that was organized by Helen, a friend of mine. To my shock and pleasant surprise, out of 35 participants, I was the only male. This was a big learning experience for me. The first night, everyone met for dinner. Keep in mind that no one knew each other. Now I had been to these first night dinners with groups of men. The first night with a group of men, you will see the following: All the men will talk about their position at work, what they do, and what monumental projects or concerns they've been involved with. They tend to boast about their successes and retell stories of how they overcame difficulties. They have all been on the worst project ever built. There is a hierarchy established from the outset. There is a pecking order. Men connect with manly hobbies like sports, hunting, fishing, and motorcycles.

The experience with the group of women was completely different. The first question out of every woman's mouth was, "How do you know Helen?" They wanted to how I came to be there. They wanted to know how I fit in with everyone else. What was my connection with Helen? Immediately they tried to establish the existing connections and networks. Connections and group harmony are paramount to many groups of women. Most of the time, there are no hierarchies established. Everyone is made to participate and feel as if they are part of the group. I think this goes back to childhood. Traditionally, little boys play games like king of the hill and follow the leader. Little girls play more collaborative games like tea and house. And if there is a girl who wants to take over and be the leader, she is shunned from the group for being "too bossy". I think these girls become the powerful women who end up in construction and engineering.

It doesn't matter of you are a man or a woman. Take note. When you know about these dynamics and try to understand these differences, you will be able to create connections with anyone in any situation and establish great relationships.

The key is to be curious, not judgmental. Seek out people and groups who are different from you and find large list of things you have in common.

Step 5: Be open, genuine, and positive

It is a choice. Smile often. It puts people at ease. Humor not only puts people at ease, it cements human relationships. Okay tough guys, I know. Smile often? What is he trying to do to us? Don't worry. Your face won't crack. I promise. Being open and genuine and positive is important, especially during those first few seconds. If you approach someone and you are closed off, unsmiling or negative, they will likely not hang around very long. Even a neutral face can be interpreted as someone who is closed off. And remember, being positive is a choice.

I have one caveat here. For all of you women tough guys out there, I understand that this may be one of those stereotypical comments from males that encourage you to smile more. That isn't what this is about. This is about making human connections. I understand that smiling may be misinterpreted by males when coming from a female. The point is to open your face and try to connect more with other humans. It's unfortunate that women in the workplace have been conditioned to put on an exterior that protects them. They shouldn't have to protect themselves. You will have to decide what that balance is.

What is your dominant style? Is it negative? Neutral? If it is not open, genuine and positive, think hard about turning that around. People like to be around positive people. And that optimism and energy can be cultivated and developed. We teach optimism to people every day. It can be learned and improved. But it starts with a choice. Read *Learned Optimism* by Martin Seligman. He is an expert in positive psychology.

To practice: First, check your emotional intelligence test (in the Appendix) and see how you scored in optimism. Do you have a pessimist profile (higher reality testing/lower optimism)? How does that affect your ability to be open, genuine and positive?

Have a positive day where you decide that everything is going to be positive. Journal how the day went. Then, have a day where everything is negative. Journal about that day. Which day went better? Were there outcomes that were affected by your positive attitude?

I have a personal story about how emotions, specifically optimism, created a desired outcome. The main thing we teach is how to manage your emotions for the best outcomes. I am known to

be overly optimistic. I score high in optimism and low in reality testing. My wife calls me "optimistic to the point of ridiculous". I was in Sweden teaching a course for a week. Keep in mind we were out in the middle of nowhere right on the Baltic Sea. On Monday evening, after a nice sauna, I jumped into the Baltic, which was around forty-five degrees, and lost my glasses. I didn't have a backup pair of glasses or a pair of contacts. This was a disaster. I couldn't see the screen to teach and had a hard time conducting the training sessions.

I called my wife and told her about my glasses, and she contacted my optometrist and had my glasses prescription sent to the conference center. In the meantime, I told my wife that I would try to find someone with a diving mask or goggles so that I could dive down into the forty-five degree water and find my glasses. Without my glasses, I was not sure I could see well enough to find them. But I was undaunted. My wife thought this was ridiculous on two levels. One, we were in Sweden. Who is going to have diving equipment? Two, the Baltic has tides. There is no way those glasses are going to be there after several days. But, I was undaunted.

I talked to the bartender at the conference center, who told me that she had just returned from a diving trip in Egypt and had a pair of diving goggles. She said that there was a small glasses boutique in the village where I might be able to get some contacts. And if I had contacts, I could use the goggles, dive down into the forty-five degree water and find my glasses. Keep in mind that time was passing. It was Wednesday now. I managed in the classroom, but could not drive into the village on Wednesday because of something we had to do as a class that evening.

I went to the glasses boutique with my prescription on Thursday afternoon and they had contacts for me. Thursday evening, I went back to the conference center with my contacts in and the diving goggles in hand. But it was too dark to look that night. I must wait until Friday.

Friday morning came, and I put on my bathing suit, my contacts, and my goggles. All the participants were seated on the deck overlooking the sea, waiting for the bus. They all told me it was a waste of time and that after four days, the glasses would be impossible to find. I dove into the forty-five degree water. It took my breath, but I swam down about twelve feet and there they were. My glasses half buried in the sand. I picked them up and triumphantly broke the surface of the water, holding them high over my head. The participants thought I had staged the whole thing to teach them a lesson about optimism and creating outcomes. Did managing my emotions and staying optimistic affect the outcome of this situation? I'm sure that it did. By staying focused on the desired outcome despite what logic and common sense told me, the outcome was a positive one. I believe that I created that reality and affected that outcome by what I chose to think and feel. Imagine the power of this in your day-to-day encounters with life's challenging situations.

Step 6: Develop compassion and genuine love or at least acceptance of other people

Accept others with all their limitations. This can be difficult. But once you accept yourself, it's much easier. I know there are a lot of difficult people out there. There are people you probably consider to be stupid, arrogant, contrary, negative, or full of angst. It's those people that need acceptance the most. Give them that grace. Give them the benefit of the doubt. Expect the best from them. You will be greatly amazed at how your attitude will affect theirs.

When you come across these difficult people, think of them as your teacher. They will teach you how to establish great relationships with any person in any situation. Also, their annoying behavior becomes less annoying. There is a great method for bridging those difficult gaps. It was developed by a man named Marshall Rosenberg and it is called Nonviolent Communication. There are four steps:

1. Observe without judgment. Be objective and evaluate the situation.
2. Notice your feelings. Check in with yourself.
3. Identify needs, both yours and theirs. What are you both trying to attain?
4. Make a request. Tell them what you want, considering their needs as well.

This is a simple and powerful way to diffuse difficult situations, but it takes practice. Try it!

When I was a project manager, we had a project with a particularly difficult owner's representative. I was having a beer with a few other project managers who had the same owner's representative on past projects.

They told me that this person was a real jerk, unreasonable, and downright mean. I conveyed to them that I got along great with him and that he was quite reasonable. They thought I was lying. But it was true. I didn't know all these negative things being said about him, so I treated him nicely. I grew the relationship and the project was easy and fun. My approach to him allowed him to act differently.

To practice: We can always use our tried and true compassion/empathy exercise, especially for those folks who are hard to love. Picture that person and that situation and go through the following statements:

- "Just like me, this person is trying to find happiness and meaning in his/her life."
- "Just like me, this person is trying to avoid pain in his/her life."
- "Just like me, this person has known heartache, loss, loneliness and despair."
- "Just like me, this person wants to be loved and connected with others."
- "Just like me, this person has people in his/her life who care about them."
- "Just like me, this person is trying to get his/her needs met."
- "Just like me, this person is trying his/her best to complete this project, make a profit, etc."
- "Just like me, this person is trying his/her best to make this project successful."
- "Just like me, this person wants to excel and be good at what he/she does."
- "Just like me, this person is learning about how to navigate through this sometimes difficult life/project/work environment."

Now that you have gone through these statements, do you see this person or this situation differently?

Step 7: The first five seconds

What are you supposed to do during the introduction? How should you act? Is it really that important? According to numerous studies, that first impression is vital. In the first few seconds, people will judge your intelligence, your socio-economic status, if you are a good person or not, whether they like you, and if you are successful or not. We utilize a process in our brain known as the adaptive unconscious. It allows us to do something called thin slicing. Malcolm Gladwell talks about this in his book, Blink. A study was done with a college professor. They asked students to rate his teaching ability after watching three fifteen second videos of him teaching. They rated the professor the same as the students who spent a semester with him. Then, they cut the video clips down to five seconds. The results were the same.

The point is, we can determine an awful lot with a minimum amount of information. This is very good for most things. The downside to this ability is stereotyping. First impressions aren't always right. And you can always overcome poor first impressions, but why should you have to? We do an exercise where I introduce myself several different ways and then ask the group to write down their impressions of me. It's amazing the assumptions they make based on a two second encounter. But they do. They will say that I am arrogant, incompetent, shy, mean, angry, or whatever they perceive for that introduction. The last introduction is a normal introduction where I relax, smile, make eye contact and use a nice, firm handshake.

So let me ask you. What first impression do you create when you meet someone? And if you don't know the answer to that question, you should find out. When you are going into a situation where you will be introducing yourself, be deliberate about what you are conveying. Be relaxed, open, smiling, and calm.

Make good eye contact and give a nice, firm handshake. Slow your mind down and be prepared to listen for the person's name. It's called "original awareness". You can't remember anything that you are not aware of. Be deliberate in your quest to remember the person's name. Repeat it, write it down, write down a short, physical description, whatever it takes to remember their name.

Many people say that they remember the face, but can't recall the name. So the trick is to associate the face with the name. Whenever I meet someone named John, I think of John the Baptist. I picture their chopped off head on a silver platter with blood and veins below it. When I see them, the name John automatically pops into my head. When I meet someone named Eric, I picture the face and put a Viking helmet and red hair on him for Eric the Red.

You can remember names by making these ridiculous associations. If you know someone with that same name, picture the two people together with a ridiculous visual image like the person you know licking the side of this person's face or putting their tongue up the person's nose. The more outrageous the image, the easier your brain will remember. There are other ways such as through sound. When I meet anyone named Jared, I picture him singing the Jared Jewelers' theme song to me. One other way to remember names is kinesthetically. When you know the person's first name, picture a movement associated with the first letter of their name. Examples are Jumping Jack, Bouncing Bob, Skating Sue, etc. When you picture that person, you will picture the movement, and the name will pop into your head.

If you want to be adept at remembering names, get The Memory Book by Harry Lorayne and Jerry Lucas. There is an entire chapter devoted to remembering names.

I was introducing emotional intelligence to a group of forty geotechnical engineers. They all filed into a large warehouse for a dinner the night before our day of work together. There was also a speaker and two caterers from a local Mexican restaurant. Everyone introduced themselves to me. At the end of the night, I asked them if they wanted a preview for tomorrow. I asked them if they knew everyone there. Since they were from several different offices, they did not. So I introduced all forty people. I also introduced the speaker and the two guys from the Mexican restaurant. They were very impressed, and it created more work for me with their company. I have recently done this same thing with a group of 112 people with similar results. Believe me, you can do this. I'm not particularly smart, and I don't have a photographic memory. It's just a little technique and a lot of practice.

At these networking events, people usually give you their business card. Don't be too quick to shove it in your pocket. In Asian cultures, the business card represents the person, so you should never write on it or put it in your pocket. They will give you their business card with both hands usually with a slight bow. They will scrutinize your card and usually make a comment on it. I'm not sure that you must bow, but I think it makes a great impression to read the card and make sure you took at the front and the back. Then, make a comment on it. Tell them it's a nice logo or ask them about their title, their position and what their job entails, their geographical location, or more information about their company.

During that short encounter, find out as much as you can about that person. Is she married? Does he have kids? What are her hobbies? What school did he go to? Then, write down some of these factoids, and later, put it into your contact database. Also, put down when and where you met them and any other pertinent facts. How many contacts do you have in your database right now that you have no idea who the person is or where you met them?

Whenever you are in conversation with a person, be fully engaged and mindful of the person who is in front of you. They are the only person in the world as far as you are concerned. Don't look at your watch or behind them or your computer screen or your phone. Don't be distracted. Be with them fully. For a coffee or lunch meeting, you may want to say to them that you are turning your phone off so you won't be interrupted. Put your laser beam focus on them. Make them feel important and valued. Make them believe that you are genuinely interested in them and what they have to say. This may be difficult with some people, but even with those difficult people, practice this full engagement. It is important.

To practice: At your next networking event, find the person in the room who is the least like you. Approach them, remember their name and find out at least three things you have in common.

Step 8: The second encounter

First, you are going to remember their name. They will likely not remember yours, so that gives you an advantage. Introduce yourself so they won't be embarrassed about not remembering your name. Then, talk about them. Let them know that you remember them and those pertinent facts. You may need to secretly refer to your phone and the contact information. That's okay. Then ask some good leading questions and let them talk. Find out even more about them. And when you gather more information, put it into your contact database. You can also put the time and place of this second meeting. Don't ever think that you will remember these details. Just document it.

Find the common threads with this person. With expanded knowledge, you can find common threads with just about anyone. The second encounter is perfect for exploring those things that you might have in common. Again, ask those questions and let them know that you know something about the things that are important to them. You don't have to agree with everything that they value or find important. The main thing is to let them know that you have a connection with them. For some people, this may be difficult, but if you are persistent, you will find something.

Step 9: Make it all about them

The key to creating a great connection with someone is to be interested, not interesting. People aren't really interested in what you are doing or saying, only in what they are doing or saying. This is the cardinal rule of being a good conversationalist. An interesting story I heard some time ago (it may be true or not) is of a lady who had the pleasure of sitting next to two British Prime Ministers at dinners on two successive weeks. The first week was Lord George, and the second was Disraeli.

After the experiences someone asked her to compare the two. Her reply was, "After sitting next to Lord George I concluded that he was the most important person in the world. After sitting next to Disraeli, I concluded I was the most important person in the world". Disraeli was intensely interested in her, not in talking about himself. When you observe successful talk show hosts on television, seldom will you find them talking about themselves. Rather, they are filled with questions for the guest of the week. Of course that's their job, but it serves as a convenient showcase to gain the feeling of being with a person who doesn't talk about themselves.

Try this magic phrase: tell me more. Be fully present and keep using that phrase. Tell me more about your family, your job, your hobbies, what you do when you aren't working, what keeps you up at night. You get the idea.

Step 10: Food and Drink

Relationships take time, but everyone, including you, must eat. By inviting people to eat or drink with you, you kill two birds with one stone. Break bread together or have a beer or cocktail together. Eating and drinking are intimate acts. Continue to talk about mutual interests. Also be prepared to talk about the interests of the other person even if they are not your own. This is a very important step in a relationship. One networker calls these FDOs (Food and Drink Opportunities). Keith Ferrazzi is a master networker. His book, Never Eat Alone, talks about being relentless in your pursuit of connections with others. And everyone has to eat and drink. And everyone likes it when you buy them lunch. Find interesting places to meet. Out of the way restaurants and coffee shops with great atmospheres are very conducive to getting people to relax and open up. Use this often to further develop your relationships.

Step 11: Create networks

Networks are powerful things. You can have formal and informal networks. Most people have the wrong idea about networking. They think it is about introducing yourself, shoving your business card in the other guy's hand and then he calls you and you get his business. WRONG! Bob Littell's book, The Heart and Art of Netweaving, takes a different approach that works quite well. He follows these steps to establish relationships. At networking events, his approach is to find out as much about the other person and their business as possible and ask them if there is anything you can do to help them or their business.

Don't sell people on yourself or your company. This is a real turnoff and a big mistake. Your encounters will avoid you like a plague. Again, make it all about them and let them know that you are there to help them and their business. Ask them what they are struggling with. Also, with your wide network of people you are amassing a great deal of expertise and knowledge. Find people that you can introduce to each other. Perhaps it's a common personal or professional interest. Or perhaps one person has a solution that the other person needs. Either way, when you solve their problem for them, they are going to remember you and recommend you to others.

Have you tried any of the online social networks? They can be a powerful way to build a large network in a very short period. I'm signed up on several of them. Although the lines between business and personal social networks are a little blurry, there are ones that are more for business like Linked In and Twitter, and there are others that are more geared toward the personal like and Facebook, Pinterest, and Instagram. There are also video sites like Tik Tok, YouTube, and Vimeo . Although I found one of my best clients through Facebook. There was a group called "People who used to work for Blount". I saw a guy there who as an co-op from Auburn on one of my first projects. I connected with him and since then, we have become good friends and have done a lot of work together.

a. The first step is very simple. Visit these websites and create a profile. If it is strictly for business and not personal, be sure to pack your profile with your accomplishments and qualifications. If it is personal, you can also add some personal information. By the way, personal information can be very beneficial in the business profiles as well. You can tell a lot about a person by where they focus their time and energy. Be sure to add a good photo. Make your profile attractive and full of good information about you and your business.

b. Start creating connections with people. Most of these sites have a feature where it will scan your contact database and find everyone on their network that is in your address book. Or you can do your own searches for individuals and ask them to create a connection with you. However you do this, you must start trolling for people. Find the ones you want to connect with and ask them to connect with you. Delve into all the companies you used to work for. Explore all the groups you have had contact within the past.

It's easy to find people now thanks to Google. I found an old boss of mine by Googling his name and the word "construction", and I had not had any contact with him for over 20 years. I found him working for a contractor in Houston, Texas. It was not only great to catch up and see what he has been up to, but this was a great business contact for me. He wanted to read my book, The People Profit Connection, which led to future work for my company.

I make connections all the time with email and phone calls. Most of the time, there is no response. Despite numerous attempts, they would not return my phone calls or emails. But when I sent out an invitation via Linked In, they accepted it quickly, usually within a few minutes. Somehow, these sites lend legitimacy to that outreach.

c. Once you have a list of people with whom you want to stay connected with, all you have to do is occasionally write a few lines about what you are doing. You may pose a question. You may post a photo or video or link to some interesting websites, videos, or articles. You can write as much or as little as you want except for Twitter, where you are limited to 280 characters.

d. You may want to program these sites to send the notifications to your mobile phone. This is very easy to do. You can always block this later if it gets to be too much.

e. You may recommend people and ask them to recommend you. You can "like" them or "follow" them and they can do the same for you. This is very easy to do. There are usually links to do that on the website. Build up your reviews in order to create credibility.

f. You may join groups or start groups. This can be helpful for networking, for best practices, for idea exchanges, support, or encouragement. Find as many groups as practical. There are many possibilities for groups: alumni groups, industry groups, special interest groups, high schools, colleges, preconstruction folks, cancer survivors, church groups, study groups, or hobbies.

g. You may use these networks internally to stay in touch with a select group of people, perhaps a project team or an internal preconstruction group. When someone posts a comment, it can be automatically sent to everyone. It's quicker than email and can be a great way to exchange information and receive feedback.

h. If you are attending a conference, you can find groups of people either geographically or an industry group that you can contact and let them know that you will be in attendance. Ask them if they would like to meet for a cup of coffee, a drink, lunch, or dinner. Use every opportunity to connect with all the people in your contacts. Check your social networks as often as possible.

i. Keep your profile updated. Send out blasts to people and look for new connections. Find some interesting things to post that will intrigue people and compel them to stay in touch with you. This is a big key. You must check these at least once per week. If people are reaching out to you and you don't reach back, they will likely drop you.

j. Start a blog. It's free, it's easy. There are numerous ways to do it. Post commentaries, ideas, and videos. Repost other's blogs. Always include a provocative headline and picture. It will increase the likelihood that someone will read it. Post your blog to all other social media.

Step 12: Follow up, follow up, follow up

Now that you have all this vital information in your contact database, use it. Send out cards for birthdays and anniversaries. Send out thank you notes. Although much of this can be done electronically, I prefer to send handwritten notes. People receive so few handwritten notes these days that they will likely read it and respond in a positive way. People are so overwhelmed by email, your message may be sent to spam or deleted without being read.

Send notes congratulating your contact on a new project, a new job, a big win for their college team, or an award. Send them links to cool websites or articles. Again, this contact should not be self-promoting. Make it all about them and send them things that they would be interested in reading or seeing.

I met an engineer at a design company. We talked briefly and he mentioned to me that his wife was the CEO of Children's Healthcare in Atlanta. He gave me his card, and I put him in my database. I remembered what he told me. A week later, there was an article in the paper saying that Children's Healthcare was named one of the top pediatric hospitals in the country. I sent him an email giving him a link to the article and said that he must be very proud of his wife. I have done a lot of work for this company.

CHAPTER 4

Common Courtesy

"Courtesy opens many doors."

~ **Fortune Cookie**

For most tough guys, courtesy is seen as weakness. But I can tell you that courtesy does, indeed, open many doors. If you utilize your courtesy skills, you can be comfortable in any situation, and people will want to be around you. They will want to work for you. It will ensure your success. Because courtesy succeeds even with people who are not courteous. And in these tough fields like construction, there are many discourteous people that you must deal with.

What has happened to common courtesy? It is much like common sense. It's not so common these days. I was raised in the South where we were brought up to be Southern gentlemen. We were taught to say "sir" and 'ma'm". We were taught to respect our elders, to give up our seats to women and older folks, to open doors, to pick up the check, and to share whatever we had. In short, our momma tried to raise us right.

But our wonderfully diverse society now seems to have a problem with these simple examples of common courtesy. This problem may stem from our increased social isolation manifesting itself in the form of too much television, video games, movies, and the internet. This causes a lack of direct social interaction and is especially true of the younger generations.

The lack of basic human support systems such as the family unit and local community organizations adds to this problem. Another possible reason for our perception of diminished courtesy may be the abundance of so many cultures with very different values. Sometimes those different values rub us the wrong way. But whatever the reasons, we need to look at these issues and make a concerted effort to re-establish common courtesy in our society. It is not only a nice thing to do, but I believe the future of our society and of our world may depend on this very simple thing.

I notice that whenever I give in to bad attitudes and rude people, whenever I become angry and rude, the situation always takes a downward spiral. But as an experiment, I tried to be nice in these situations. I tried to be overly nice. I tried to turn the other cheek. And most of the time, whenever I was nice and courteous, the outcome was markedly different. Most situations ended positively.

A younger man asked an old man the secret to his long marriage. The old man replied, "Well, son, let me tell you. You can be right, or you can be happy." That is true for most of the difficult situations we encounter. Don't try to be right. You don't need to be right. All you need to do is make things work out in a positive way. This is not just about getting what you want. It's also about karma. I know, tough guy, you think karma is something for the soft and weak.

Think about it. In the weeks following September 11th, everyone was genuinely nice to each other, not just in the US, but all over the world. I was in Prague during the 9/11 attacks. After the attacks, the airports were shut down. We could not get home even if we wanted to. The hotel where I was staying offered to house all Americans for free until they could return home. Every restaurant I went into would not let me pay for my meal when they heard my US accent. There was an outpouring of humanity and common courtesy. They were being nice to me, and it made a tremendous difference.

Imagine for a moment if we could sustain that level of courtesy. We would be so busy being nice, that many of our global ideological conflicts would be put into perspective and our divisive societies and countries would come together. Courtesy would transcend culture, religion, politics, and language. Our work would become more joyful. Our relationships would be more satisfying. Then, we could begin to build bridges of understanding throughout the world.

The Tools

1. Use the Magic words

As a small child, I watched the Captain Kangaroo show every day. On that show, the magic words were "please" and "thank you". You could get almost anything you wanted by using these words. On the other hand, if you didn't use those words, you never received what you asked for. It was like magic. It may sound too simple to be true, but this is the foundation for courtesy. Use these words often and with sincerity, and you will be surprised how the magic will begin to work. One other very important magic word is "sorry". You can diffuse many volatile situations by saying "I'm sorry". You can also say "bless you" when someone sneezes. Variations of this phrase are used in many cultures after a sneeze. In Southern Europe and parts of South America, they say "salut", in Sweden, "prosit".

Whenever someone does something nice, write them a thank you note. If possible, make this a handwritten note. People receive a lot of emails, and your e-card may get lost in the shuffle. But people very rarely receive snail mail anymore. They will open and read your note. My wife is the queen of thank you notes and writes them often. This is a tangible "thank you" and is always appreciated.

2. Be Sincere

You can't just use the magic words. You must mean them. My wife encountered a situation with an airline where the company did not deliver what they promised. In each piece of correspondence, they apologized profusely and vowed to correct the situation. The only problem was that they never corrected anything. The apologies became a source of frustration instead of a bridge to understanding. So be sincere and follow through. Some folks in the programs think that keeping track of personal details in your phone and computer is somehow insincere. Keith Ferrazzi, the master of creating relationships says, "Just because it's intentional doesn't mean it's insincere."

3. Use the Platinum Rule

We all know the Golden Rule. Do unto others as you would have them do unto you. But do you know the Platinum Rule? Treat others the way they want to be treated, which, in some cases, may be different than the way you want to be treated. Of course, there are times that we don't always practice either of these rules. There are predictable times when we forget it. By keeping the Platinum Rule in the back of your head, you will be surprised at how effective you can handle most situations. Take a moment and ask yourself, "If I were sitting behind that counter or in that toll booth, or across from me at this table, how would I want to be treated?"

4. Use Empathy, walk around in their shoes for a while

Ian MacLaren said, "Be kind, for everyone you meet is fighting a hard battle." Always try to put yourself into the shoes of the person with whom you are dealing. The next time you are in a fast food line or returning an item, consider the person behind that counter. They are in a low-paying, fast-paced, high stress job, and they often encounter frustrated, angry, rude people. Perhaps they are in a poor economic situation, lack higher education, or are immigrants who speak very little English.

Would it improve the situation if you asked them how their day was going? Or told them that you thought they had a difficult job and appreciated their efforts? You may also talk about some skill they possess that you admire. I am always impressed by skilled receptionists who can greet visitors and answer dozens of phone calls at the same time. If I had to be a receptionist, I know I would be a terrible one. I simply don't possess those skills. Let people know that you appreciate them for the skills they possess. If you establish this connection with them, you will be more likely to receive excellent service. Service employees should remember that customers may be angry and upset. If you simply smile, use a clear voice, see their point of view and use "please", "thank you" and "I'm sorry", it is often possible to disarm their anger. As Emily Post, the guru of etiquette, said, "Manners are a sensitive awareness of the feelings of others. If you have that awareness, you have good manners, no matter what fork you use."

5. Speak Clearly

One thing that destroys personal encounters faster than anything is basic communication. Many times, people don't speak clearly, distinctly, or with the proper volume. This problem may be cultural, it may be a personality trait or it may be a problem with the language.

If you speak slowly, distinctly, and loudly enough to be heard, many of your encounters will go more smoothly. In addition, since communication is up to 95% non-verbal, overt sign language may help. I was in a Big Lots recently, and a young woman was asking for a product. She spoke to one of the Big Lots representatives, who was Russian. The woman asked if they had a "stawa". That is exactly what I heard from her mouth, "stawa".

In addition to that pronunciation, she said it in a very soft voice. The Big Lots representative did not understand and asked her to repeat it several times. Finally, the exasperated woman stormed out. The Russian woman was at a loss. I finally figured out that the young woman was saying "stop watch". If she had spoken slowly, distinctly, with the right amount of volume, or if she had mimed using a stopwatch, the Russian woman probably would have understood what she wanted.

A similar thing happened at a local jewelry store. An older man wanted to "get a clas put on this hyere braylet". There were several stares from the woman behind the counter, who was from Cuba. The man decided that she didn't speak English well and asked to speak to someone else. Another woman came from the back, who was from India. The man rolled his eyes and looked exasperated. Now he had to speak to another "foreigner" who also would not understand him. He asked her if the jeweler could "put a clas on the braylet". I finally understood and told the Indian woman that he wanted a clasp put on his bracelet. The man seemed relieved to have a translator available to make his wishes known.

You can see from these examples how important it is to simply be heard. So, speak slowly, distinctly, and with proper volume. Do your best to communicate well. It will go a long way. If English is a second language or you have a strong regional dialect, this is even more important. In these cases speak as clearly as you can. And if you are listening, listen carefully and ask people to repeat if necessary.

If you encounter someone who doesn't speak clearly, tell them that you are hard of hearing and ask them to speak up and speak slowly. This will put all the blame on you, but it will get them to communicate better, and it's more courteous than saying, "I can't understand you." or "Why don't you learn to speak English?" or "Would you quit mumbling?".

6. Call them by their name

If they have name-tags, call them by their name. When people hear their name, they are pleasantly surprised. As Dale Carnegie says, everyone likes to hear their own name. This can put a person at ease instantly. Of course, you don't want to overdo this and come across like a bad salesman.

7. Smile!

The world is not such a serious place. This is the number one thing I have to keep reminding my participants, to smile more. A smile transcends all languages and cultures. Even if you are feeling tired, frustrated, or impatient, you can smile and put the other person at ease. This will make your encounter more pleasant no matter what the circumstances. This is especially true when you speak over the phone. People can hear the smile in your voice.

8. Use humor if you can

Humor can diffuse tough situations and give you perspective on things. Here are a few examples:

I was returning a close-out item to an office supply store. The store policy was that close-outs could not be returned. But this item was missing a part that was essential to its operation. I repeatedly explained this to the woman behind the counter, and she repeated that it was their policy that they could not accept this as a return. I explained myself several times, and she quoted the policy several times. Finally she asked, "Are you an idiot?" I answered in a very polite and non-sarcastic way, "Why yes, as a matter of fact, I am an idiot. I come from a long line of idiots. My father was an idiot and his father before him. And before we came to this country, my great- great-grandfather was the village idiot. It's sort of a family tradition." She laughed and the tension was gone. She apologized and told me that she had not slept the night before and had a very rough day. She gave me a store credit despite the "company policy".

I was on the phone with a bank. They were trying very hard to understand, but the point was not getting across, and we were both getting a bit frustrated with the situation. They didn't seem to understand that I had two American Express Accounts. They had electronically paid one on time, but the other one was late and I was assessed a finance charge. Finally I said, "Thanks for being patient with me. I'm sure I have some responsibility in this situation. Perhaps I put the electronic payment request in too late." This softened them up a bit, and they said that perhaps they had some responsibility in the matter. Then, I said to them, "Wait a minute. I'm a little confused about one thing. Aren't you a big bank? Aren't you supposed to tell me that it is all my fault and transfer me to ten different people?" We all had a good laugh, the tension was gone, and we resolved the situation. They ended up paying the finance charge for me.

9. Children and Pets

If you have children and/or dogs, cats, birds, gerbils, or fish, please keep one thing in mind: nobody loves them as much as you do. You may not mind that your pets jump on you or lick your face or put their nose up your crotch. But other people do mind. You may not mind your children being loud or jumping on you or covering your head with whipped cream. Be aware that your friends, neighbors, and relatives may mind these things. Keep your children and pets well-behaved.

10. If someone needs help, offer to help them

If you see someone broken down on the highway, looking lost or having a problem with a copier, a vending machine, or ATM, offer to help if you think you can do so safely. There are exceptions, of course. If you are alone and see a man with a bloody hockey mask and a chain saw on the side of the road, you should probably keep driving. When you do stop and help someone, do this without any expectations of payment or being thanked. This spreads good karma. Sometimes the person needing help will offer to pay you for your trouble. If they do this, you may want to tell them that they should do something nice for someone else and use the "pay it forward" concept.

One time, I helped an elderly couple change a tire on the interstate highway. They had been waiting for someone to help them for four hours, and they told me I was their guardian angel. When they offered to pay me, I said, "We don't use money in heaven".

Be diplomatic, especially if the person has a disability. Avoid the word "need". Instead of saying, "Do you need help?", try saying, "May I help you with that?" You should not help the person without asking. It allows them the option to accept your help. If you see someone struggling to open a door, simply open it for them. It's nice to open a door for someone even if they don't "need" it. They usually appreciate it. When you go through a door, look back and see if you can hold the door for the next person.

11. Be on time

We are all busy. Most of us are extremely busy. But we should not use that as an excuse for being late, especially with GPS apps. Sometimes there are circumstances beyond our control, but those are very rare. If you plan for those things that can go wrong, you will rarely be late. To be late shows disrespect for the other person's time and begins any encounter on a bad note. So be on time, start meetings on time, and pick people up on time. And if you do have to be late, call them, let them know you are going to be late, tell them you are sorry, ask them to please forgive you, and thank them for being so understanding. If you don't start a meeting on time, you will actually encourage people to be late for the next meeting.

Furthermore, it penalizes those who are on time. One time my wife asked a subordinate why he always came late to meetings. He replied that there were several others who were always late, so he didn't want to arrive too early. With this attitude a downward spiral occurs. The people arrive late, then the meeting starts later, then the people start arriving later, then the meeting starts even later, and so on and so on.

There are exceptions to this. When I did a program in Argentina, I found that everyone was consistently fifteen to thirty minutes "late". Being on time is not part of their culture, and you must be aware of those differences.

12. Turn off your mobile device!

In public places, be aware of other people and put your mobile telephone on vibrate. That loud ringing is annoying and distracting, especially in public places such as movies, libraries, parks, and restaurants.

Our phones now beep and chirp when email arrives. Turn them off or put them on vibrate. This can also be a time management issue. If you turn these devices off for periods of time and check them in batches, you can make more efficient use of your time.

If you ever have a one-on-one meeting with someone such as a business meeting or lunch, it is good courtesy to turn your mobile phone off during these times. There are rare exceptions, of course such as a pregnant wife or an illness in the family that requires monitoring. If you have an exception, tell the person beforehand that you may have to answer your phone. But these circumstances are very rare. I don't know many people or circumstances that have that level of importance.

For the development program I mentioned before, we also had the champagne rule. If anyone's mobile phone rang during a session, that participant had to buy a round of drinks for everyone in the group. And since the group had as many as 30 people, absent-mindedness became quite expensive. Another mobile device rule was that if yours rang during a session, you had to sing a song for the group. This worked quite well until we had a Dane in the group who loved to sing. We would ask people to call him so he could perform for everyone. One time a phone was on vibrate, vibrated across the table and fell on the floor. Even though it didn't ring, it distracted the group, and we charged that participant with the champagne penalty.

13. Don't be in a rush if you can help it

If you're rushing around, pressed for time and think that you are going to zip in and out to renew your license or return that piece of merchandise, then you are setting yourself up to fail. You are putting yourself in a situation that will most likely have a poor outcome. If you don't have the time for potentially time consuming tasks, then put them off to a later time. Plan so that you are not rushed as the deadline approaches. When you are not rushed, you will be able to relax and think about the concepts in this book.

14. Be aware of cultural differences

There are many different cultures in the USA, and most have different values. Some cultures seem more tolerant of things like waiting or profanity. Some of these values are drawn along socio-economic lines. Remember this and act accordingly. In many cases, the people you are dealing with are not attempting to annoy. They may be acting as their culture or socio-economic background dictates. In these cases, you must be more diligent with your courtesy. Many times, when we become angry at these people, and they happen to be from a different culture, we resort to stereotyping. Imagine if we could get beyond that stereotyping and make a true connection with these people. What a difference that would make.

Cultural differences don't only happen with people from other countries. We have definite cultural differences right here in the USA. The South has a different pace and different rules than the North. In the Public Agenda survey, it was found that there was a big split on the use of profanity from North to South. Three out of four Southerners said it is always wrong to take God's name in vain, while half of those surveyed from the Northeast said that there is nothing wrong with it or it falls in the gray area. There is also an East coast, West coast split. Just because people live their lives at a different pace and have different beliefs, tolerances, prejudices, and priorities, doesn't mean you can't make a connection with them. Find the common thread and use it to build a relationship.

Be aware of things like eye contact, personal space requirements, and physical contact because they vary from culture to culture. These cultural differences are usually discussed in travel books. Please pay attention to them and respect them. Asian cultures have different personal space requirements and rarely look you in the eye for any period of time. Americans like that strong handshake, but this can be misconstrued in some cultures as an act of aggression.

If you can learn a little about other people's culture and learn a few key phrases in their language, you can deal with any situation much more effectively.

The Situations

1. Returns/Checkouts/Restaurants/Fast Food/Retail

In the Public Agenda survey, nearly half of those surveyed had walked out of a store in the past year because of "poor customer service". When dealing with service personnel, remain patient and calm while in line. You may want to bring a book, an audio book, or some music to pass the time in case there are delays. Personally, I take this type of opportunity to go over some positive affirmations.

Smile when it is your turn and ask how the person is doing today. Calmly explain what you would like. Remember, this person may encounter angry, impatient people all day long. Fill the conversation with "please" and "thank you" and call the person by name. Never demand. Use phrases like "I'm sorry to bother you" or "Can you do me a favor?" This usually gets better results than being demanding.

If they make a mistake, don't be too quick to point it out. Instead of saying, "Hey, I ordered this with no pickle!", perhaps you could say something along the lines of "I'm sorry, I may be wrong, I probably am, but I thought I ordered this without pickles. Would it be too much trouble to make me another sandwich?" You can usually gain a lot by saying "It's probably my fault" even if it isn't. But to place blame sets up a confrontation and resistance. While this may appear self-deprecating, it usually gets results.

When checking out at the grocery store, please don't get in the express lane unless you have the right number of items. If you see someone with only a few items, let them go ahead of you. Think how pleased you are when someone does that for you. When you aren't in a rush, you can afford this courtesy.

2. Being pulled over

When you are pulled over, the first thing to do is relax. If you have done something wrong, you are likely to get a ticket. Remember, police officers put their lives on the line for you every day. Imagine that you are a police officer and you are paid very little to do a difficult job. The last thing you want is a citizen who is angry at you because they broke the law. If you didn't break the law, you will always have the opportunity to explain it in court. Don't take it out on the officer. You can talk to them about how difficult their job is and how they don't get paid enough. A good thing to do is apologize for breaking the law. Don't offer excuses. It doesn't help. Smile and be nice. You would be surprised at the number of tickets that are dismissed.

I had this happen to me recently. I was pulled over for speeding in another neighborhood. We are always trying to get people to slow down in our neighborhood, but there I was doing 50 in a 25. I told the officer that I appreciated everything that he did for us, and that I was glad he pulled me over. I told him that I had become one of those people that I dislike, speeding through a residential area. He was quite shocked. He still gave me ticket, but reduced the speed I was traveling and told me how to plead nolo contendre so that it would not show up on my driving record. After that, I made a conscious effort to slow down and drive the speed limit, especially in residential areas.

There is a glaring exception to this rule. I facilitated a panel discussion on diversity and inclusion, and the discussion led to the differences that African Americans face in some situations that white people take for granted. As a middle-aged white male, when I get pulled over, I don't have to be too concerned with a potentially violent encounter. But one of our panelists, an African American male, made it clear that his experience of being pulled over was far different than mine, and his approach to this situation was to be very deliberate and careful.

3. Work situations

First, be on time for all meetings. For breaks and lunches, use only the allotted time and no more. Just because you are being paid doesn't mean that you don't have to be nice. People respond to nice. Say please and thank you, especially to subordinates. Write thank you notes. This is a tangible way of using the magic words "thank you", and it is always appreciated. On one project, I wrote a thank you note to all the mechanical, electrical, and plumbing superintendents. The plumbing superintendent told me that in 20 years, he had never received a thank you note. He took it home and showed his family. His wife put it on the refrigerator next to their kids' artwork. Whenever I needed anything, this super- intendent was there for me. I have also given massage certificates to subordinates for a job well done. These kinds of tangible thank yous create loyalty and increase performance.

Well-placed humor is also appreciated in the workplace. A subordinate came to me upset about the way a certain project was progressing. The deadline loomed nearer and nearer, and she was hitting brick walls at every turn. In addition, her personal life was difficult as she was going through a divorce. She was nearly in tears when she came to me, overwhelmed by everything. I told her not to worry. I was going to help her. She looked relieved. Then I said, "The first thing we must do is . . . go and get a cup of coffee." She looked at me incredulously and laughed. "Are you serious?" she asked. "Yes", I replied, and we went to a local coffee shop.

By getting away from the office and relaxing a bit, she was able to get some perspective on the problem. When we returned to the office, she tackled her project with renewed vigor and completed it on time. All she needed was to break the tension and loosen up a bit.

The Platinum Rule should always be in effect at work. Be aware of how co-workers feel and talk to them about things that are important to them whether it is work-related or not. I had to motivate a project team to do something, but could not get through to the project leader. One day, I found out that he liked bowling and was on tour as a professional bowler at one time. From then on, I started all conversations with how is your game? After that, the project proceeded smoothly.

4. Be a good audience member

When you go to a concert or theater or movie, there are some things you should keep in mind. If you are late, sit in the back. Don't go down front and walk over people who are trying to enjoy the event. If you are a tall person, have big hair or wear a hat, be mindful of where you sit, especially if you are in a theater that does not have stadium seating. Don't block other's line of sight. Turn off your mobile device. Don't talk during the performance. If you are one of those people who go to the restroom or to buy refreshments during the show or performance, sit on the aisle and in the back. Don't bring young children to the show unless it is something like Sponge Bob on ice. They can be annoying to others in the audience.

One of the greatest stories of audience courtesy I have ever heard was a told by Leonard Slatkin, the famous conductor. The orchestra was in Japan. One of the patrons started to cough. When he knew he couldn't control his cough, he covered his mouth, crouched down and ran up the aisle and out of the auditorium so as not to disturb the other patrons. Mr. Slatkin said that in the USA, when the concert is over, several dozen people exit the auditorium quickly without clapping in order to beat the traffic. In Japan, not only did the entire audience clap for the orchestra, but they waited until all the musicians had left the stage before leaving the auditorium. They did this to show respect and courtesy.

5. A sign won't do it

We've all seen the signs: DON'T HANG TOWELS OVER THE BALCONY, NO SWIMMING AFTER 10 O'CLOCK, LOADING AND UNLOADING ONLY, EXPRESS LANE-MAXIMUM 12 ITEMS, PLEASE WASH YOUR COFFEE CUP AFTER EACH USE.

The problem with signs is that they just don't work very well. Don't think you will fix a problem by installing a sign. In general, people ignore signs. Part of the problem is our independent nature here in the USA. We tend to think that the rules are for all those other people. There are also problems with literacy and English as a second language. In some large cities, over 200 languages are spoken. Even if you have a sign in Spanish and English, people still may be unable or unwilling to read your well thought out, well-intentioned, problem solving sign. If you want a problem resolved, the best way to do it is face-to-face.

6. Phone orders/solicitations/phone courtesy

Phone conversations create definite impressions and we should pay more attention to them. Call five businesses from the phone book and see if you can understand the name of the business. From personal experience, most of the time, the name of the business cannot be understood. We tend to mumble, hold the receiver away from our mouths, talk too, fast, and not really listen.

Use your communication skills when you are on the phone. Talk slowly and distinctly. Make sure you truly listen when you encounter voicemail. The message may give you all the information you need. When leaving a message, always leave your number even if you know they have it. Say it slowly and say it twice so that the other person doesn't have to look up your number to call you back. They may be checking their messages remotely and not have your number with them.

If you don't need for them to call you back, say that on the message. It is frustrating to play "phone tag" when a clear, concise message could convey all the necessary information. You may also want to leave some windows of time to return the call. By making this window clear, you may get more returned calls. Return your messages promptly. Make your outgoing message an interesting one. The same old "sorry we can't be here to take your call . . . " message is boring and lifeless. Be creative. A sample message from my business line (it changes often) is "I can't take your call right now because I am out saving civilization as we know it by training new leaders." If your message is varied and interesting, people are more likely to listen and leave a message. How many times do you hear the answering machine kick in and the caller hangs up before the outgoing message has been completed?

Be especially nice and courteous over the phone because you are only communicating through your voice. Tone, quality, and articulation are essential. Smile when you talk on the phone. The person on the other end will be able to hear when your smile. One company I called answered, "Having a great day at . . . ." What a wonderful way to answer the phone. Also, when I asked for someone there, the receptionist said, "It's my pleasure to connect you." This can be shortened to "my pleasure" if time is an issue.

When receiving calls from telephone solicitors, please don't get angry. There is no need to ruin your evening or theirs. Simply tell them "sorry, but I'm not interested" and hang up. Another approach is to tell them you are not interested and ask them to remove you from the call list. This isn't the best job in the world, and they probably encounter all kinds of personal attacks before they make a sale. In the past, I used an idea from an episode of Seinfeld. I asked the solicitor for his home phone number and told him that I would call him later that evening. When he refused to give me his number, I said, "so, you're telling me that you don't like people to call you at home in the evening?" This worked okay most of the time, but one time the solicitor gave me his phone number and asked me to call him at home any time. This made me realize that these people are just trying to make a living. How can we fault them for that?

If you call a wrong number, please don't hang up or mumble something unintelligible. Simply say, "I'm sorry. I have the wrong number." Then, hang up. If it is very late or very early, apologize for disturbing them.

7. Dealing with Annoying People

Sometimes we encounter rude and annoying people; that surly server or retail sales person, the guy talking in the movie, the person who cuts in line. How do we deal with these people? Sometimes we ignore them and sometimes we get angry at them. Sometimes we say something and sometimes we let it go. What if we overwhelmed them with nice? Most of the time, being nice works. What if the next time you encountered a surly server you said, "Are you having a bad day? I'm sorry if you're having a bad day."

For the line cutter, you can start by saying to them, "Excuse me. I'm sorry to bother you. Perhaps you didn't know the line started back there. Because I know you wouldn't cut in front of everyone like that because that wouldn't be fair, now would it?"

For the movie talker or cell phone answerer, you can say, "Excuse me, but I wonder if you wouldn't mind turning off your cell phone or stop talking please? I'm really into this movie and each time I hear you talk or answer your cell phone, it pulls me out of it. Thanks for your consideration."

Remember to consider their situation. Sometimes people aren't being rude. There may be circumstances that you don't realize. That man cutting in line may have a pregnant wife in the car about to deliver a baby. My wife and I had season tickets to the symphony, and the woman in front of us always left early. This annoyed me and my wife. Before one concert, we were chatting with her, and she told us that her husband was bedridden and this was her only time to go out. She always snuck out early because she didn't want to be away from him for too long. That was a good lesson for both of us.

8. Dealing with Scammers and Panhandlers

If you are approached by a panhandler, you don't have to be rude. You can say something along the lines of "I'm sorry, but I don't have any money to give you right now." Even if you have money in your pocket, you are not telling a lie. There are some people who are scamming for money. They give you a long story about trying to raise enough money for gas and that their family is waiting in the car. Again, you can be nice, but not give in.

Some panhandlers say they want to work, but really only want you to give them money. When I worked for a contractor, I used to give my business card to the people with "will work for food" signs and tell them to call me if they wanted a job. After handing out dozens of cards, I received a phone call from a guy who was a skilled mason. I arranged for him to go to work for our masonry division, where he worked for several years.

9. Driving/Road rage/Handicapped parking

Public Agenda's survey said that six drivers in ten regularly see other people driving aggressively or recklessly. More than one-third admitted to occasional bad driving themselves. These road rage incidents, which seem to be on the rise, are dangerous. If you are stuck in traffic, or someone cuts you off, let it go. They may be desperate to get somewhere for a legitimate reason. If you make a mistake or cut someone off, tell them you are sorry. Shrug your shoulders and hit yourself in the head.

Don't drive in the HOV lane unless you have a passenger. Don't drink and drive. Don't pull past the lane lines or pedestrian lines at intersections. They are there for a reason, so pedestrians can walk and cars can make turns more easily. If you are past the line, the turning cars have a difficult time and the pedestrians cannot walk across the street. If you are broken down or in an accident, unless there are laws prohibiting it, remove your car from the road. If you see someone broken down, give them plenty of room. Go wide around them, in the left lane if possible. Don't drive while talking on the phone unless you can do it hands free and safely. Let people merge. Let people pull ahead of you. Give people plenty of room. Don't block intersections. If you miss a turn or an exit, don't stop and block everything. Keep moving and turn around. Use your turn signals. Don't drive slowly in the fast lane. Slow down in parking lots.

Try this next time you are at a toll booth. Pay for the person behind you. Tell the attendant to tell the next person that you already paid for them and to have a nice day. You never know where small acts of kindness like that may lead.

As for handicapped parking, don't be too quick to judge someone who is trying to take advantage of those coveted parking spots. I know someone who yelled at a person for parking in the handicapped space because they walked normally when they got out of their car. As it turned out, the woman had Multiple Sclerosis that came in episodes. Sometimes she could walk fine. Other times, she needed a cane or a walker. For those of you who don't know, that wide area between handicapped parking spaces is not a parking space. They are areas set aside so that people with handicapped vans will have the room to open their door and deploy their ramp. Please don't park there.

One final note on the use of the word "handicapped". Most people with disabilities find this word offensive. They prefer the term "disabled" or having "special needs". They do not like the euphemisms that use the words "impaired" or "deficient". Deaf people don't believe that their deafness is a handicap and prefer not to be referred to as disabled. Blind people generally prefer the word "blind". They are not "vision impaired" or "deficient in sight".

10. Waiting room at doctor/dentist/hair appointment

If you are a reader, remember to bring a book to read or listen to an audio book. This may help with your patience. If you have the time, and you are at a particularly good part of the book, tell them to take the next person. Be patient and be on time. Part of the reason for backups at these places is that so many people are not on time. Don't pick a time when you must be rushed.

I did try one thing with a doctor that worked well. I waited for over two hours past my appointed time. When I received my bill, I deducted my billable rate for two hours from the bill and sent it back to him. I did end up paying for the full price of the visit, but I think the doctor got the message. I never waited more than ½ hour after that.

11. Tipping

If please, thank you, and sorry are magic words, tipping is a magic act. It is especially useful when it is not expected. One time my luggage was lost, and they had a delivery service bring it to my home. I noticed that the delivery guy did this on the side because he used his own car. Perhaps it was a second job. He probably encountered hostile people most of the time. The airlines misplaced their luggage, but the customers probably took it out on him. He pulled up to the curb at my house, which sets up on a hill. My trip was a monthlong business trip, so the suitcase was huge and heavy. I walked down to the curb, he unloaded my suitcase, and I gave him a ten dollar bill. I thanked him for bringing my suitcase to me. I'm sure that with most people, he is eager to drop the suitcase quickly and leave before the yelling begins. But he offered to take the suitcase up to the door and into the house. He thanked me several times and told me to have a nice night.

Another example is when my wife and I went to a restaurant with complimentary valet parking. When we left the restaurant, it was pouring down rain. We saw several people in front of us getting their cars, and not one gave the valet a tip. After all, the sign said "free". The valet was soaked to the skin, but used a towel to keep the car seat dry. To my embarrassment, I found that I didn't have any cash to give him a tip. I told him I would give it to him later, and he gave me that look. The one that said, "Yeah, right, buddy." We drove to an ATM and withdrew some cash. We drove back to the restaurant and gave the valet a ten dollar bill. He gave us a broad smile and said, "You have restored my faith in humanity." And we did that all for only ten dollars.

12. If you are a host or guest in someone's home

It is not difficult to be a good host. Make sure your guests are comfortable. They should have nice place to sleep complete with a few extra pillows and an extra blanket. A reading light is a nice touch as well. Make sure your guests have plenty of towels, wash cloths, toilet paper, shampoo, and other essentials. We keep a basket of soaps and shampoos from hotels for our guests. It is also nice to have some room in the closet for hanging clothes as well as one of those small stands to set a suitcase upon. Let them know that they are welcome and to "make themselves at home".

If you are a guest, you should always leave things better than when you arrived at your host's home. Make your bed. Do your laundry. Do their laundry. Buy groceries and cook a meal. Clean the house or pay to have it cleaned. Be courteous with watching television or listening to music. Always ask if it is okay. Don't monopolize the time with these entertainment centers. Don't use all the hot water. If you have special dietary needs, take care of them yourself. Don't expect your hosts to accommodate you. Thank you notes are nice after a stay with your host along with a small gift if appropriate.

You've probably seen the house rules sign in a summer beach house or mountain cottage. I think there is some old fashioned wisdom and courtesy in these rules:

13. Basic House Rules:

If you open it, close it.
If you turn it on, turn it off.
If you unlock it, lock it up.
If you break it, admit it.
If you can't fix it, call in someone who can.
If you borrow it, return it.

If you value it, take care of it.
If you mess it up, clean it up.
If you move it, put it back.
If it belongs to someone else, and you want to use it, get permission.
If you don't know how to operate it, leave it alone.
If it's none of your business, don't ask questions.
If it ain't broke, don't fix it.
If it will brighten someone's day, say it.
If it will tarnish someone's reputation, keep it to yourself.

14. Borrowing someone's car

After borrowing someone's car, you should fill the tank with gas. It would also be nice to take the car through a car wash or buy some nice thing for the car such as an air freshener or a tire gauge. If you want to be nice, you can have the car serviced or detailed.

15. Public Transportation:

When you ride the bus or a train, always give up your seat to the elderly or disabled. In fact, you should give up your seat to any woman regardless of age. This seems to work everywhere except New York where the women may be reluctant to take your seat. This is a cultural difference that you may not been able to overcome. Let people off the train or bus before trying to pile in. If people want to be left alone and read a book or listen to music, honor their isolation.

16. Airplanes

For domestic flights, stay on the lookout for people who need help finding their seat or putting their luggage in the overhead bins. Let people know when you are leaning your chair back so that you don't slam their knees or pinch their feet. For international flights remember there are around 300 people on the plane and only a handful of bathrooms. Keep your time in the bathroom short. One time I waited 20 minutes for a bathroom. When the young man came out, he looked like he had taken a shower, and the bathroom was a complete mess.

17. Foreign travel

We are known as the "ugly Americans" in other parts of this world. Much of the world perceives us to be loud, aggressive, and rude. When you travel to other parts of the world, you start to understand why we have this reputation. For the most part, we tend to project that image although I hope not intentionally.

Most Americans think that the French are rude, so we have these negative expectations when we travel to France. But if you learn some rudimentary French and speak it wherever you go, you may be surprised. You don't have to know proper French. Preface your conversation by asking the person in French if they speak English. I tried this when I traveled to Paris, and I did not encounter any rudeness from the French people whatsoever. In fact, they were lovely people and treated me kindly.

I did see a French person be "rude" to an American. It was because the American started their encounter by speaking very loudly in English as he asked directions to the Louvre. The Frenchman simply shrugged his shoulders half way through the American's oration and left. And of course, the American said something along the lines of, "All these damn frogs are rude as hell!" Many Americans labor under the delusion that if you speak English loudly enough and slowly enough, all "foreigners" will be able to understand you. We tend to call them "foreigners" even though we are guests in their country.

I think the problem may lie in the fact that most Americans believe that everyone does or should speak English. This simply isn't true. With that attitude, most Americans approach people in other countries and start speaking English, and most of the time, their voices are loud and their tempos are slow. Think for a minute if a French person came up to you on the street in the USA and started speaking very loudly and very slowly in French. And when you acted as if you did not understand, he became angry and spoke even louder. When you think about it that way, perhaps you can see how the term "ugly American" came into being. It's no wonder that Americans receive rude behavior in return. So, learn a few phrases in the language of the country you are visiting and always ask if they speak English-in their language if possible. And if you do have to resort to English, please speak it slowly (but not too slowly), distinctly, and without volume.

Familiarize yourself with the local customs concerning methods of greeting and phrases, actions, and other things to avoid. All the basic travel guides have this information. Avoid doing something that would be considered rude or forward. Remember this: When you are traveling to a foreign country, you are an ambassador for the United States. Please act accordingly.

There is a joke that goes something like this: What do you call someone who speaks three languages? The answer is trilingual. What do you call someone who speaks two languages? The answer is bilingual. What do you call someone who speaks one language? The answer is American. If you do nothing else, learn "please", "thank you", "sorry" and "excuse me" in the language of the countries you are visiting. Those words work their magic in any language or culture. There are thousands of websites that offer translations for these words and phrases in hundreds of different languages.

When checking into a hotel, it may speed things up if you present your passport, business card, or other identification. Saying your name may not help as your pronunciation will likely not match theirs. They will be grateful and you won't have to go through the exercise of repeating your name. Many people learn their English as British English, not US English. The pronunciations are markedly different

18. The Chain of Courtesy

Because we are all connected, when we are discourteous, it can begin a chain of rudeness that can spread like a horrible virus. If one of us is late for an appointment, it not only inconveniences the person we are meeting, but it may make both of us late for our next appointment. Then we have three more people who are inconvenienced. When we are rude to someone, they may take it out on several others. These others, in turn, may be rude to more people throughout the day. This could go on for quite a while until we have a long line of angry people. But the opposite is also true. If we are kind to people, if we are courteous and on time for our appointments, it can set off a chain of courtesy that is palpable. Remember the rampant courtesy after September 11th? That is a perfect example of this chain of courtesy.

19. No good deed ever goes unpunished

There will be times when you do a good deed, and it will backfire on you. This happened recently to me. I walked up to an ATM and saw a debit card sticking out of the machine. I took the card and waited for around fifteen minutes, but no one came. I called information and tried to find the person on the card to no avail. I finally called the number on the back of the card and told them the situation. They took my name and number. The next day, the woman called me and thanked me. She was from out of town and desperately needed her card. I arranged to meet her the next morning at the bank.

The next morning, she called me and said she couldn't get to the bank and wondered if I would bring the card to her. I told her I couldn't because I had a doctor's appointment that morning that could not be changed. She called me back and told me that she had arranged for someone to meet me at the bank, but asked if I could come a half hour earlier. I told her that I could. I waited for ten minutes past the time. After no one showed, I called her back and told her that I would be happy to mail her the card. I took her address and went to the doctor.

During my appointment, she called eight times. Finally, I was able to answer, and her friend asked if he could come to the doctor's office and retrieve the card. I told him that he could. He came in, took the card and thanked me. Even if these frustrating things happen occasionally, don't let it discourage you from being nice and courteous.

20. When something good happens

When you receive good service or have a good encounter with someone, celebrate it. Tell the person's supervisor, write a thank you note to let them know that you appreciate what they have done for you. We all tend to want to report things when they go wrong. We are less likely to report when things go well.

A friend of mine was in a small diner and received very good service and a great meal cooked just the way he liked it. Before leaving, he asked to speak to the manager. "Is something wrong?", the waitress asked. "Please get me the manager", he replied. And she did. When the manager came, he extolled the virtues of his server and the cook and left a big tip. If we celebrated our encounters with good service, we would have more and more experiences where people strive to be courteous.

When someone does something nice for you, point it out and say thank you. If someone lets you merge or turn in front of them, thank them and give them a friendly wave. Celebrate all that is good.

21. When all else fails

There will be times when old patterns will take over and you will become frustrated with a situation. You may have tried all the common courtesy tips to no avail. During those encounters, take a deep breath and ask yourself, is it worth the price of the anger? In the grand scheme of things, is this so important that you must get angry and raise your blood pressure and stress levels? Most of the time, the answer will be a resounding "no". So when you feel yourself starting to get angry, step back and take some deep breaths. If necessary, end the transaction, walk away, and do it another time.

22. Turn things around

Have you seen those individuals who are mean to others? When these mean people are in a group, the meanness seems to escalate. Couples get into the habit of being mean to each other and talking badly about each other. But you can do something about this. You can reverse these negative emotions. It has been clinically proven that emotions are contagious. Your attitude, whether positive or negative has a profound affect on others. Remember that the next time you see people being negative. Turn it around with your positive emotions.

23. Be good to one another

In this fast-paced world in which we live, we get stressed and frustrated and we tend to take it out on each other. But remember that we are all human beings and we all like to be treated nicely. That will go a long way to improve our day-to-day dealings with each other. Let us all do our best to get back that civility and gentility that we experienced during the few weeks past September 11th, 2001.

We used to greet each other by saying, "Your servant." Use this concept and submit to each other. Ask yourself, "How can I love you, serve you, accommodate myself to you?" If we do this, we will be able to bring common courtesy back into common usage. And who knows, if we take this to the extreme, perhaps we can save the world. Never underestimate the power of one. As the saying goes, "If everyone swept in front of their home, the whole world would be clean." It all starts with you.

Final thoughts

If you think that you aren't good at developing and maintaining relationships, you are absolutely right. But I can tell you that this is a skill just like any other skill. The first thing you must do is get your mind right. Tell yourself you are good at relationships. Practice the twelve steps. Put into practice the tenants of common courtesy. Before long, you will be a master at relationships. You will no longer feel awkward at networking meetings or large gatherings. You will feel comfortable because you possess the knowledge to cultivate relationships. Relationships drive business and personal success. Remember, relationships give you ideas, encouragement, and energy. Stop your isolation and tap into this energy. You will be glad that you did.

CHAPTER 5
Stress Management

"I was a little excited but mostly blorft. "Blorft" is an adjective I just made up that means 'Completely overwhelmed but proceeding as if everything is fine and reacting to the stress with the torpor of a possum.' I have been blorft every day for the past seven years."

~ Tina Fey, Bossypants

Introduction

This part of the book is all about managing your stress, an area where most tough guys fall short. In fact, the construction industry has the second highest suicide rate of any industry according to the CDC. If you or someone you know is struggling, please visit *www.preventconstructionsuicide.com* for risk assessments and more information.

First, you should take the emotional intelligence test and see if you are in burnout. Second, we talk about what stress and your lifestyle choices are doing to you. Third, we cover a step-by-step process and practical tools to use that will reduce your reactions to your stressors. We also cover lifestyle tips that contribute to a healthier and happier life. In the Appendix, there is a Body Battery Inventory and Performance Plan that will show you where you are in terms of stressors versus recovery activities. You will create a performance plan to build in recovery activities to recharge your body battery before, during and after stressful events.

When you embrace these concepts and practice these exercises and tips, you will begin to have a better, more satisfying life. This book may even save your life and prevent you from developing some horrible, stress related disease. Also, think about how stress affects safety and workforce development. You can't make good decisions and think clearly if you are running on adrenaline. And because of the high stress levels, many young folks are staying away from the industry.

Companies can also promote this agenda of managing stress and promoting wellness and good mental health by having a wellness program, talking about mental health and suicide prevention, pay for gym memberships, have weight loss and tobacco cessation programs, and by putting more fun into work. Cianbro is a great model for wellness program and has saved millions of dollars in insurance costs and lost productivity with healthier, happier more productive employees.

But for this to benefit you, you have to keep an open mind. As the founder of Dewar's whisky said, "Minds are like parachutes. They only work when open."

What is stress and your lifestyle choices doing to you?

The effects and symptoms of stress

We live in a hectic society. We work longer hours and more days than any nation on earth. We also have the fewest paid holidays and vacation on earth. Did I sense a little swell of pride there, tough guy? I thought I did. You like to work. And there's nothing wrong with that. Stress doesn't kill anyone. We need a certain amount of stress to perform well. Stress is an everyday occurrence. It's part of our lives. And for the most part, we can't control those things that are happening around us. But we do have 100% control over how we react to those situations. And it's that reaction to stress that may be killing us. According to Kelly McGonigal, the fear of stress, not the stress itself, is what kills us. In a study that she did, people who were under a lot of stress, but didn't see stress as a negative, had a lower death rate than people with low levels of stress who thought stress was harming them. So the first thing I want you to do is reframe your stress. Be thankful that you have such a challenging, interesting job that is interesting and a life that keeps you busy.

Let's look at what you reaction to stress is doing to you.

Did you know that according to the CDC, 80-90% of all illness in developed countries is lifestyle and stress-related? That's right, tough guy. That is what your reaction to stress is doing to you. Making you sick. The USA is number one in stress-related illnesses. Hurray! We're number one! Doesn't it make you proud? Stress and burnout are epidemic.

According to the American Psychological Association (APA), 75% of Americans say that work has a significant impact on their stress levels. It is estimated that US companies lose hundreds of billions of dollars per year in stress-related illnesses and lost productivity. That's billions with a "B".

The following statistics are from the CDC (Centers for Disease Control) website:

Chronic Diseases: The Leading Causes of Death and Disability in the United States

Chronic diseases and conditions—such as heart disease, stroke, cancer, diabetes, obesity, and arthritis—are among the most common, costly, and preventable of all health problems.

As of 2020, Six out of ten of all adults have one or more chronic health conditions. Four in ten adults have two or more chronic health conditions.

Seven of the top ten causes of death in 2017 were chronic diseases. Two of these chronic diseases—heart disease and cancer—together accounted for nearly half of all deaths.

Obesity is a serious health concern. During 2017–2018, the obesity rate was 42.4%, or about 140 million people. In 2008, the estimated annual medical cost for obesity was $147. Obesity rates are higher in non-whites and lower socioeconomic groups.

Arthritis, an autoimmune disease where the body attacks itself, is the most common cause of disability. Of the 54.4 million adults with a doctor diagnosis of arthritis, more than 22 million say arthritis causes them to have trouble with their usual activities. The CDC estimates that by 2040, 26% of US aged adults will have arthritis.

Diabetes, another autoimmune disease, is the leading cause of kidney failure, lower limb amputations other than those caused by injury, and new cases of blindness among adults. Currently (2020), 34.2 million people have diabetes. This is expected to almost double by 2030. It is estimated that 88 million people are currently pre-diabetic (elevated glucose levels).

Health Risk Behaviors that Cause Chronic Diseases

Health risk behaviors are unhealthy behaviors you can change. These health risk behaviors—lack of exercise or physical activity, poor nutrition, poor sleep, not managing stress well, tobacco use, and too much alcohol and drug use cause much of the illnesses, suffering, and early death related to chronic diseases and conditions.

In 2020, almost half (47%) of adults aged 18 years or older did not meet recommendations for aerobic exercise or physical activity. In addition, 76% did not meet recommendations for muscle-strengthening physical activity.

About half of US adults (47%) have at least one of the following major risk factors for heart disease or stroke: uncontrolled high blood pressure, uncontrolled high LDL cholesterol, or are current smokers. Ninety percent of Americans consume too much sodium, increasing their risk of high blood pressure.

In 2011, more than one-third (36%) of adolescents said they ate fruit less than once a day, and 38% said they ate vegetables less than once a day. In addition, 38% of adults said they ate fruit less than once a day, and 23% said they ate vegetables less than once a day.

In 2018, more than 34.2 million adults (14 out of every 100) said they currently smoked cigarettes. In the US, smoking related deaths number 480,000. Worldwide, cigarette smoking accounts for more than 7 million deaths each year. On average, smokers die 10 years earlier than non-smokers. And the latest studies show that vaping is not any better.

Drinking too much alcohol is responsible for 88,000 deaths each year, more than half of which are due to binge drinking. In 2018, about 26.45 % of US adults report binge drinking in the past month, and have an average of 8 drinks per binge, yet most binge drinkers are not alcohol dependent.

The Cost of Chronic Diseases and Health Risk Behaviors

The majority of US health care and economic costs associated with medical conditions are for the costs of chronic diseases and conditions and associated health risk behaviors.

Seventy-five percent of all health care spending in 2020 was spent on chronic medical conditions and is estimated to cost $5,300 per person in the US per year.

- The total costs of heart disease, the leading cause of death across the world, stands at 647,000 people annually (2014-2015) were estimated to be $219 billion.
- Cancer care cost $174 billion in 2020 (estimate).
- The total estimated cost of diagnosed diabetes in 2017 was $327 billion.
- The total cost of arthritis and related conditions was about $140 billion in 2020.
- Medical costs linked to obesity were estimated to be $147 billion in 2008.
- Smoking is estimated to cost more than $300 billion a year.
- The economic costs of drinking too much alcohol were estimated to be $175.9 billion.

These are sobering statistics. Keep them in mind. All these illnesses are caused by or made worse by stress and your lifestyle choices. Cardiovascular or heart disease is the number one killer in this country and around the world. In the US, one in three will die of heart disease. That includes women. Okay tough guy, I know what you're thinking. You have a genetic pre-disposition to these diseases. Yes, genetics do factor into the equation. But if you have a genetic pre-disposition to these diseases, shouldn't you be even more careful? A friend of mine, after his first heart attack, told me that he is eating anything he wants to eat because his dad died young from a heart attack and there was nothing much that he could do. Wrong! This book will teach you lifestyle choices that can alter that outcome and techniques that have been proven by the Harvard Medical School to change the expression of those genes and help to prevent disease and slow down aging. Interested now, tough guy?

Tobacco and Drug Use:

What about those bad habits that you have? If you smoke, tough guy, quit now. Quit as you are reading this sentence. Vow to put that cigarette down and never pick one up again. Smoking is without a doubt, one of the worst things you can do to your body. I know because my dad smoked for 50 years. He died from COPD (chronic obstructive pulmonary disease) and had terrible quality of life before his death in 2009. He was on oxygen and had chronic infections in his lungs. On one trip to the hospital for pneumonia, he caught something called pseudomonas, which is an antibiotic resistant bacterial infection that basically never goes away. He said to me, "If I thought I would have lived this long, I would have taken better care of myself."

I don't care what you need to do, you must quit now. Do the patch, the gum, the pills, get hypnotized, but stop it now! Did you know that according to one WHO (World Health Organization) study, smokers under 40 are five times more likely to have a heart attack than non-smokers? Did you know that according to another WHO study, 80% of all people ages 35-39 who had heart attacks were smokers? Smoking in this group was judged to be the cause of 65% of all the non-fatal heart attacks in women and 55% of all of the non-fatal heart attacks in men.

Drugs (including recreational, over the counter, and prescription) alter how the body works. The healthy body is a self-healing, self-regulating organism. Too much use of drugs can put the body in danger of developing a disease. Many of the over the counter medications and prescription drugs were developed for short term use only. Read the labels. Many drugs are poisons that tax the liver. Some work by decreasing the immune response, which leaves the body wide open for other diseases. Read the side effects carefully. The rules for bringing a drug to market give the drug companies a lot of leeway, and for some classes of drugs these requirements are modified significantly or waived altogether. Many drugs that come to market have significant side effects and are not much better than placebo.

Obesity and Weight:

Are you overweight? Obesity is another one of those epidemics that we are facing. If you are overweight, you must act now. We'll talk about specifics later, but make a vow right now to get that weight off and keep it off. Did you know that there is a possible link to stress and obesity? We are the most stressed nation on earth and the fattest nation on earth. I believe that there is a correlation. Recent National Institute of Health studies have linked chronic stress with keeping weight on.

Many of you have poor eating habits with lots of frozen foods, fast food, and pre-packaged dinners. You have sedentary lifestyles. You sit a lot and watch a lot of television. Our screen time has ballooned up to 11 hours per day on average. By the age of 65, we will have watched a screen for 30 of those years. We don't exercise as we should. And what is the cost? Being overweight contributes to all these illnesses. It is the main cause for the increase in diabetes.

So what is our nation doing about this epidemic? We spend billions on diet and exercise fads. Look at magazines and television. There is a new miracle weight loss pill out each week. We also spend billions on cosmetics and plastic surgery in order to look younger. We are obsessed with youth and thin bodies and unwrinkled faces. Everyone is looking for magic bullets and quick answers to their weight issues. But there are no easy answers and no quick fixes.

Fight, Flight or Freeze

Let's look at stress first and see how it affects your body. There is a book called Why Zebras Don't Get Ulcers by Robert Sapolsky. It's about how mammals have the fight or flight response built in. It's in the very primitive part of our brain, the limbic system. When we are faced with danger, our brains start pumping out cortisol. Our body pumps out adrenaline. The blood flows away from our middle and to our arms and legs. Our fists clench. Our jaws tighten. Our heart rate and respiration rate increase dramatically. We are ready to fight, freeze or flee.

So where do Zebras come in? All mammals have this fight or flight response. When a zebra sees a lion, its body does the same thing. Since it cannot fight a lion, it prepares to run. And when the danger is over, the zebra's body goes back to normal within a short period of time. He either escapes the lion or is eaten. Either way, the danger has passed. The problem with human beings is that we experience this fight or flight response all day long.

Are you hearing me, tough guy? As human beings, when we experience stressful moments, our body acts the same as if our lives were in danger. It starts the fight, freeze or flee response. It pumps out cortisol and adrenaline. It prepares us to fight, freeze or flee. So your alarm clock doesn't go off and you get a shot of adrenaline and cortisol. You walk outside and see that you have a flat tire. More adrenaline and cortisol. You are late, so you are now stuck in traffic. More adrenaline and cortisol. And this happens all day long.

How many of you have been involved in a near death experience like an accident or rescue? There is story after story about men lifting cars off people. That adrenaline rush helps us to do those kinds of superhuman things. But ask yourself or ask anyone who has been through such ordeals. How do you feel afterward? Exhausted, right? So is it any wonder that you are exhausted at the end of the day? Your body has been in fight or flight all day long. So once you hit that La-z-boy and relax, you collapse in a heap. Many people in our programs say that it is all they can do to eat dinner, spend a little time with the family, and go to bed.

Here's another phenomenon that I see quite a bit. You see, tough guy, adrenaline is a marvelous thing. It can keep you going, keep you performing, keep you from getting sick. But there is a cost. It wears your body out. How many of you get sick when you go on vacation? This is quite common for stressed out people. Because the adrenaline is flowing freely, you keep going. You keep pushing. You stay at it non-stop. But after the first few days of your vacation, especially if you don't check in at the office, your body gets the message that there is no longer a lion waiting to eat you, so it stops pumping out the adrenaline and cortisol. And when those stop, your body collapses and falls into dis-ease. That's when you get a cold. It's not very fun to have a cold and to have that big physical let down on vacation. Some of the tough guys I work with are addicted to adrenaline. They need it. They tell me, "I love to work!" But they don't look at the costs. Some can't get enough adrenaline at work so they take up hobbies like skydiving and bungee jumping. Okay. I want you to hear me tough guy. If you don't build in recovery for your body, you will wear your body out and die at an early age. Is that clear enough?

One other thing about adrenaline. Guess what it does to your brain? This fight, freeze or flee response comes from the limbic system. This is the primitive part of your brain and this response is for pure survival. But what it also does is shut down the neocortex or the thinking part of your brain. Because when you are being chased by a lion, it is not in your best interest to over-analyze the situation. So not only are you stressed, but your thinking brain isn't working as it should. Therefore it takes you much longer to work through any cognitive processes that you are trying to accomplish.

There is another phenomenon with this adrenaline production all day long. Because you are getting those little shots of adrenaline with each annoying thing that happens (note it is your reaction to these things, not the things, that is causing this), there is a buildup of adrenaline throughout your day. It is common that one little thing can set you off. It's like you have a cup that is almost full, and when that last little annoying thing happens such as your spouse saying something snotty or your kid leaving his toy out for you to trip over, you explode. Your cup has run over and you are out of control.

You experience what is known as an amygdala highjack. The emotional part of your brain takes over, and you go off like a rocket before the thinking part has a chance to process the information. Then you feel badly about it. It's as if you were out of your own body. Like you had no control. This is adrenaline overload, and you never know what is going to set you off.

What is all this stress doing to your body? You know that the long-term effect of stress is disease, but what does it do prior to the disease showing up in your body? There are physical symptoms of stress. It is your body's way of telling you that something is wrong.

These are at least twelve symptoms that are related to stress:

1. Headaches

Half to three quarters of adults worldwide have had a headache in the past year. In 2015, the medical cost of treating migraines was more than $5.4 billion and the estimated cost of lost productivity is $36 billion annually. If you have more than a couple of headaches per month, this could be a symptom of stress. There are different kinds of headaches. There are stress headaches that start in the back of the neck and by the end of the day is a full-blown, debilitating headache. There are sinus headaches and migraines. All these headaches are caused by or made worse by stress. Most headache sufferers accept this as normal. It is common, but far from normal. If your body is working properly, you should not be getting headaches.

2. Pain

If you have any kind of chronic pain such as back pain, joint pain, fibromyalgia, or any other kind of pain, this may be a sign of stress. People with chronic pain are usually drained at the end of the day. It takes a lot of energy to function with pain. Again, pain is common, but not normal. A normally functioning body should not be experiencing pain. Pain may be a sign of more serious auto-immune diseases as well.

3. Fatigue and Depression

We talked about being exhausted at the end of the day. Some folks have Chronic Fatigue Syndrome or Yuppie Flu. If you have a hard time finding the energy to get through the day or if you are exhausted when you get home in the afternoon or evenings, this could be a symptom of stress. Don't you want to address this symptom so that you have more energy for yourself and your family? Also, if you have feelings of depression or melancholy or if you lack motivation, this may be a symptom of stress.

4. Difficulty sleeping

Do you have difficulty falling asleep or do you wake up in the middle of the night and find that you can't go back to sleep? You are not alone. Usually ½ to ¾ of our program participants have trouble getting a good night's sleep. Are your sleep patterns all over the place? Do you only fall asleep from exhaustion? This could be a sign of stress. Keep in mind that the CIA uses sleep deprivation as torture. Lack of sleep can cause psychosis. At the very least lack of sleep makes you less efficient and can cause other health issues. According to sleep researcher, Matthew Walker lack of sleep is related to accelerated tumor growth, heart disease, constipation, diabetes, obesity, depression, anxiety, stomach ulcers, diminished cognitive performance, memory loss, dementia, Alzheimer's, and a weakened immune system.

Several of my clients have sleep apnea and require a CPAP (continuous positive airway pressure) machine in order to get a good night's sleep. They tell me that the difference in the way that they feel when they use their CPAP is like night and day. They feel so much better when they get a good night's sleep. They also tell me that when there is less stress in their lives, they are less dependent on their machine. They sleep better naturally.

5. Stomach problems

Acid stomach, Acid reflux, Chron's Disease, Irritable Bowel Syndrome, Ulcers. If your stomach isn't working as it should, if it is not performing its duty of processing and digesting food properly, it could be a sign of stress. When you are in fight or flight, your body removes the blood from your internal organs including the stomach. So if you eat while you are stressed, your stomach is unable to properly digest your food. And acid reducing medications only make things worse. Without the proper acid to digest your food, you don't get the nutrition you need. And when the body doesn't get the proper nutrition, it has to work that much harder. There is not enough fuel to do the things you need to do, and you are exhausted at the end of the day.

Did you know that many original onsets of Chron's Disease immediately follows a stressful episode in a person's life? Did you know that irritable bowel syndrome is greatly helped with stress management? Stress has been shown to make all these stomach issues worse. Recent studies have found a bacterial link to ulcers, but the studies also show that existing ulcers are more painful when the patient is experiencing emotional stress. You wolf down fast food and work through lunch in a mad race to get more done. Is it any wonder that your stomach rebels?

6. Irritability

I know. Tough guys never get irritable. But for those of you who do, for those of you who lose it when someone pulls out in front of you or a subordinate doesn't perform to your liking or someone cuts in front of you in line, this may be a physical sign of stress.

7. Problem turning off your mind

Have you ever gotten that song stuck in your head and couldn't get it out? Did you ever wake up in the middle of the night thinking about something and could not turn those thoughts off? This could be a physical sign of stress. At the very least it is a physical sign of being overwhelmed.

8. Sinus problems, allergies, and asthma

Many people suffer with these physical signs of stress. These are all auto-immune maladies. It is the body attacking itself. When you think about it, there is no good reason why the body should start pumping out histamines because of dust or pollen. These substances aren't dangerous to our bodies, but our bodies react as if they were. A friend of mine is an asthma specialist. He told me that there is one thing that has reduced emergency room visits from his patients. He gave them his cell phone number and told them to contact him any time of day or night. Just knowing that he is there for them reduces their anxiety and stress and therefore reduces their attacks that warrant a trip to the emergency room. If you have any of these auto-immune symptoms, you may be under stress.

9. Skin problems

Rashes, hives, shingles, outbreaks of psoriasis and eczema. Most of these episodes are brought about by stressful circumstances. If you experience these symptoms, you may be under too much stress. Healthy skin, our largest organ, is a good sign of overall health.

10. Diminished sex drive

This is a big issue for tough guys. It is a fact that the older we get, the less drive we have for sex. But stress can accelerate this process. Again, this may be common, but not normal. Healthy men should be able to have sex well into their sixties and perhaps even seventies. If you are experiencing this, you may be under too much stress.

11. High blood pressure and cholesterol

These are classic symptoms of stress. You can tell the stressed out guy with the red face who yells a lot. It's a cliché. He will likely have issues with blood pressure. It's even made it into our lexicon. We say, "Boy that sure raised my blood pressure." And stress raises bad cholesterol levels as well. There also may be a link between high stress and poor lifestyle habits such as diet and smoking, and these will also contribute to higher cholesterol.

12. Diminished immune response, frequent colds or flu

If you are sick often, you may be under too much stress. It also may be because of the adrenaline response to fight or flight. Whenever you let go and relax, over the weekend or going on vacation, your body gets sick. And your immune system is compromised, so you can't fight it off very well. If you get more than one or two colds per year, this is not normal.

So there you have it, twelve symptoms of stress. They are your body's way of telling you that something is wrong. It's trying to get your attention. It's like a light going on in the dashboard of your car. So you're traveling down the road and a light comes on. What do you do? Do you put a piece of tape over it? You hear a loud knocking coming from under the hood. Do you turn the radio up? No. You probably take your car into a mechanic to see what is wrong and get it fixed. But your body is giving you those warning signs and what are you doing about them? You are probably ignoring them or covering them up. Most of us treat the symptom, not the underlying cause, which is the stress itself. And most of us treat our cars better than we treat our bodies.

The drug companies have figured this all out. They not only have drugs for the diseases caused by stress, they have drugs that will alleviate all the symptoms of stress. For headaches and other kinds of pain, there are a wide variety of pain relievers and prescription drugs. The drug companies have recently come out with pills that treat combinations of these symptoms. They now have pain pills with a sleep aid that you can take at night. And in the morning, you can take a special pain pill for morning pain and stiffness.

For fatigue, there are prescription drugs and over the counter remedies galore. There are dozens of "energy" drinks such as Red Bull and 5 Hour Energy to give us a boost in energy, which is usually short lived and followed by a crash. For difficulty sleeping we have Ambien, Rozerem, and Lunesta, and a variety of over the counter sleep aids although the latest data is hard to find. In the US, 50-70 million people suffer from sleep issues.

For stomach problems, we have Nexium, Protonics, Prilosec, Prevacid, Pepcid, Zantac, Reglan, Carafate, and Aciphex, and several of these have been linked to various cancers. There are specific drugs for Chron's and irritable bowel, and a wide variety of over the counter antacids such as Rolaids, Maalox, Mylanta, Rennie, Pepto Bismol, and Tums.

I used to visit the shiny white first aid kit in the jobsite trailer to pop a couple of aspirin and antacids as a pre-emptive strike on my daily acid stomach and stress headache. For irritability we have a variety of antidepressants which even out our moods. Between 1988-1994 and 2005-2008, the use of antidepressants increased by 400% (National Center for Health Statistics). Frequent colds and flu are treated with thousands of over the counter cold medications.

There are dozens of drugs for sinus problems, allergies, and asthma. We treat most skin irritations with drugs as well. For diminished sex drive, we have Viagra and Cialis among others with shots of testosterone thrown in for good measure. There are dozens of drugs that treat high blood pressure and cholesterol, and now there is one that treats your high blood pressure and your high cholesterol at the same time.

Here is an interesting fact: our bodies need cholesterol to manufacture testosterone. When we take cholesterol lowering drugs, many times it lowers our cholesterol so that we aren't manufacturing as much testosterone. Guess what? That lowers our sex drive so that we need to take another drug.

In 2019, the sales of prescription drugs was estimated at $844 Billion (Statista). Most of these drugs treat the symptoms of stress, but they never address the underlying causes of the symptoms, which is the stress itself. We spend more than any nation on earth on healthcare, but we are one of the sickest nations on the planet. Don't get me wrong. I'm not demonizing drug companies or doctors. My niece would be dead without her daily doses of insulin. All I am saying is that doctors are trained to treat symptoms with poisons.

Most doctors do what they are trained to do, treat symptoms. They are not trained to look at the root causes. What do you think the symbol for doctors means? It is the Rod of Asclepius that has a snake wrapped around a staff. The snake represents the poisons that are given to patients in the correct amount to alleviate their suffering.

According to the journal ACS Chemical Neuroscience, in 2019, there were 4.38 Billion prescriptions filled in the US. That's over 12 prescriptions per year for every man, woman and child in the US. That's staggering! Many people I know who are in their fifties are on at least three or four different drugs treating symptoms like high blood pressure, high cholesterol, depression, sleep aids, and erectile dysfunction). And when one drug causes another symptom, most doctors just prescribe another drug to treat THAT symptom. And there is no way to test for drug interactions with every other drug. According to the Organization for Economic Cooperation and Development (OECD) our per capita spending on healthcare (which should be called sick care) in 2018 was over $10,000. No other country comes close. We are the sickest nation on the planet.

We live in this fix-it society. We are overworked, and we can't slow down. We don't get enough down time to stay healthy. We want a quick fix. We want to alleviate the symptoms so we can keep going. I remember in college when I was elated when they came out with Dayquil. Now I could take Nyquil at night and sleep, then take Dayquil all day to keep going, even when I was sick. Can I get a witness, tough guys?

So now we see it in black and white. We are stressed and our bodies have these symptoms. It's trying to tell us to pay attention, to take some action and do something about the underlying cause, which is our reaction to the stresses in our lives. So how do we do that?

How to deal with the stresses in your life: Recovery and Lifestyle Choices

If you don't take drugs to cover up symptoms and you want to address the underlying stress that is causing these symptoms, what do you do? The answer is simple, but not easy. You have to do all of those things that you know you are supposed to do to lead a healthy life. What are the simple things you can do to turn your health around?

1. Always eat breakfast

Many of the tough guys I work with don't eat breakfast at all. Breakfast for them is usually a cup of coffee grabbed on the run. If they do eat breakfast at all, it's usually a carbohydrate loaded breakfast sandwich that they have purchased in a fast food place or break truck. Either that or a sugar loaded donut or Danish. What happens when you don't eat breakfast? You're telling your body to shut down your metabolism because there may not be any food coming for a while. And when you eat those carbohydrates, your blood sugar spikes, which sets you up for a crash later in the morning. I'm sure you've had those mid-morning comas where you needed more sugar and a jolt of caffeine to keep going until lunch.

2. Eat five to six small meals per day

When you eat large meals, especially those loaded with carbohydrates, you spike your blood sugar. This is followed by a crash, and you must spike it again. Each time, your crash is lower and you need more sugar and caffeine to recover. By the end of the day, you are exhausted. But if you eat five to six small meals a day and make sure you include some protein with each meal, your blood sugar is more stable. Protein is a slower burning fuel. You get some fluctuations in blood sugar, but you don't get those highs and lows. This blood sugar stabilization gives you more even energy throughout your day and you aren't exhausted at the end of it. Eat lighter as the day goes on. The saying is "eat like a king in the morning, like a prince at noon, and like a peasant in the evening."

3. Eat foods as close to their natural state as possible

Nutrition is a huge issue in this country. Food companies have one mission: to get us to eat as much food as possible. This increases profits. They do this in a variety of ways. They advertise heavily. They offer incentives to eat more food and larger portions. They strip out all the nutrients through processing and then add back nutrients and call it "fortified".

Food companies have food scientists who use fat, salt, and sugar to create cheap, good tasting foods that people will buy and eat. When one ingredient gets a bad name, they substitute other ingredients to achieve the same result. For instance, when sugar became a "bad" ingredient, the scientists started substituting dextrin, maltodextrin, sucrose, dextrose and other sugars. Some of these ingredients have higher glucose indices than sugar. Those kinds of deceptive practices are leading us toward an obesity epidemic. It is also an epidemic of poor nutrition.

I believe that the food companies of today are like the tobacco companies in the 1950s. How many people do you know who have died from a disease related to smoking? Those numbers are high. And tobacco companies knew that cigarettes were bad for you. Do you think food companies know that these foods that are stripped of nutrition and filled with fat, sugar, and salt are bad for you? Of course they do. But they are doing everything within their power to get you to buy more and eat more food.

Nutrition is a key for good health, for proper energy, for proper cognitive function and proper emotional function. First Corinthians tells us that our body is a temple that houses the Holy Spirit. But most of us don't treat our bodies like temples. We treat them like trash bins, depositing garbage food that leaves us empty in many ways.

Minimize the processed foods that you eat. Eat organic and locally grown whenever you can, especially meat and dairy. If you can't buy organic fruits and vegetables, wash them thoroughly with a vegetable wash. Just put one tablespoon of lemon and two tablespoons of vinegar in a spray bottle and spray all your fruits and vegetables before you eat them.

Processed foods, frozen dinners, and other convenience foods are usually stripped of nutrients, are high in sodium and calories, and are generally not good fuel for your body. Read labels and avoid products with high amounts of sugar, sodium, and fat. As we said before, food companies have food scientists who create processed food using fat, sugar, and salt that tastes good and is cheap to make. If you want to be safe, shop on the perimeter of the grocery store and include meats, fruits, and vegetables in your diet.

Food companies are deceptive in their approach to selling food. They call these frozen food products things like Healthy Choice and Lean Cuisine and Weight Watcher's Smart Ones. When we go to McDonald's, we know what we are getting, but when we buy something called Healthy Choice, we assume that it is healthy to eat. I bought a Healthy Choice Chicken and Broccoli Alfredo meal. The front of the package said "Good Food, Good Life" and "Healthy Choice prepares meals that meet the highest quality and nutritional standards," so what do you think would be in this delightful, healthy, nutritious meal? Look:

Ingredients: Vegetables with Water (Peas, Broccoli, Carrots, Water), Water, Cooked Enriched Fettuccini (Water, Durum Semolina [Enriched with Niacinamide, Ferrous Sulfate (Iron), Thiamine Mononitrate, Riboflavin, Folic Acid], Egg Whites), White Meat Chicken with Binders (White Meat Chicken, Water, Modified Food Starch, Isolated Soy Protein, Rendered Chicken Fat, Dextrose, Maltodextrin, Salt, Chicken Flavor [Yeast Extract, Maltodextrin, Chicken Flavor (Contains Xanthan Gum, Disodium Inosinate and Disodium Guanylate), Salt, Rendered Chicken Fat, Citric Acid, Natural Flavor], Soy Lecithin [Nonfat Milk, Soy Lecithin, Partially Hydrogenated Soybean Oil], Sodium Tripolyphosphate, Xanthan Gum, Flavoring), Cherries, Brown Sugar, Vanilla Crunch (Bleached Wheat Flour, Sugar, Palm Oil, Salt, Soy Lecithin, Natural and Artificial Flavors, Baking Soda), Parmesan Cheese (Part-Skim Milk, Cheese Culture, Salt, Enzymes), Cherry Juice (Contains Malic Acid), Contains 2% or Less of the Following: Alfredo Sauce Mix (Cream, Cheese Blend [Cheddar, Parmesan, Blue (Pasteurized Milk, Salt, Culture, Enzymes)], Dried Whey, Butter [Cream, Salt], Nonfat Dry Milk, Modified Cornstarch, Buttermilk, Flavor, Maltodextrin, Salt, Cultured Whey, Wheat Flour, Disodium Phosphate, Lecithin, Partially Hydrogenated Soybean Oil, Lactic Acid, Citric Acid, Tocopherol, Ascorbyl Palmitate, Ascorbic Acid), Modified Food Starch, Soybean Oil, Alfredo Cheese Blend (Parmesan, Cheddar, and Romano Cheeses [Pasteurized Cow's Milk, Cultures, Salt, Enzymes], Water, Nonfat Dry Milk, Enzymes, Disodium Phosphate, Salt, Trisodium Citrate), Whey Protein Concentrate, Salt, Chicken Broth Powder (Maltodextrin, Chicken Broth, Salt and Flavors), Garlic Powder, Onion Powder, Locust Bean Gum, Disodium Phosphate, Mono- and Diglycerides and Datem (Emulsifier), Almond Extract (Almond Oil and Other Natural Ingredients, Water and Alcohol), Spice, Alfredo Seasoning (Maltodextrin, Dextrin).

Doesn't that make you hungry? This food product is full of hidden sugars, transfats, artificial colors and flavors, and chemicals. Start reading labels and make better choices. A pretty good rule of thumb is if you can't pronounce it, you probably shouldn't eat it. That goes for hygiene products as well. Make sure your soaps, shampoos, conditioners, shaving creams, and lotions have as few chemicals as possible. These chemicals are absorbed through your skin and must be eliminated as toxins through your liver.

4. Minimize Fast Food and Eating Out

Look at the following list: college, computers, software, cars, movies, books, magazines, newspapers, music and videos. Guess what we spend more on than all these things combined? The answer: Fast food. I like fast food. I really do. But I minimize my intake of fast food and use it as a treat occasionally. Fast food tastes good. It's comfort food. I remember in college my favorite hangover meal was a cheeseburger, fries, and a coke. If you have any trouble giving up fast food, watch the films Fast Food Nation or Super Size Me. They are eye openers.

If you must eat fast food, do it in moderation. Order a salad and a small cheeseburger instead of a Super-Sized Quarter Pounder with Cheese Meal. If you must eat out, order things that are minimally processed and nutritious. Ask the chef for healthy alternatives. Probably the best meal to eat out is sushi. It is minimally processed and contains dense nutrition. You need carbohydrates to maintain serotonin and the even mood it produces. But don't overdo the carbohydrates and always include some protein. Keep bars handy with a good protein/carbohydrate balance. And if you eat carbohydrates, make them complex carbohydrates, not refined sugar. Eat more fruit and whole grains. Avoid processed, carbohydrate loaded snacks, which are mostly just empty calories.

5. Reduce simple sugars

Avoid processed sugars and sweets altogether and if you must have them, minimize the intake. Americans eat 165 pounds of sugar per year (Department of Health and Human Services). Sugar has been linked to heart disease and has been shown to decrease your immune response. It has been shown to excite the same centers of the brain as cocaine, It is highly addictive. It's not a good thing to eat too much. Skip dessert, and if you need something sweet, go for the fruit instead. Also, keep an eye on starches like pasta, rice, and potatoes. These starches will convert directly to sugar in your body.

Be on the lookout for sugars in ingredients in all the foods you eat. High fructose corn syrup is a common sweetener and has been used to induce diabetes in laboratory rats. Anything ending in "ose" is a sugar: fructose, sucrose, lactose, dextrose. Food companies have caught onto this sugar aversion. They now have many names for sugars and many substitutes for sugar. We mentioned maltodextrin before. It is a common sweetener and has a 50% higher glycemic index than sugar. It's WORSE than sugar. A participant brought us a bag of candy he bought for his kids. On the front of the package in large letters was SUGAR FREE! The first ingredient was maltodextrin.

Also avoid these sugar substitutes like sugar alcohols (maltitol, erythritol, sorbitol, xylitol). The jury is still out on these and they can cause bowel issues like cramping and diarrhea. Also avoid artificial sweeteners like aspartame. Aspartame has been linked to several health issues such as memory loss and saccharin is another artificial sweetener that may not be the best choice.

There are some natural alternatives to sugar and these other sweeteners. Agave has a lower glycemic index than most sweeteners. Stevia is a plant with a glycemic index of zero. We grow it in our garden and use it to sweeten our tea. Be aware that some stevia products also contain erythritol. Look at the label and make sure it just says "stevia".

Of course, honey, molasses, and maple syrup and more natural forms of sweeteners, but beware. Although they are probably better for you than some of these other sweeteners, they can still raise your glycemic index. Be educated and read labels. Don't get fooled by the food companies.

6. Stay hydrated

Drink plenty of water, filtered if possible. Our bodies are around 70% water. We can go approximately 70 days without eating food, but without water, we die within a week or two. Everyone needs different amounts of water, but the general rule of thumb is to drink half your weight in ounces per day. Water keeps things moving in your digestive track, it lubricates things, it keeps your brain functioning properly, it gets rid of toxins in your body. It keeps your skin, the largest organ in your body, healthy.

Did you know that headache is one of the first signs of dehydration? If you drink lots of water, it can also cut down on what you are eating because you will feel full. Don't drink water or other liquids while you are eating. Wait until you are finished with your meal prior to drinking and only drink a few ounces. Drink between meals if you can. This helps with your digestion. When you drink too much during a meal, you dilute the stomach acids that are vital for the first stages of digestion.

7. Use caffeine, nicotine, and alcohol in moderation or not at all

If you can cut out nicotine altogether, that's probably best. But if you can't, cut down. Caffeine is like a whip on your nervous system. All that coffee and all those Red Bulls and 5-Hour Energy Drinks will keep you going, but there are consequences. There is a moment of reckoning where everything crashes. I love my coffee in the morning, so what we've done is gradually made the beans ½ decaffeinated and ½ caffeinated. This way, I can drink more coffee without the guilt. And I change to decaf or herbal tea in the afternoon. Some studies show that an occasional alcoholic drink can be good for you. But don't overdo it. A six-pack every evening is probably not a good way to deal with the stresses of life.

8. Exercise

What if I told you there was a secret, ancient miracle remedy that has been proven to be effective in reducing pain from arthritis, slowing the progression of dementia, reducing anxiety and depression, decreasing hip fractures and reducing the progression of diabetes. It is the number one treatment for fatigue and is guaranteed to improve your quality of life. What is this miracle remedy? Exercise!

I know, tough guy. This is a difficult one, but it is essential for good health and for dealing with stress. Don't over-commit. The first thing to do is to find an exercise that you love. If you do something that you hate, you will likely not do it on a regular basis. Yoga is a great exercise. So is swimming. Walking is also good. And this is something you can do with the family. Start slowly. Even ten minutes of walking or yoga a few times per week will yield results. Find an exercise partner. You can hold each other accountable and make sure each of you sticks to the commitment.

9. Quiet Your Mind

I cannot stress this one enough. Build in quiet time for yourself each day. Peter Senge says that everyone pursuing personal mastery practices some form of meditation each day. You must have down time. You can call it reflection time, pondering time, prayer time, meditation time, personal time, quiet time, vision time, whatever. And it doesn't have to be long. It can be ten minutes a day before the family gets up or ten minutes after they've gone to bed. Maybe you can find time to get away during the day and have that quiet time. Find what works for you. Listen to some nice music without any lyrics in order to calm your mind. Take a walk. On your commute, turn off talk radio and reflect. If you could only commit to one thing, this is it. Quiet your mind every day.

10. Seek rest and recovery every 90 to 120 minutes

"Doing nothing is very hard to do. You never know when you are done." Leslie Nielsen

This is a tough thing for most tough guys. It's hard to stop and take a break. You want to push and push until it all gets done. But it's never done, is it? You will be much more productive if you will learn to stop and take a break and build in recovery activity every 1-1/2 to 2 hours. It doesn't have to be much. It could be some deep breathing or a walk or listening to music. Did you know that working while you are stressed and tired increases your problem solving time by up to 500%?

We do an exercise in our stress management class where half the room holds out a full soda can. These are the tough guys. They can take it. The soda can represents stress. And it's not much. They must hold the can out continuously. The other half of the room holds out their can, but they are the Zen masters. They are wise and know to take breaks. I give them short breaks where they can put the can down on the table. Then they pick them up again. After about five minutes, the tough guys are starting to strain. That little can of stress is starting to get heavy. I ask the Zen master group how long they could do this. They reply, "All day long." I then ask the tough guys how long they can do this. Many of them reply, "All day long." But they know it's not true. How many times have you pushed through your fatigue and completed something only to have to redo it the next day? Take breaks, tough guys, and get a lot more done. Check out the body battery inventory at the end of the book so that you can create your stress/recovery plan.

11. Get the Sleep You Need

a. Everyone needs different amounts of sleep and everyone has different sleep patterns. Eight hours is a good rule of thumb. If you have trouble with sleep, you can do the following from Matthew Walker's *Why We Sleep* to help you get a better night's sleep:

b. Sleep regular hours if possible. Go to bed and wake up within ½ hour either way each day.

c. Lower the temperature in your bedroom. 65 degrees F or cooler is optimal.

d. Sleep in the dark. No night lights.

e. Get rid of electronics and things that make noise. Use earplugs and a sleep mask if necessary.

f. Don't drink before bed and be sure to use the bathroom before bed.

g. Eat a high protein snack and a piece of fruit a few hours before bed.

h. Take a hot bath or sauna before bed.

i. Don't watch TV before bed.

j. Read something inspirational before bed.

k. Listen to relaxation music or sleep meditations before bed.

l. Meditate before bed.

m. Do yoga before bed. There are poses that are conducive to sleep and relaxation.

n. Write in a journal. Get all those random thoughts out of your head so they don't enter at 3 am.

o. Avoid alcohol, caffeine, and any foods that don't agree with you.

p. Take melatonin before bed (short term only).

r. Avoid prescription sleep drugs at all cost. They are highly addictive and interfere with your natural circadian rhythms.

s. Naps can recharge. There was a recent study in Greece that showed that naps significantly reduced the chance of heart attacks. I used to go out to my car during lunch and grab a quick, 10 minute power nap. It made my afternoon productive.

t. When I was working for a contractor, I gave them the suggestion to put in a nap or quiet room, but the idea was ridiculed. I learned recently that Skender in Chicago has put in quiet rooms. I feel like it is a personal victory. But the more we learn about naps, the more we know that naps could really be beneficial for us as individuals and for companies. Are your tough guy instincts kicking in? Do you think it's wimpy to want to take a nap? Keep thinking that way. I'm sure you can take some good naps while you are recovering from your heart attack.

12. Mindfulness

There is a way of approaching life called mindfulness. I remember seeing a cartoon in the New Yorker. Two guys are at a bar and one turns to the other and says, "Do you dwell on the wasted years behind you or the terrifying years ahead?" It's so true. Think about it. Most of our stress comes from dwelling on the past or worrying about the future. If we are completely in the moment, in the present, mindful of everything going on around us, we experience less stress. This is empirically true. There is a researcher named Jon Kabat Zinn who studies mindfulness and the effect it has on the body.

Zinn did a study with two groups of researchers. One group was taught mindfulness techniques and learned to be fully in the moment without judgment. They were also taught proper breathing techniques. The other group did their usual work in their usual way. All measures of stress both physical and emotional showed much less stress in the group that practiced mindfulness. They had lower blood pressure, lower cortisol production, and increased DHEA, the youth hormone. It's a simple thing, but quite frankly, not easy. The fast pace of life and work causes us to get caught up in the race, and we lose the present moments.

I recommend that you start with being mindful during your meals. Fully experience your meals with all your senses. Slow down, tiger. Take your time. Chew each bite. Fully smell and taste the food. Be fully present in that moment. Then you can build on this practice and let it flow into other areas of your life.

13. Minimize your exposure to media, violent images, and news

A lot of tough guys watch a lot of news, listen to a lot of talk radio, and are glued to the media. The media usually focuses on creating fear, which increases our stress levels. It's the old garbage in/garbage out theory. Minimize your exposure to those fearful and violent images, minimize the violent video games, adrenaline pumping movies, and violent stories. Stop checking the stock market ten times a day. This will decrease your stress and increase your satisfaction. Take a media break for a week and see how differently you feel. Then, you can build in media free days or weekends.

14. Take your vacations and holidays

Did you know that the USA is the only industrialized nation on earth without a paid leave law? Employers are not legally responsible to provide paid vacations to their employees. They only do it because they feel they must in order to attract and maintain employees. In China, if you work at the McDonald's, you get a minimum three weeks of paid vacation guaranteed by the government. Americans very rarely take the full two or three weeks. And when we do, we are constantly checking our emails and answering our phones. That is not a vacation. Most of us take these days off in increments of three or four days. The time we take off is in long weekends. I know, tough guy, you don't need a vacation. Many folks I work with brag that they haven't had a vacation in ten years. But what is the cost? In one study, taking a yearly vacation reduced the risk of heart attack by 30% in men and 50% in women.

European countries have anywhere from 18 to 32 days of vacation and legal holidays. Some people I know have nine weeks of paid vacation. In the US, we have around 16 days on average. The whole country of

Sweden takes three weeks off during the summer. If you lived in Sweden, you would know why. They have long, dark, cold winters, and the summer is a time of celebration. The Swedes tell me that they need the three weeks because the first week, they are still thinking about work. The second week is a week of total decompression. The third week, they are thinking about all the things at work that they will have to do when they return.

If you want to live a long, healthy life, you must build in recovery. Vacation and time off is a way to do that. Be sure to take your vacation. Don't work every weekend. Use it as an opportunity to train people underneath you. I know this will come as a shock, but when you are gone, work goes on pretty much the same. The earth doesn't stop revolving on its axis. If you use this vacation time to develop people underneath you, you will also develop the skill of delegation, which is essential to great time management.

15. Breathing, meditation, and yoga

We talked about being able to go for months without food and weeks without water. But you can only go for a minute or two without breathing. Breath is life. And, as adults, I think that most of us have forgotten how to properly breathe. Proper breathing is essential for good stress management. Put one hand on your upper chest and one hand below your belly button and take a deep, deep breath. Which hand moved the most? If it was the chest hand, then you have become a chest breather. That is not a natural way to breathe.

Look at a baby or an animal. Watch how they breathe. It's as if there whole body moves during inhalation and exhalation. As adults, we wear tight clothes, pull our belts tight, and hold our guts in. We even resort to "slimming" tee shirts, girdles, control top panty hose, and "slimming" pants. But what is that doing to your breathing? You probably only use the top 25% to 30% of your lungs. This reduces the oxygen in your body. It is estimated that most of the toxins removed from the body on a cellular level are expelled through carbon dioxide on your exhalation breath. Also, remember the old fight or flight response and what happens to your breathing? It gets shallow. What you are telling your body by breathing that way is that there is a lion nearby. Your body starts pumping out cortisol and adrenaline.

In our classes, we teach full, diaphragmatic breathing. Take a deep breath and fill the bottom part of your lungs first. Your lower belly should rise as you breathe. Then work your way up and top off your lungs by filling your entire lungs with air. Then reverse that process. Deep breathing does all kinds of wonderful things in your body. It initiates the relaxation response, lowers your heart rate and your blood pressure. It oxygenates your brain. It makes your body function better. It reduces your stress.

There is a whole practice that involves breathing and energy called Pranayama. It takes this breathing practice to the next level. This technique is thousands of years old, but Navy Seals have adopted it and in the West, we call it box breathing. When a Navy Seal is storming a compound, he must keep his nervous system relaxed, heart rate and respiration rate down and blood pressure and adrenaline and cortisol low. He doesn't want his body to go into fight or flight. It's a very simple technique. Breath in for a count of four, hold for a count of four, breath out for a count of six and hold the exhale for two, then repeat for three to five minutes. Try it and see how you feel.

One other breathing technique called alternate nostril breathing, is a simple way to calm the mind and nervous system. Put your index and second finger on your "third eye" between your eyes. Your thumb will be on one side of your nose and your third and fourth finger will be on the other side. Close the left side of your nose and breathe in for eight counts, hold for eight counts, then breathe out on the same side for eight counts. Then close off the right nostril and repeat. Breathe in for eight, hold for eight, breathe out on the same side for eight. Switch back to the first side and alternate sides. Continue for three to five minutes. See how you feel.

If you want to take this relaxation response one step further, I highly encourage you to give meditation a try. Meditation is like training your brain. Think of it as conscious sleep. You get all the benefits of sleep such as shutting down your mind and resting, but you are conscious the entire time. For those who get thoughts or songs stuck in your head and you can't get them out or wake up in the middle of the night and can't go back to sleep because you can't turn off your mind, meditation can really help. These runaway thoughts indicate that your brain is out of control. It's like a spoiled child, vying for attention. It doesn't have discipline. What if I told you that you can train your brain just like you train your body and control those thoughts?

That's where meditation comes in. And it's very simple. But it takes practice. In fact, that's what they call it, the practice of meditation. Try this simple meditation practice and see what you think. If this doesn't work for you, I encourage you to try different kinds of meditation because everyone reacts differently to these different techniques. Some people are highly visual, others aural, others are experiential. See what works best for you.

Sit in a comfortable position or lie on your back and start breathing deeply. Don't try to control your breath. Just take deep, natural, diaphragmatic breaths. Breathe in and when you breathe out, think the number one in your mind. Then breathe in and when you breathe out, think the number two. Then breathe in and breathe out and think the number three. Then breathe in and breathe out and think the number four. Then start the process over beginning with number one. Do this for three to five minutes. Set a timer if you must.

What you will notice is that other thoughts will enter your mind and occupy your brain. This is your spoiled child, and you must discipline him. Don't get upset or angry about these thoughts, just politely dismiss them and go back to your breathing and counting. You will find that, at first, you will have many thoughts trying to invade your brain and take over. The yogis call this chattering monkey brain. But, over time, those thoughts will diminish, you will be in control, and you will be able to focus. This will help you when you need to focus on a task at hand or calm your thoughts in order to sleep. There is also a great visual meditation called candle concentration. You stare at a candle for three minutes, then lightly place the palms of your hands over your closed eyes. Most of you, but not all of you, will see the negative image of the flame, much like a flashbulb ghost. Keep that image for as long as you can. You will find that it will fade and float away, but your concentration will keep bringing it back.

We teach meditation by focusing on sound as well. You can breathe and listen to a nature sound or a mantra. Focus entirely on the sound and dismiss the thoughts that float through your mind. Some people love this sound meditation and prefer it over the others.

The final meditation we teach is a guided meditation. You can purchase my guided meditation mp3 from www.brentdarnell.com. We have three music tracks and four guided meditations and visualizations. There is also a progressive relaxation where you start at your feet and work your way up your body relaxing each part as you go. For some people, these guided meditations are the best form of meditation. There are thousands of these out there. Explore them. Find one that works for you.

The more you meditate, the easier it comes to you. You will find yourself better able to focus and better able to shut off endless loops of thought. After you have gained some mastery, the next time you wake up at 1:00 in the morning and can't shut your brain off, try one of these meditation techniques. It really works once you have developed the discipline. It allows you to be more focused. This will make you more productive and efficient.

But that's not all. Meditation affects you on a much deeper level. Harvard Medical School has been studying this phenomenon for a while and they have now found that the "physiologic state of deep rest induced by practices such as meditation, yoga, deep breathing and prayer—produces immediate changes in the expression of genes involved in immune function, energy metabolism, and insulin secretion." This means that regular mediation practice helps to increase your immunity, increase your metabolism, and decrease inflammation (the source of many diseases)." Wow!

We have finger-like projections on our chromosomes called telomeres. When we age, our telomeres shrink. A regular deep rest practice like meditation lengthens our telomeres, so it reverses the aging process!

For many of these programs, we also do yoga. Now I'll admit that yoga isn't for everyone. But I highly recommend that you try it. Almost half of the participants in my classes who try yoga continue to do it. Why? Because it is so beneficial. I have been practicing yoga since 1977. I am a certified yoga instructor and use many of these techniques in our leadership programs.

Yoga increases lung capacity, cardiovascular function, strength, and flexibility. It reduces stress and allows your body to recover. It's low impact. It decreases injuries and joint issues. It strengthens your back. You don't need any special equipment. You can do it anywhere, even when you travel. You can purchase your own yoga mat if you want. I have purchased something called Yoga Paws and take them with me when I travel. Instead of taking a whole yoga mat, I take Yoga Paws instead. You wear them on your hands and feet, and the material is a non- slip, padded material, so you can do yoga on just about any surface without slipping. This is especially helpful in Europe where most of the floors are wood or tile.

There are a few simple forms of yoga that can be quite beneficial. There are several websites on desk yoga that will give you basic yoga moves that you can do at your desk each day. There is a very simple series of yoga moves called the Sun Salutation. Again, a simple Google search can show you these moves. The Sun Salutation stretches every muscle in your body and makes you feel great. A few rounds of Sun Salutations in the morning will make your day much better and you will have more energy at the end of the day. And it only takes a few minutes.

16. The Three-Minute De-Stressor

We teach a quick, three-minute de-stressor, which is very effective. Here are the steps:

a. Check in with how you are breathing. Is your breathing shallow? Can you help yourself by taking a few deep, diaphragmatic breaths?

b. Smile. It creates all kinds of positive, physiological changes immediately.

c. Figure out what you are thinking. Are there thoughts that trigger these stressful episodes? If so, deal with those thoughts or minimize them.

d. Strike a Power Pose for two minutes (see Amy Cuddy's Ted Talk).

e. Place the tip of your tongue on the gums just behind your front teeth. Martial artists use this technique to break boards. This is an acupuncture point that allows for energy to flow through your body.

f. Count your blessings. Think of all the things you are thankful for. It's impossible to be thankful and stressed at the same time.

Things that contribute to your exhaustion at the end of the day

Nervous habits and useless movements such as tapping your feet or fingers, chewing gum or tobacco, chewing your fingernails, moving without purpose, clenching your jaws.

Holding muscles in tension. In yoga and meditation, we teach participants how to do a body inventory. They start at their feet and work up their bodies, finding areas where they are holding tension. Then they give a gentle command to those areas to relax. It takes energy to hold a muscle in tension. That drains your body battery. I see many tough guys with their shoulders up around their ears by the end of the day. No wonder they are exhausted.

Endless loops of useless thought. It takes energy to think. And when you are thinking about non-productive thoughts and those thoughts that continue to go over and over in your mind, you are wasting energy. Meditation techniques will help you focus your thoughts, be more productive, and use less energy.

Being around "energy vampires." My friend, Jon Gordon, wrote a book called The Energy Bus. In it, he talks about energy vampires. You know who they are. Those are the people who suck the life force right out of your body. When you leave them, you feel exhausted. They are feeding on your energy. Minimize your time with these people. And if you can't do that, find ways to recover your energy either before or after your encounters with them.

Not building in recovery activities and time. You must learn to take breaks and recover. Eat something, drink something, change channels mentally, get up and walk around, or listen to music. Exercise, meditate or do pranayama. If you can develop a habit of doing this, you will be much less tired at the end of the day.

Not having proper nutrition. Eating foods that are nutrition dense will make you perform better mentally and physically. Good nutrition throughout your day will maintain even blood sugar levels and feed your brain and body with everything it needs to function at its best.

Think of your body as a battery. It's charged up in the morning, but by the end of the day, you are depleted. The first thing is find ways to recharge your battery throughout the day. Build in recovery time and activities. Take breaks. Restore yourself. Keep an eye on the things

that are depleting your battery. If you are doing activities that are robbing your energy, but not allowing you to be productive, that is a problem. Take the Body Battery Inventory in the Appendix to see how your body is doing regarding dischargers and rechargers.

Sitting is the new smoking.

According to the Mayo Clinic, "Research has linked sitting for long periods of time with a number of health concerns. They include obesity and a cluster of conditions — increased blood pressure, high blood sugar, excess body fat around the waist and abnormal cholesterol levels — that make up metabolic syndrome. Too much sitting overall and prolonged periods of sitting also seem to increase the risk of death from cardiovascular disease and cancer.

During your breaks every 90 to 120 minutes, be sure to stand and move. Get a standing desk and alternate standing and sitting all day. Do some desk yoga (GTS) and stretch throughout your day.

Doing it all when you get busy

a. Exercise whenever you can. Most hotels have gyms, but you should have an exercise you can do anywhere. A few exercise options are yoga, walking and working out with bands. These band workouts are easy to do and you can shove bands in your suitcase. They travel well.

b. Always wear good shoes and comfortable clothing.

   When you are walking through airports and traveling, it is important to be comfortable so that you can relax. A good pair of shoes makes a huge difference in the energy you expend while walking. Make sure your foot is supported and the shoes feel good on your feet.

c. Walk as much as you can. Park far away, walk instead of taking the train to the concourse when possible. If you have time, walk up and down the concourse prior to your flight. Take stairs wherever you can and find ways to walk during your trip. When you get to the hotel, instead of turning on the television or eating, take a nice walk.

d. Invest in good luggage. I see people all the time wearing heavy garment bags on one shoulder and a heavy computer bag on the other. This will wear you out quickly. Even backpacks, which evenly distribute the weight, can become heavy during travel. Find luggage that bears no weight on you. The best are those four-wheeled jobs that glide along with very little effort. Second to that are the two-wheeled kind. Avoid those pieces of luggage on two wheels that you have to lift off the ground. They become heavy very quickly. You would be amazed at how much energy you expend on poor luggage. Invest in good luggage and feel better at the end of your trip.

e. Eat the best food possible. Always carry food with you if possible. Take some good bars with some protein, some good fruit or nuts or other healthy snack. Most plane food is carbohydrate loaded. Make sure you have some protein to mix with it. Probably the best choice if you must eat out is sushi. It has the least amount of processing. If you must eat fast food, eat a salad and a small burger or sandwich instead of the Quarter Pounder with Cheese Supersize Meal.

f. Stay hydrated. Drink plenty of water and avoid caffeine, especially when you are on airplanes. When you arrive, take a quick shower to rehydrate your skin.

18. Live to be 100!

Do you want to live a healthy life until you are 100 years old? It's possible. There was a study done of people all over the world who lived to be 100 or more. They looked at all kinds of factors such as diet, exercise, genetics, water sources, etc. What they found out is that no matter the type of diet or the lifestyle, there were three things in common: They ate 1/3 of the calories that we eat. They ate around 1,200 calories a day. The average American eats 3,600 calories per day. The second thing is that they all had family or community support. They were not isolated. They interacted with people on a daily basis. And the third thing was that they were thankful each day. They counted their blessings and had spiritual component to their lives. It is physiologically impossible to be stressed and thankful at the same time. Take note tough guys. If you want to live to be 100, follow this recipe.

19. Involve the Entire Family

Several participants have brought their whole family in on the process of being better and getting healthier in something they call the eight-week family makeover. The family agrees on the things they are trying to accomplish together as a family such as exercising more, watching less television, playing less video games, eating healthier meals, losing weight, quitting bad habits, etc. The family keeps a log for each member on how they have done on these agreed upon initiatives. There can be prizes for the family members who accomplish the most. This is a great way for the family to support each other in this healthy endeavor. And most of the time, these habits last beyond the eight weeks.

20. Ignoring stress has its consequences

I worked with a person who was very driven, a typical type "A" personality in his mid-thirties. He was placed as a project manager on a very difficult project. There was a huge penalty for not finishing the project on time, and there was a lot of pressure. My friend worked ungodly hours for months on end. Then, one day, he started developing something called cluster headaches. These headaches are some of the worst kind that you can get. The people who experience them say it's like having a hot poker thrust through your eye. Drugs are not very effective. They call them cluster headaches because they come on like clockwork.

My friend needed to keep working, so he went to the doctor to find some relief. He never thought about slowing down his work schedule or taking some time off. The doctor prescribed Prednisone, a steroid. He would start off with a large dose, then gradually diminish the dose each day. This, the doctor said, would get rid of the headaches. My friend took the first dose and went to bed. The next day, he had severe pain in his hip joints. He couldn't get out of bed. He went to the hospital and was diagnosed with aseptic necrosis in his hip joints, which meant that the hip bone was dead. He was now faced with hip replacement surgery and the possibility of being disabled.

He has learned to cope with this situation. He tried some vascular surgery to help the bone, but it was not successful. He is now in constant pain. The question that keeps going over and over in my mind is what if he had stopped working and addressed his stress levels? Would this have even happened to him? I can't say. But I do know that health issues for men in their forties and fifties can be life altering. How many people do you know that are having heart attacks and the onset of diseases like diabetes and arthritis? Don't be a victim. Take responsibility for your health right now. This very moment. Don't let your tough guy attitudes lead you to an early grave. Pay attention or face some pretty dire consequences. And if you aren't willing to do it for you, then do it for your family. They probably want you around for a long time.

CHAPTER 6
Time Management Using Lean Principles

"I kept wanting you to give me the silver magic silver bullet so that I could manage my time better. Then, I realized that the magic silver bullet was me."

~ **John W.** *Project Superintendent*

Time management has nothing to do with managing your time. It's about managing yourself, your values and your energy. Do you spend time and energy on the things you don't value? The likely answer is yes. This chapter is devoted to finding those tasks and closely examining them with lean in mind. Lean is a production system used by manufacturers and now the construction industry to streamline processes and eliminate waste. When lean concepts are employed, you are constantly asking if there is a better way to do something. You get rid of the waste and ask yourself if it adds value or not. If it doesn't it can be modified or eliminated.

Because I work with a lot of construction folks, we take the same approach as creating a schedule for a project. There are simple steps:

a. When is the end?

The Big Picture

When is the project to be completed? What is the end date? You must know when the client expects his building. It's no different with your life. What is your end date? When will you be done? By "done", I mean dead. Now none of us know exactly when we're going to die, but we can look at statistics and get close. Think about it. You have around 4,000 weeks on this planet. You probably have around 2,000 left. What are you going to do with those 2,000 weeks? One other way to look at this is to put a 25' tape on the ground to around 80 inches. The average lifespan is around 80. Put a post it by your age and see if there is more tape to the left or to the right.

b. Lay out the mission.

What are your general philosophies for your project (your life)? Many projects write down their mission or general plan for the project. They go something like this: "Our mission is to build a quality project on time, within the budget, with zero accidents and zero defects." So what should go in your mission statement? I'll share mine with you: "To make the world a better place. To make a positive difference in people's lives the world over and help them to develop their potential in order to change their lives for the better. To work until I'm 90 and grow old gracefully alongside my wife. To create massive wealth and give most of it back to family, friends, my community, and the world."

c. Set your milestones.

What are your milestones? What are the major things you want to do or accomplish before you die? Write these milestones down. It might be specific goals or general things. Pay for the kids' college, learn a language, become a great mom or dad or wife or husband, build a mountain home, attend church more, start another career, travel more, work less. What are those milestones? Be sure to write them down. Make a list. Keep in mind all the different hats that you wear in life and you may have some milestone goals for each of those.

d. Make a schedule.

Once you have all this preliminary work done, you must start on your actual schedule. You have things that you want to accomplish. You have an end date. Now what activities must you schedule to attain all your goals? Contractors do this very practically. If they have 1,000 pieces of precast to set in 100 days, they know they must set 10 pieces per day to reach that goal. If you want to learn a language, you must schedule a class or time to work through language tapes. If you want to pay for your kids' college, you must make a budget and set aside money each month. If you want to become a better wife, you must schedule dates and time with your husband. Those things don't just happen. You must schedule activities that propel you toward those goals.

Daily schedules don't work as well for the day-to-day work things that pop up all day long. This time management method simply does not work any longer. But schedule the things that are important to you. Schedule the things that you value. In addition, schedule your week like a four-day workweek. Don't schedule anything on Fridays unless you are forced into it. This may not work for some weeks, but for most weeks, this is probably feasible. That way, you can use Fridays as your overflow day, your catch-up day, so that just maybe you will avoid coming in on some Saturdays. This is a time management principle known as Parkinson's Rule. You tend to use all the time you have allotted to complete tasks.

e. Work your plan.

Once you have your schedule, you must work your plan. This takes discipline and accountability. Find that accountability in your spouse a good friend, or a support group. However, you need to do it, do it. Without the accountability, this is all for naught. Make this happen. Stephen Pressfield says, "Never forget: This very moment, we can change our lives. There never was a moment, and never will be, when we are without the power to alter our destiny. This second, we can turn the tables on resistance. This second, we can sit down and do our work."

Steps to better manage your life and work

1. Find out how you are spending your time right now.

Do a time log for a week (see Appendix). How do you spend a typical week? Write down everything you do and how you are spending every minute of every day for a week. Don't just put "work" or "home". Write down exactly what you were doing in as much detail as possible. At the end of the week, review how you are spending your time. Are you doing the activities that are propelling you toward your goals? Are you spending time on the things you value? Or are you doing a lot of activities that are wasting a lot of your time? When I did this, it was a real eye opener. I have my own business, and when I did my time log, I found out I was spending 60% of my time doing administrative crap. I was spending most of my time doing things that made me no money. So the next day, I hired an administrative assistant and gave her all of that stuff to do. It's made a tremendous difference.

My wife and I now say, "If it doesn't bring us joy or make us money, we will get someone else to do it." We are really into outsourcing our lives. We outsource work tasks, the cleaning of the house and the maintenance of the yard. The other day, she asked me to order some glass so that she could reframe a picture. I dropped the picture off and told the frame shop to do it.

2. The four immutable rules of time management.

Note, some of these concepts are from David Allen's book, Getting Things Done, which I highly recommend.

a. Empty your head. Get everything out of your head and onto pieces of paper. Use one piece of paper for each thing. When I did this, I had a stack of papers a foot high. Martial artists use this concept. They empty their mind and focus so that they are ready for anything. When you have a million things on your mind, you can't have good time management.

We have made this process easier with our Time Management Worksheet in the Appendix. Instead of stack of papers, you dump everything onto an Excel spread sheet. The first step is to do a total mind dump and literally list EVERYTHING YOU DO on the sheet. I mean everything! Everything from the time you wake up in the morning to the time you go to bed at night. Everything you do daily, weekly, monthly, annually. Anything that takes mental or physical energy should be listed from eating breakfast to taking out the garbage to paying bills to filing taxes to making dinner to buying Holiday gifts to commuting. I MEAN EVERYTHING! Then follow the instructions and work through this giant list. There should be hundreds and perhaps thousands of items that you can examine to see if you can look at it in a different way. You ask yourself, should I do it (if it takes a small amount of time), delegate it, defer it, or redefine it?

The questions continually asked when reviewing this list are:

Does it focus on the people in your life? Does it bring you joy? Does it eliminate waste? Does it embrace continual improvement? Does it take energy, give you energy, or is it neutral? Does it add value to your life and work?

Some Examples: I used to take the garbage out every week. But it's a huge can and only me and my wife. So I started taking it out once a month. That cut out 75% of my time to do that one thing. I save around 3 hours per year on that one item. I hired someone to cut my grass an average of twice per month. That saves me forty-eight hours a year. Imagine adding up all the time you can save from these hundreds or thousands of items. The time saved could be tremendous!

b. Put these things in a system that you like. There are several good systems out there. Put it into a system where you know it won't get lost.

c. According to David Allen, you should use outcome thinking. What outcome do you want? The next question is what next physical action do I need to take to propel that thing toward that outcome? This is a very important distinction. I changed from "to do" lists which seemed to just repeat to a "next actions" list with a focus on outcome thinking per David Allen. It has made a huge difference.

d. You must review your system at least once a week. Go through everything and take items off that have been completed. Update everything with a detailed review. I usually do mine on Monday mornings.

Time Wasters

1. Lack of delegation.

This is one of the biggest time wasters in business. We tough guys think that we are the only ones who know how to do things properly, so we end up doing a lot of the work ourselves. This is great for the ego, but terrible for time management. Also, this is the biggest stumbling block to getting to the next level of your career. What you should be doing is developing five of you underneath you. Those are the people who get promoted. Do you get caught up in all those little things that don't get you big returns? Have you trained your people that they can dump problems on you and you will step up and solve them? You are allowing them to let you solve their problems for them. Again, this is very good for the ego, but not very good for time management. There are lots of reasons we don't delegate:

a. Fear of losing control. This is a big issue with a lot of tough guys.

b. Thinking you can do it better.

c. Fear that they may do it better.

d. Fear of overburdening staff. This is silly. One guy told me that he worked most Saturdays because his staff had families. I asked him if he had a family. After a pause, he said, "Yes." Duh.

e. Inexperience with delegating. This takes practice.

f. Insecurity.

g. Being suspicious.

h. Lacking trust.

i. Being too busy. I hear this one often. By the time I explain how to do it, I could just do it myself. Sure. That time. But think of it as an investment in time. The next time that same situation comes up, that person will be able to do it and you can spend your time doing other things.

If you have the "control/perfectionist" emotional intelligence profile, you may have a hard time delegating. You must work on your flexibility first. Start thinking like a CEO. They spend 30% of their time creating the vision, 30% of the time re-evaluating, 30% of their time developing others, and 10% of their time with those little things that clog up their day.

2. Meetings

Meetings can be a huge time waster. One quote I saw said, "When I die, I hope it's in a meeting. The transition from life to death will be barely perceptible." So how can you make meetings more efficient?

a. a. Prepare. Don't walk into meetings without preparation. Know what is to be accomplished.

b. b. Don't forget the food. This not only improves attendance, but keeps people's brains full of nutrition so they can think. Try complex carbohydrates or some proteins instead of donuts.

c. c. Have an agenda. If you can't make an agenda or you don't have one, don't have a meeting. In my opinion, meetings over one hour are a waste of time and energy. Your agenda can be a timed agenda as well. Allocate certain time slots for certain topics. And stick to it.

d. Have a Timekeeper and Facilitator. This can be the same person, but you must have someone that makes sure the agenda is followed. Cut down on the rabbit trails and the personal stuff. If items come up during the meeting that are important, but not part of that meeting, put it in a parking lot. Assign someone to follow up and set up a future meeting to address it.

e. Begin on time. One time I asked this person why he was always late for meetings and he said, "We never start on time anyway." If you begin on time, people will get the message.

f. Have etiquette rules. Don't have everyone talk at once. Raise your hand to speak. No mobile phones.

g. Involve everyone.

h. End on time.

More meeting ideas:

a. You can play a game called Holy Crap Bingo (see Appendix). This usually engages everyone. Create a 5 X 5 grid and write down all those buzz phrases for meetings for your industry in each square: things such as win-win, sports analogies, synergy, think outside the box, revisit, out of the loop, proactive. During the meeting, if you hear one of these phrases, mark it off. When you have all the squares filled across, up and down, or diagonally, you yell, "HOLY CRAP!" It's probably not good for a client meeting, but for an internal meeting, it can be great fun. And it gets people to pay attention.

b. Think about the topics that are covered at most meetings. Do you focus on positive, productive issues such as teambuilding, vision, relationships, celebrations of milestones, celebrations of project goals, and other human aspects of the project? Or do you focus more on the crises and problems such as conflicts between contractors, owner and architect problems, non-performance issues, poor communication, relationship issues, and cover-your-ass posturing?

If most of your meetings are taken up with the latter, you may want to take a different approach. If you work to improve the people side of your project that promotes great relationships and positive communication, you will spend less time on the problems. Take a different approach to meetings. Start with something fun. Make sure you put into the agenda some of the Quadrant II items (important, but not urgent). This will make meeting more productive and enjoyable. In addition, if you start with something fun, the meetings are more likely to be full of energy and engagement.

c. You may want to also try Lean Coffee meetings:

It's a very simple meeting process based on the Lean model.

All you need is Sharpies, sticky notes, and a timer (a phone will do)

Step 0: if folks don't know each other, create name tags. Or you could ready the chapter in The 12 Steps to Great Relationships to learn how to remember names.

Step 1: Create a kanban (a Japanese method to show a sequence with the use of visual cards). Set up an area on the table to place all sticky notes so everyone can see them.

Step 2: Generate topics. Everyone will take a sticky note and write down a topic. You can guide folks with a general topic or it can be wide open. Everyone will introduce their topics to the group.

Step 3: Everyone votes on the topics. Everyone gets two votes. You can vote on one topic or two. The topics with the most votes will be discussed during the meeting. Everyone will agree on the length of time to discuss the topic and the length of time for continuation of a topic.

Step 4: Create 3 areas: To Discuss, Discussing, Discussed

Step 5: Take the first topic, put it in the Discussing pile, and discuss. At the end of the time, everyone votes on whether to continue (thumbs up, thumbs down, flat hand for neutral). If there are enough positive votes, continue to discuss the topic. If not, put it in the Discussed pile. If you continue, when you have completed the continuation, put it in the Discussed pile. Go to the next topic.

Step 6: Save time at the end of the meeting for everyone to voice their takeaways and the topics they would like to discuss later. If there are deliverables, make sure everyone knows who is responsible and when the deliverable is due.

d. Have no meeting Wednesdays (or another day).

e. Cut all meeting times in half. See how it goes. If they work, cut them in half again.

f. Have standing meetings. It usually cuts down on meeting times.

g. Have walking meetings. Try Gemba walks to assess the real field conditions. Gemba means "the real place" and is used to access what is really taking place in the field. Go to where the work is and talk about any issues.

3. Phone calls.

This is a big time waster. But I have found a secret that not many tough guys know. There is an OFF button on your smartphone. I'm serious. Now all you need to do is turn them off. There are times when you should turn them off. During vacations and holidays, for instance. But there are other times during the day when you could silence them. When you really need to focus and get some things done, turn the darned thing off!

You can batch your calls and return all the messages. And since you are likely to get voice mail and get put on hold, you can be checking emails at the same time. I worked with a company that had the policy that the phones were to be on 24/7. This was because they wanted to give great customer service. I question the logic of this. One guy answered his phone five times during an hour-long meeting that we were having. This may be good for customer service, but horrible for time management.

4. Emails

Emails are a real problem. Email has become a chat room, and people expect an immediate response. People can receive hundreds, sometimes thousands of emails each day. The expectation from others is that you are sitting there waiting to see their email and answer it immediately. So it is up to you to create a different expectation.

The first thing you need to do is turn off that bell that dings when an email hits. Don't you feel compelled to open it and read it? Have you become a Pavolv's dog to email? Do you salivate as well? Again, don't answer emails as they come in. Turn off your Outlook and do other things. Answer your emails in batches. And if your company doesn't have email rules to cut down on the crap, talk them into it. No personal emails with baby announcements and birthdays.

Never check your email first thing in the morning. Always start with the important things that you must accomplish. How many times have you started with emails first thing and you look up and it's noon. Resist that temptation to check emails first thing in the morning. That way, you won't wind up on everyone else's agenda.

There was a fantastic idea from The 4-Hour Work Week by Tim Farriss. I tried it and it really works. If you want to reduce the email in your inbox by 50%, do the following: First, send out an auto-responder for a few weeks that says that in order to serve your clients better, you will only check your email twice per day, at noon and at 5:00 pm. Tell them if they really need to get in touch with you, please call or text your mobile phone. I did this and reduced my emails by 50% without a huge increase in texts or phone calls.

If you have key clients or personnel, call them directly and let them know what you are doing. You created an expectation of immediate response. This is a process to create a different expectation. In addition to this, create rules for all incoming emails. You can automatically send emails to subordinates from certain people and let them handle it. For those emails that you like to read, but aren't critical, put them into a read file. When you get busy, you can delete these without even looking at them.

There was a project manager that said he could never do this. He said he had to look at every email on the project. I told him that would be great for keeping an eye on things, but horrible for time management. Then, his child became ill and he travelled with him to a hospital out of state. While he was there, he couldn't check emails very often, so he tried the auto-responder. It worked like a charm and he reduced his emails by 40%. And the project didn't fall apart.

Also, I have a few email rules that make emails faster and easier to read. First, put something interesting in the subject line, maybe even the whole email. That way people won't even have to open it. Make it clear when no reply is needed. Don't send one word "thanks" emails. Don't write an email that you have to scroll down to read. Keep them short and sweet. Nobody reads those thirty page emails. Don't add any attachments unless expected or warranted. No one opens attachments.

One other issue for email are those annoying threads that can be 20 emails long. One of our participants told us how they handle these. When the email gets to the third thread, that person is responsible for resolving the situation. They can't extend the thread, but they must resolve it and send out a resolution emails to all interested parties.

5. The Myth of Multi-tasking

Some people think they are great multi-taskers. But they would be wrong. Mutli-tasking is a myth. The brain can only do one thing at a time. Some folks are adept at multi-switching. They can switch back and forth between tasks quickly. Try this. Spell MULTITASK out loud and time yourself. Now count to 18 by twos. Time yourself. Now switch back and forth between the two. M-2-U-4-L-6-T-8 etc. Which is faster? It's much more efficient to work in blocks (email, phone calls, schedule, budget) than to switch among these all day long.

6. Drop in visitors.

We've all heard it. Have you got a minute? But is it ever a minute? When someone says this, first, ask them what this is about. Then tell them how much time you can give them and stick to it. Or tell them that you don't have time right now. This is a great approach. Tell them you don't have time and that they should figure this out themselves. Tell them if they can't figure it out by 4:00 today, to come back and you will help. 90% of the time, they never come back.

If they don't get the message to leave, stand up and walk toward the door. Put no extra chairs in your office. That will keep people from staying so long. Have you seen the guy who comes in, sits down, and puts his feet up only to talk about his personal life for an hour? You can also have designated office hours for drop-in visitors. The last resort is to hide so that no one knows you are in your office.

7. Personal clutter.

Are you holding on to things that don't help you attain your goals? Does it take you a long time to find things in your office? If your house or office burned down, what would be irreplaceable? We hold onto way too much stuff. We are in the electronic age and most of our documents aren't paper. Yet we still experience clutter. There are some schools of thought on organization that say you should only handle a piece of paper once. David Allen, the author of Getting Things Done, says that if something takes less than two minutes, you should just do it. Do a de-clutter day once a week or once a month and if you haven't touched something in a month, throw it away. One person told me that they throw their paper away in a recycling box so that if they needed it later, they can always go back through the recycling.

Do you have folders within folders within folders? If you have this setup you have increased the number of places where something isn't. Simplify your filing system to alphabetical order for all files. A great file naming protocol is the date, initial of who created it and a name. Example: 2020-5-28-BD-Tough Guy Survival Kit.

8. Procrastination.

Do you put things off? Is this an issue for you? Most people put things off for two reasons: either they hate to do this thing or they are not good at this thing. If you're not good at something, get the training to be good at it. If you don't like doing something, do it first thing in the morning. When you have accomplished that thing that you hate to do, the rest of the day feels like a vacation. You can do easy hard or hard easy. Start with those difficult tasks that you hate first, then the other things will be so much easier. If you save those big things for the end, they tend to never get done.

9. Just say no.

Learn how to say no. Set limits. I know this is hard for all of those get-r-done tough guys, but you must learn to say no. Or as my wife says, "I just can't say yes to that at this time."

10. Idle talk and gossip.

I know tough guy, you will probably tell me that you don't do this. But I don't believe you. How many trash talk sessions do you have per day. How many bull sessions are on your agenda? These sessions can be fun and useful for relationship building, but they are horrible for time management. They waste a lot of time. Don't do it.

11. Screen Time

Again, some estimates say that we are in front of screens for 11 hours per day on average. With that average, by the age of 65, you've been in front of a screen for 30 years.

Television is probably the biggest time waster on the planet. In the USA, we watch 4-1/2 hours of television per day on average. I watch an average of one hour per day, so someone out there is watching eight hours of television per day. And for those of you who say you watch less than 4-1/2 hours per day, think about ballgames, car races, ESPN, and Sports Center. With that average of 4-1/2 hours per day, by the age of

65, you've watched 12 years of television. Imagine what you could do with those twelve years. Let's add commute time (The Atlanta average is 48 minutes per day. Your commute time may be longer.), internet surfing, calls, other "wasted" time (2 hours per day). Without even figuring in holidays, weekends, and vacations, you "waste" 107 full 24 hour days each year on these kinds of activities.

What if you took ½ that time or 53 full 24 hour days and used it for yourself and your family. Which would bring you greater happiness at the end of the year? Do you sit in your car during a commute when you could be listening to some book on tape that will help you? Or some nice music? Or use that as productive, reflective time? The time is there if you just utilize it in a better way.

There's an app for that:

Remember, if it doesn't bring you joy or make you money, someone else can do it. There are many apps that do things with a few clicks that used to take us hours: Note Vault (automatically generates daily reports), Out of Milk (groceries), banking apps, and apps that reduce your time on your phone like Forest. There are sites like Fiverr and Upwork where freelancers will do work for you. Get into the wonderful world of apps and see what you can find to save time and energy.

CHAPTER 7
Work/Life Balance

"Remember that work and life coexist. Wellness at work follows you home and vice-versa. The same goes for when you're not well, fueled, or fulfilled. Work and life aren't opposing forces to balance; they go hand-in-hand and are intertwined as different elements of the same person: you."

~ **Melissa Steginus**, *Self Care at Work: How to Reduce Stress, Boost Productivity, and Do More of What Matters*

This is the shortest chapter of the book for a reason. The simple fact is that work-life balance is a choice. You can have better work-life balance if you choose to do it right now. No one has ever said on their deathbed, "I wish I could have worked a little more."

I saw a cartoon once with a man and his family sitting around a table. The caption reads "Before we begin our family meeting, how about we go around and say our names and a little something about ourselves." One participant told me that he was commuting once a week and sometimes every other week. One week, he came home, and his two-year old daughter was afraid of him. She didn't know who he was. That was a big wake up call for him. He vowed to get home more often.

Have you noticed something about those successful folks? They seem to have pretty good work/life balance. Now, they may have sacrificed that balance at times in their careers. That's understandable. But they have learned valuable lessons. They have learned what the true definition of success is. And it's not working your ass off until you have a heart attack at age fifty.

What is your work/life ratio? Ideally, the ratios should go something like this: 33% work, 33% family, and 33% personal. For most of us, it's 70-80% work, 10-20% family, and 0-10% personal. I don't know of anyone who has reached this ideal, but it's something to keep in your mind. Most tough guys sacrifice themselves first. This isn't a very good strategy because if you don't take care of yourself, you're no good to your employer or your family. So the first thing to do for good work/life balance is to schedule more time for you. Make sure you have your daily reflection time.

Who suffers when your life is out of balance? I'm sure there is some personal suffering, but the family also suffers. I know, tough guy, you work hard because you love your family and you want to provide for them. But ask them what they would rather have. I think you know the answer. No one has ever said on their deathbed that they wish they could have worked a little more and spent less time with their families. My classes are filled with older tough guys who have real regrets over not spending more time with family, especially their children. Tough guys take note. Don't be full of regret at the end of your life and career. Start working toward better work/life balance.

Don't get me wrong. It's not easy. This is probably one of the hardest things you will ever do. But the payoff is tremendous. And the smart employers want you to have good work/life balance as well. They want you making money for them for a long time, not just until your health fails from burnout.

Final thoughts:

There will be three challenges that you will face when you start to pay attention to life balance and time management. The first is guilt. You will feel guilty when you start working less hours. But the great feeling you get by spending more time with your family will offset this guilt. The second thing is misunderstandings from others. They may think that you are becoming a slacker. They may ridicule you in your new approach. This is to be expected. They probably are going down a bad road themselves and want to take you with them. Don't let them.

The construction industry is the only industry I know where you can work 80-hour weeks for six months and when you decide to take off a Friday afternoon to see your kid's ballgame, your boss gives you grief, looks at his watch, and says, "Boy, I wish I could keep those banker's hours like you." It's insane. The third thing you might experience is painful insights. You may find that you aren't a very good husband. You may find that you are a video junkie as I did. These insights are just ways to grow. Embrace them and overcome them.

BIOGRAPHY AND CONTACT INFORMATION

Brent Darnell is the pioneer in bringing emotional intelligence to the construction industry. He began teaching it in 1999 before the AEC industry knew they needed it. In 2012 he was awarded Engineering News Record's top 25 newsmaker's award for his record-breaking program that "transforms Alpha males into service focused leaders". In 2017, he also won the volunteer of the year award for AGC Georgia for his work in training and development.

Brent is a third generation construction guy. He grew up walking projects like the Plaza Tower in New Orleans with his Dad. He graduated with a mechanical engineering degree from Georgia Tech in 1981 and spent 18 years managing projects such as the Brooke Army Medical Center and housing for athletes in the Olympic Village in Atlanta. The impact

The impact of Brent's unique programs spans the globe to 20 countries from the US to places such as New York, Stockholm, Copenhagen, Oslo, Cape Town, Helsinki, Buenos Aires, Moscow, Prague, London, and as far away as Hong Kong.

His clients include Skanska, Balfour Beatty, The Beck Group, Jacobsen, McCarthy, Manhattan, Clark, Heery, J.E. Dunn, Kiewit, Barton-Malow, Batson-Cook, Brasfield & Gorrie, and Granite.

He has also worked at the national level with AEC support organizations like the AGC, ABC, DBIA, CURT, COAA, CMAA, and LCI among others and is a sought after speaker at their regional and national conferences.

He is an adjunct professor at such notable universities as Auburn, Penn State and Virginia Tech to ensure that young people come into the industry with much needed people skills.

He has authored many books geared to the construction industry such as The People Profit Connection and The Tough Guy Survival Kit. His books have sold over 100,000 copies worldwide.

Brent has recently developed the world's first online e-learning courses on emotional intelligence and soft skills for the AEC industry. He is a true Renaissance man. He is a mechanical engineer, actor, playwright, musician, poet, yoga instructor, and book publisher.

If you wish to contact Brent Darnell concerning this emotional intelligence work, please visit www.brentdarnell.com.

APPENDIX

Body Battery Inventory

Many stress management seminars talk about reducing the stress in your life. I'm sure there is something to that. But work and life can be very stressful. We take a slightly different approach. Imagine that your body is a battery. There is stress and other things that discharge your body battery and deplete your energy. Those things will always be there. There are also things you can do to recharge your body battery and replenish that energy. So, do your best to decrease the things that are depleting you and increase things that recharge your battery. Adjust how you react to stressful situations. If you can build in more ways to recharge your body battery throughout your day, you will have much more energy and be much less stressed at the end of the day.

Fill out the following body battery inventory & plan and see where you are.

Take the tests by placing an "X" on your choice.

Step 1:
Go to pages 237 and 238 to determine your body battery dischargers. If you are taking a drug that masks a symptom, fill this out as if you are not taking the drug.

Step 2:
Go to page 239 to determine your body battery rechargers.

Step 3:
Go to page 242 to see your score of the body battery rechargers minus the body battery dischargers. Fill in for Score 1.

Step 4:
Go to pages 244-246 and fill out your body battery performance plan for daily and occasional stressors and how you will recharge your body battery before, during, or after that stressful event. We include many ways to recharge yourbody battery throughout your day.

Step 5:
After some time of working on your stress and recovery, fill out pages 240-242 (Re-Tests) and put the second number on page 242 (Score 2). What has changed?

Step 6:
Tweak your Body Battery Performance Plan for better results next time.

Discharge Body Battery

		NONE	SOME	MODERATE	A LOT	INSANE
	Point Value	0	1	2	3	4
1	Work Stress					
2	Personal Stress					
3	Emotional Stress					
4	Travel/Commute Stress					
5	Physical Stress (like training or exercise)					
6	Family Stress					
7	Health Stress (colds, illness, fatigue, etc)					
	Cigarettes per day	0	1-5	6-10	11-15	16+
8	I use nicotine					
	Drinks per week	0	2	4	6	8+
10	I drink alcohol					
	Overweight by lbs	0	5	10	10	16+
12	I am overweight					

Total number of points for dischargers (Add all points): [ ]

Physical Symptoms of Stress and Stress Related Illnesses: Put an 'X' next to all that apply to you. These discharge your body battery and deplete your energy.

☐ Headaches: 40 million chronic sufferers

☐ Pain: back, joint, chronic, Fibromyalgia Syndrome

☐ Difficulty sleeping: falling asleep or waking up and can't go back to sleep

☐ Stomach Problems: Acid Stomach, Acid Reflux, Ulcers, Chron's, Irritable Bowel, constipation, diarrhea

☐ Irritability, feeling on the edge, explosive nature, chest pains

☐ Allergies, Asthma, sinus problems

☐ Skin problems (dry skin, eczema, psoriasis, rashes, hives, shingles)

☐ Depression or anxiety: melancholy, no drive, or anxious feelings

☐ Frequent illness, frequent colds or flu, diminished immunity

☐ Cognitive impairment: can't think clearly, memory issues

☐ Diminished sex drive

☐ Diabetes

☐ Arthritis

☐ Cancer

☐ High Blood Pressure

☐ High Cholesterol

☐ Pancreatitis, Lupus, MS, other autoimmune

Multiply the number of physical symptoms/illnesses by 4:

Total number of points for stress related symptoms/illnesses: [ ]

If you have had a major life shift or transition in the past twelve months:

☐ Death of a loved

☐ A physical move

☐ Graduation

☐ A new job

☐ Being let go from a job

☐ Bankruptcy, a failed endeavor

☐ Major or life threatening illness

☐ Marriage or divorce

☐ Any other major life transition or major life stress

Multiply the number of major life shifts by 5:

Total number of points for major life shifts: [ ]

Total number of points: Dischargers, Physical Symptoms of Stress, and Major Life Shifts: This is your Body Battery Discharge Number: [ ]

Recharge Body Battery

		NONE	RARELY	SOMETIMES	MOSTLY	ALL THE TIME
	Point Value	0	1	2	3	4
1	I sleep well and awake refreshed:					
2	I take naps or have complete down time daily:					
3	I have passive recovery times daily [reading (no news or violence), television (no news or violence), movies (no violence or upsetting movies), video games (no violence or upsetting images), music (hopefully soothing and relaxing), radio(no talk radio, news, or violence)]:					
4	I do relaxation exercises for recovery daily (meditation, yoga, breathing, massage):					
5	My diet is filled with nutritious foods and limited simple sugars:					
6	My diet is many small meals spread throughout my day:					
7	I eat only around 1,500 to 2,000 calories per day:					
8	My day has fun in it every day:					
9	I have at least one hour of personal time just for me each day:					
10	I find time for reflection (prayer, meditation, quiet time) each day:					
11	I connect with family, friends, and community daily:					
12	I am grateful and thankful each day:					
13	I take my full two weeks of vacation without checking in at the office:					
14	I have down time every weekend without checking in at the office:					
15	I am positive each day:					
16	I seek rest and recovery every 90 to 120 minutes:					

This is your Body Battery Recharge Number: ☐

Discharge Body Battery 2		NONE	SOME	MODERATE	A LOT	INSANE
	Point Value	0	1	2	3	4
1	Work Stress					
2	Personal Stress					
3	Emotional Stress					
4	Travel/Commute Stress					
5	Physical Stress (like training or exercise)					
6	Family Stress					
7	Health Stress (colds, illness, fatigue, etc)					
	Cigarettes per day	0	1-5	6-10	11-15	16+
8	I use nicotine					
	Drinks per week	0	2	4	6	8+
10	I drink alcohol					
	Overweight by lbs	0	5	10	10	16+
12	I am overweight					

Total number of points for dischargers: _____

Physical Symptoms of Stress and Stress Related Illnesses: Put an 'X' next to all that apply to you. These discharge your body battery and deplete your energy.

☐ Headaches: 40 million chronic sufferers

☐ Pain: back, joint, chronic, Fibromyalgia Syndrome

☐ Difficulty sleeping: falling asleep or waking up and can't go back to sleep

☐ Stomach Problems: Acid Stomach, Acid Reflux, Ulcers, Chron's, Irritable Bowel, constipation, diarrhea

☐ Irritability, feeling on the edge, explosive nature, chest pains

☐ Allergies, Asthma, sinus problems

☐ Skin problems (dry skin, eczema, psoriasis, rashes, hives, shingles)

☐ Depression or anxiety: melancholy, no drive, or anxious feelings

☐ Frequent illness, frequent colds or flu, diminished immunity

☐ Cognitive impairment: can't think clearly, memory issues

☐ Diminished sex drive

☐ Diabetes

☐ Arthritis

☐ Cancer

☐ High Blood Pressure

☐ High Cholesterol

☐ Pancreatitis, Lupus, MS, other autoimmune

Multiply the number of physical symptoms/illnesses by 4:

**Total number of points
for stress related symptoms/illnesses:** [   ]

If you have had a major life shift or transition in the past twelve months:

☐ Death of a loved

☐ A physical move

☐ Graduation

☐ A new job

☐ Being let go from a job

☐ Bankruptcy, a failed endeavor

☐ Major or life threatening illness

☐ Marriage or divorce

☐ Any other major life transition or major life stress

Multiply the number of major life shifts by 5:

Total number of points for major life shifts: [   ]

Total number of points: Dischargers, Physical Symptoms of Stress, and Major Life Shifts: This is your Body Battery Discharge Number: [   ]

Recharge Body Battery 2

		NONE	RARELY	SOMETIMES	MOSTLY	ALL THE TIME
	Point Value	0	1	2	3	4
1	I sleep well and awake refreshed:					
2	I take naps or have complete down time daily:					
3	I have passive recovery times daily [reading (no news or violence), television (no news or violence), movies (no violence or upsetting movies), video games (no violence or upsetting images), music (hopefully soothing and relaxing), radio(no talk radio, news, or violence)]:					
4	I do relaxation exercises for recovery daily (meditation, yoga, breathing, massage):					
5	My diet is filled with nutritious foods and limited simple sugars:					
6	My diet is many small meals spread throughout my day:					
7	I eat only around 1,500 to 2,000 calories per day:					
8	My day has fun in it every day:					
9	I have at least one hour of personal time just for me each day:					
10	I find time for reflection (prayer, meditation, quiet time) each day:					
11	I connect with family, friends, and community daily:					
12	I am grateful and thankful each day:					
13	I take my full two weeks of vacation without checking in at the office:					
14	I have down time every weekend without checking in at the office:					
15	I am positive each day:					
16	I seek rest and recovery every 90 to 120 minutes:					

This is your Body Battery Recharge Number: ☐

	Score 1	Score 2
Body Battery Recharge Number	☐	☐
-		
Body Battery Discharge Number	☐	☐
Body Battery Total Number	☐	☐

If this Body Battery Total Number is positive, keep up the good work. If it is negative or nearly equal, it is recommended that you either find more ways to reduce your body battery discharges or find more ways to recharge your body battery.

See below for your Body Battery Performance Plan. You likely have battery dischargers that deplete your body battery: things such as a daily commute, a daily or weekly meeting, weekly or monthly travel, an annual report, tax time, monthly progress or accounting, bill paying time, stressful family gatherings, encounters with difficult people, etc. These dischargers may be daily or occasional.

Put down the activities that are discharging your body battery and depleting your energy, then fill out what recharging activities you will do before, during, or after to recharge your body battery. The list of 85 battery rechargers are below.

Body Battery Performance Plan:

Daily body battery dischargers	Recharging activities

Occasional body battery dischargers	Recharging activities

Sample Body Battery Performance Plan:

Daily body battery dischargers	Recharging activities
commute	music, make weird noises
deadline driven project	positive attitude, take breaks
stressful daily situation	be conciously thankful, smile
meetings, stress at work	deep breathing, turn negative talk into positive

Occasional body battery dischargers	Recharging activities
Monthly or Quarterly reports, Meetings	massage, nap, quiet my mind
Paying Bills, April 15th	spend time with my pet, stay hydrated
Holidays	dance, laugh, connect with family
Annual Physical	exercise, drink water, tell jokes

Sample Body Battery Performance Plan:

1. Eat Breakfast and 5 to 6 small meals per day
2. Eat 1,500--2,00 calories per day
3. Have daily connection and support from family, friends and community
4. Be consciously thankful most days
5. Find time to laugh and have fun every day
6. Stay hydrated throughout my day
7. Don't eat many simple, refined sugars
8. Sleep regular hours most nights and get plenty of sleep
9. Take naps when I need to in order to recharge
10. Use caffeine, nicotine and/or alcohol in moderation
11. Exercise regularly (at least 3 times per week)
12. Quiet my mind each day with meditation/prayer/etc
13. Seek rest and recovery every 90 to 120 minutes
14. Take my vacations and enjoy my weekends without checking in at the office or project
15. Maintain a positive attitude even during stressful times.
16. Take five deep breaths.

17. Think of something you are grateful and thankful for.
18. Drink water.
19. Do something silly. Make a face or stick out your tongue.
20. Start a laugh club and laugh daily.
21. Put Scotch tape on your face and distort it.
22. Play hopscotch on the sidewalk.
23. Play a game with kids.
24. Do something extremely physical.
25. Go to an amusement park.
26. Yell at the top of your lungs.
27. Sing or hum a song.
28. Smile. It creates physiological changes.
29. Take a nap.
30. Spend some time with your pet.
31. Go make someone's day with a surprise visit.
32. Change your body.
33. Throw your shoulders back
34. Stretch your arms over your head, then touch your toes
35. Plant your feet firmly on the ground. Feel the heaviness.
36. Feel yourself as you become assertive and powerful.
37. Turn your negative self-talk around.
38. Create a mantra and repeat it.
39. Visualize yourself being relaxed, calm, and full of energy.
40. Dance around the room.
41. Go to a different place physically.
42. Work out with weights or do something that gets your heart rate up.
43. Shake all over like a dog.
44. Get some protein either in shake or bar form.
45. Go for a walk in nature.
46. Call someone who is supportive and talk to them.
47. Look at cool videos or your mind movie.
48. Ask for a hug.
49. Zone out with music.
50. Watch a sitcom or standup comedy show.
51. Take an acting class or a dance class or an aerobics class.
52. Get a massage, acupuncture, reflexology or Reiki.
53. Take an improvisation class.
54. Play nonsense song on the musical instrument of your choice even if you can't play a musical instrument.
55. Tell a joke.
56. Open a window and get some fresh air.
57. Go to some funny websites with jokes or funny videos.
58. Look at a photo of someone you love.
59. Explore your feelings.
60. Doodle, draw a picture.
61. Do the two minute de-stressor: Notice your breath. How are you breathing? Breathe deeply. What are you thinking? Are there thoughts that cause this stress? Think of things you are grateful and thankful for. Tap the tip of your tongue on the gums just above the top front teeth.
62. Look in Stress Tolerance section of the Total Leadership Program Resource book.
63. Read a kid's book.
64. Look at fish in an aquarium.

65. Look at birds, squirrels and other animals near your house.
66. Look under a rock and observe what is there.
67. Go to a museum or aquarium.
68. Help someone in need.
69. Visit an assisted living place and sing a song for the residents.
70. Have lunch at Chucky Cheese or other kid's restaurant.
71. Have a mindful meal that lasts at least one hour.
72. Make faces in the mirror.
73. Give yourself a massage on your shoulders and face.
74. Take a Jacuzzi.
75. Run as fast as you can.
76. Try to not think about zebras.
77. Put on some disco and do the robot.
78. Pretend to be someone else.
79. Make weird noises.
80. Do a puzzle.
81. Make a prank phone call.
82. Eat an ice cream cone or frozen yogurt.
83. Get a mani pedi (that's manicure and pedicure).
84. Gargle sing a song or burp the alphabet.
85. Strike a Power Pose (hands on hips, hands up in the air, spread yourself out and take up a lot of space) for 2 minutes. This will increase your testosterone by 20% and decrease your cortisol (the stress hormone) by 15% from the baseline. For more information, Google Amy Cuddy Ted Power Pose.

Time Log Exercise

Don't just put "work" or "home". Put exactly what you are doing in as much detail as possible throughout your week. See sample time log on page 225.

Time log	Sunday	Monday	Tuesday	Wednesday	Thursday	Friday	Saturday
time							
5							
6							
7							
8							
9							
10							
11							
12							
1							
2							
3							
4							
5							
6							
7							
8							
9							
10							
11							
12							
1							
2							
3							
4							

EVALUATION AND ANALYSIS

Role	Hours/week
Family	
Health	
Work	
Community	
Learning	
Personal Growth	
Personal	
TV	
Entertainment	
Eating	
Travel	
Recovery	
Sleep	
Exercise	
Reflection	
Meetings	
Other	
Other	
Other	
Total	**168**

List the top 5-10 things you value the most in your life and work!

1 _____
2 _____
3 _____
4 _____
5 _____
6 _____
7 _____
8 _____
9 _____
10 _____

Does your time allocation per week match the things you value?

_____
_____
_____
_____
_____

Time Allocation =
168 hrs per wk

SAMPLE TIME LOG

Time log	Sunday	Monday	Tuesday	Wednesday	Thursday	Friday	Saturday
time							
5	sleep	morning routine	morning routine	commute	morning routine	commute commute	sleep
6	exercise	commute	commute flat tire	commute	commute		sleep
7	family breakfast	emails/calls		emails	budget meeting	paperwork	commute
8	watch TV	daily huddle/walk			budget meeting		update project
9	watch TV	accident at project	catch up calls	OAC meeting	budget meeting	emails/calls	
10	Sunday school		team meeting		budget meeting	emails/calls	
11	church			walk project	budget meeting	emails/calls	
12	church			lunch	lunch	project chase	lunch
1	Sunday meal out	catch up emails	lunch	project updates	project visit		kid's games
2	Sunday meal out	catch up calls	plan meetings				
3	work around house	lunch			owner meeting	weekly meeting	
4	work around house	CO meeting		interview folks			
5	Watch TV		emails/calls			commute	time w/family
6	Watch TV	commute	paperwork		commute	commute	Watch TV
7	family dinner	family dinner	paperwork	commute	Watch TV/family	Watch TV/family	Watch TV/family
8	Watch TV	Watch TV	paperwork	Watch TV	Watch TV/family	Watch TV/family	Watch TV/family
9		Watch TV	commute	read	read	read	read
10	sleep	sleep	sleep	sleep	sleep	sleep	sleep
11	sleep	sleep	sleep	sleep	sleep	sleep	sleep
12	sleep	sleep	sleep	sleep	sleep	sleep	sleep
1	sleep	sleep	sleep	sleep	sleep	sleep	sleep
2	sleep	sleep	sleep	sleep	sleep	sleep	sleep
3	sleep	sleep	sleep	sleep	sleep	sleep	sleep
4	sleep	sleep	sleep	sleep	sleep	sleep	sleep

morning routine: reading, meditation, exercise (walk), breakfast, shower, dress

TIME MANAGEMENT WORKSHEET

CONTINUALLY ASK: DOES IT?:
Focus on the people in your life? Bring you joy? Eliminate waste? Embrace continual improvement? Take energy, give you energy or is it neutral? Put " + " if it adds energy, " - " if it takes energy, and " **n** " for neutral. Add value to your life/work, take away value, or is it neutral? Put " + " if it adds value, " - " if it takes away value, and " **n** " for neutral. If it does not add value, but you ned to keep doing it, Put " * ". We filled out the first few for examples.

Fill out ALL THAT YOU DO: All the things on time log, all things on to do list, everything from the time you wake up in the morning until you go to bed at night.
ALL OF THE THINGS THAT YOU DO EVERY day, EVERY week, EVERY month, EVERY year including: morning routine, shower, eat breakfast, commute, all work items
including all meetings, phone calls emails, etc. Drop the kids off, kids' games, church, watch TV, family dinners, buy groceries, do laundry, pick up dry cleaning, pay bills, prepare taxes, work around house (specific tasks), yard work, exercise, clean house, make dinner, coach kids' team, vacation, travel, holidays, buy presents.

Things I do now (EVERYTHING)	perfect outcome	first step	Do it	Delete	Delegate	Defer	Redefine	Energy?	Value?	hours saved/ mo
Dentist appt	cleaning and exam	call and make appt	done					-	+	
garbage out weekly	less time doing it	take it to the curb					monthly	-	*	2
cut grass weekly	less time doing it	call to arrange			hire kid			-	+	4
weekly OAC	less time doing it	prepare for meeting					monthly	-	*	
Reorganize files	files done	schedule some time				Spring		n	+	
Get PE License	obtain license	start studying		don't need				-	n	
Volunteer for HOA	become a volunteer	call and volunteer		NO				-	-	
Work out regularly	3 to 5 x per week	join a gym	done					+	+	

TIME MANAGEMENT WORKSHEET

Things I do now (EVERYTHING)	perfect outcome	first step	Do it	Delete	Delegate	Defer	Redefine	Energy?	Value?	hours saved/mo

Holy Crap Meeting Bingo

Before (or during) your next meeting, prepare your "Holy Crap Meeting Bingo" card by drawing a square — I find that 5" by 5" is a good size — and dividing it into columns — five across and five down. That will give you 25 1-inch blocks.

2. Write one of the following words/phrases in each block:

cleanup
composite crew
manpower
overtime
son of a bitch or *sumbitch*
RFI
delay
Owner
delivery
safety
fall protection
Architect
tie off
problem
two blocked
layout

behind
out of the loop
benchmark
value-added
proactive
win-win
think outside the box
fast track
crap
at the end of the day
touch base
mindset
client focus(ed)
ballpark
game plan

Check off the appropriate block when you hear one of those words/phrases.

When you get five blocks horizontally, vertically, or diagonally, stand up and shout "HOLY CRAP!"

www.ingramcontent.com/pod-product-compliance
Lightning Source LLC
Chambersburg PA
CBHW060312240426

43661CB00059B/2741